T2-CRY-070

The Master's Perspective Series
Volume 2

The

Master's Perspective
on
CONTEMPORARY
ISSUES

ROBERT L. THOMAS
general editor

kregel
PUBLICATIONS

Grand Rapids, MI 49501

Library of Congress Cataloging-in-Publication Data
Thomas, Robert L.
   The Master's perspective on contemporary issues / by Robert L. Thomas, editor.
      p.   cm. — (The master's perspective series)
   A collection of previously published articles that appeared in The master's seminary journal.
   Includes bibliographical references and indexes.
   1. Theology, Doctrinal.   I. Thomas, Robert L.
II. Master's seminary journal.   III. Series.
BT80.M37   1998   230—dc21   98-27365
                                                  CIP

ISBN 0-8254-3181-6

Printed in the United States of America

1 2 3 4 / 03 02 01 00 99 98

Table of Contents

Foreword

My son, if you receive my words, and treasure my commands within you, so that you incline your ear to wisdom, and apply your heart to understanding; yes, if you cry out for discernment, and lift up your voice for understanding, if you seek her as silver, and search for her as for hidden treasures; then you will understand the fear of the LORD, and find the knowledge of God. (Proverbs 2:1–5 NKJV)

The grand promise of that passage is that the Eternal God has a storehouse of wisdom which He reveals to the "godly" so that they may know what is the time and right "course" of life in every circumstance. The responsibility of that revelation is the Scripture which, when carefully examined and clearly understood, establishes the path for every believer in every place and time.

Understanding that cause fulfills the will of God in providing Scripture. Such fulfillment, however, demands skilled interpretation and discernment.

Paul commanded the church to engage in such thoughtful and careful interpretation: "Examine everything carefully; hold fast to that which is good; abstain from every form of evil" (1 Thess. 5:20–21 NASB). That is the clearest call in the New Testament to discernment and a necessary admonition in every age, particularly this one.

The place of biblical discernment has been largely ignored and its priority placed last because of several current evangelical perspectives: (1) depreciation of doctrine and the place of sound theology; (2) disdain for any teaching that is perceived to divide Christians; (3) disregard for antithetical thinking that separates what is true from all false interpretations regardless of who it offends; (4) displacing of careful exegesis with mystical, intuitive, and personal approaches to understanding Scripture and God's will; (5) dominance of personalities and organizations that lack solid doctrine, scholarly skill and depth, but have wide exposure for their teaching.

These are more than trends. They are established features of contemporary evangelicalism that militate against clear explication of the Word of God on the issues of our time.

In *The Master's Perspective on Contemporary Issues,* scholars from The Master's Seminary who have honed their skills in discerning the meanings of God's Word, by experience through many years of searching the depths of Scripture, address some of the most crucial issues of our day with clarity.

I am grateful to share some grace with these men and confident their work will help you to "discern the fear of the LORD, and discover the knowledge of God" (Prov. 2:5 NASB).

John F. MacArthur Jr.

Introduction

Paul wrote to the Corinthian church, "I hear that divisions exist among you; and in part, I believe it. For there must also be factions among you, in order that those who are approved may have become evident among you" (1 Cor. 11:18b–19). As it was in Corinth, so it has been with the body of Christ throughout the centuries of the Christian era. "Peculiar opinions" have arisen and continue to arise causing divisions within the body. Deviations from sound doctrine have occasioned repeated responses from those who cherish the inspired Word of God above all else.

The Master's Perspective on Contemporary Issues has selected a number of such peculiar opinions to respond to, in hope of setting the record straight for Christians who find the mixed signals they are receiving confusing. The issues dealt with include the following:

1. How the integration of psychology with the Bible has misled Christians regarding principles of Christian living.
2. How the proposal about fallible prophecy in contemporary Christianity has misinterpreted the New Testament.
3. How a respected scholar has misrepresented a dispensational system of thought.
4. How theonomists have proposed an early dating of Revelation to preserve their postmillennial scheme of eschatology.
5. How a former cessationist has switched to noncessationism and now sharply attacks cessationists.
6. How present-day Christians have misunderstood the legitimacy of Christian involvement in Freemasonry.
7. How evangelical feminist proponents have misconstrued grammatical-historical principles of interpretation.
8. How respected Christian leaders have sent the wrong signal about rapprochement between evangelicals and Catholics.
9. How Progressive Dispensationalism has departed from dispensational principles of literal interpretation.

10. Why evangelical attempts to respond to the extremism of the Jesus Seminar have been fruitless.
11. Why those who place limitations on God's love for humanity have misread the Bible.

Each chapter measures one of these issues by biblical standards and attempts to clarify what is a proper perspective.

The resolving of each question is the proposal of the contributor and does not necessarily represent the opinion of The Master's Seminary, its administration, or its faculty. Each one, however, is a solution that is recommended for consideration by readers of this volume.

English translations used in this volume are those of the authors of individual chapters unless otherwise indicated.

I want to express my thanks to Mr. Dennis Swanson for his help in compiling the indexes for this volume.

Robert L. Thomas
Editor

About *The Master's Seminary Journal*

For those unfamiliar with *The Master's Seminary Journal,* a word of introduction is in order. *TMSJ* began publication in 1990 with the following statement of purpose:

> With this issue, *The Master's Seminary Journal* launches its career as a medium for the publication of scholarly articles dealing with the biblical text, Christian theology, and pastoral concerns. As you have noted, or will note, it also contains reviews of current and significant books and, occasionally, of articles, relating to these issues. With these emphases in mind, technical articles dealing with such issues as the philosophy of religion, linguistics, or archaeology will not be included unless they clearly, directly, and significantly contribute to the understanding or application of God's written revelation—the Holy Bible. The editors desire that all articles be understandable, not only by seminary professors and other professional scholars but also by pastors and, indeed, by any serious students of Scripture.
>
> While most of the articles will be contributed by the faculty members of The Master's Seminary, the editors will solicit articles and reviews from recognized evangelical scholars, will evaluate voluntary contributions for possible inclusion, and will occasionally include outstanding historical selections from the public domain.
>
> It is our fervent prayer that our Lord Jesus Christ will be honored and exalted, either directly or indirectly, on every page of this publication, and that every article and review will contribute to the understanding or application of the Holy Scriptures as we await His return. (Excerpted from "Editorial," *TMSJ* 1, no. 1 [1990]: 1–2)

The *Journal* has continued without interruption since that time, endeavoring to fulfill the purpose established at its beginning. Those interested in a subscription to *TMSJ* may contact Professor James F. Stitzinger, *The Master's Seminary Journal*, 13248 Roscoe Blvd., Sun Valley, CA 91352, or by e-mail at the address jstitzinger@mastersem.edu.

To the following pages of *The Master's Perspective on Contemporary Issues*, volume 2 (1991) of *TMSJ* has contributed two chapters (chaps. 1 and 2), volume 3 (1992) has provided one chapter (chap. 3), volume 5 (1994) was the source of four chapters (chaps. 4, 5, 6, and 7), volume 6 (1995) has furnished two chapters (chaps. 8 and 9), and two of the chapters (chaps. 10 and 11) appeared in volume 7 (1996).

Contributors

F. David Farnell
Associate Professor of New Testament
The Master's Seminary

Eddy D. Field II
A southern California businessman and longtime friend of
The Master's Seminary

Eddy D. Field III
Th.M. Alumnus, The Master's Seminary
Adjunct Professor of Biblical Education,
Philadelphia College of Bible
Ph.D. student, Westminster Theological Seminary, Philadelphia

Paul W. Felix Sr.
Th.M. Alumnus, The Master's Seminary
Pastor
Berean Bible Church
Denver, Colorado

John F. MacArthur Jr.
President, Professor of Pastoral Ministries
The Master's Seminary

Richard L. Mayhue
Senior Vice President and Dean, Professor of Pastoral Ministries and
Systematic Theology
The Master's Seminary

Robert L. Thomas
Professor of New Testament
The Master's Seminary

CHAPTER ONE

Psychology

The Psychology Epidemic and Its Cure[1]

John F. MacArthur Jr.

The church's right to counsel from the Bible has been reconfirmed in court rulings of recent times. Yet in many instances the church has surrendered that right and responsibility because of the "professionalization" of the counseling ministry among Christians. This is tragic because the behavioral sciences are not, as is commonly believed, scientific. Neither have they proven effective in changing the human heart. "Christian psychology," with its claim of a secret knowledge about dealing with people, has made deep inroads into the church, but it is no more than a duplication of its secular counterpart with Scripture references occasionally interspersed. A reliance on Christ, the "Wonderful Counselor," and God's sufficient Word as dispensed by spiritually gifted Christians to one another is the church's only solution in meeting the spiritual needs of its people.

* * * * *

In 1980, Grace Community Church became the object of a lawsuit charging that the pastors on staff were negligent for trying to help a suicidal young member of the church by giving him biblical truth. It was the first clergy malpractice case ever heard in the American court system. The secular media had a field day as the case dragged on for years. Some nationally aired tabloid-type programs even alleged that the church had encouraged the young man to kill himself, teaching him that suicide was a sure way to heaven. Of course, that was not true. He knew from Scripture that suicide is wrong. We urged him to let the Word of God lead him to intimate knowledge and appropriation of the resources available in the One who wanted to heal his troubled mind. Tragically, he refused our counsel and took his life.

One of the key issues the case raised was the question of whether churches should have the legal right to use the Bible in counseling troubled people. Many would argue that giving someone advice from Scripture is a simplistic approach to counseling. The Bible may be fine as an encouragement to the average person, they say, but people who have *real* problems need the help of a psychological expert.

Therefore, this lawsuit contended, church counselors are required to refer seriously depressed and suicidal people to the mental-health professionals. To attempt to counsel these troubled people from the Bible amounts to irresponsibility and negligence for which church counselors should be held morally and legally culpable.

The truth that came out in court received little or no coverage on the network news. Testimony showed that this young man *was* under the care of professional psychiatrists. In addition to the biblical direction he received from the pastoral staff, he had sought psychiatric treatment. Moreover, the staff had seen to it that he was examined by several medical doctors to rule out organic or chemical causes for his depression. He was receiving every kind of therapy available, but he chose to end his life anyway. We did all we could to help him; he rejected our counsel and turned his back on his spiritual sufficiency in Christ.

Not only did the courts view the issue as a First Amendment right of religious freedom into which government should not intrude, but all three times Grace Church won the case, the judges also expressed the opinion that the church had *not* failed in its responsibility to give him proper care. Their judgment was that the staff had more than fulfilled their legal and moral obligations by trying to help this young man who had sought our counsel. Eventually the case was appealed all the way to the United States Supreme Court. The High Court refused to hear it, thereby letting stand the California State Supreme Court's ruling, which vindicated the church. Most important of all, the case affirmed every church's constitutional right to counsel from the Bible, establishing a legal precedent to keep secular courts from encroaching on the area of counseling in the church.

THE PROFESSIONALIZATION OF THE COUNSELING MINISTRY

Unfortunately, the privilege of counseling people with biblical truth may be in jeopardy anyway, not because of any legal barrier imposed from outside the church, but because of the attitude toward Scripture within the church. During the trial, a number of "experts" gave testimony. Most surprising were the so-called Christian psychologists and psychiatrists who testified that the Bible alone is not sufficient to meet people's deepest personal and emotional needs. These men were arguing before a secular court that God's Word is not an adequate resource for counseling people about spiritual problems! What is truly appalling is the number of evangelicals who are willing to take the word of such "professionals" on this subject.[2]

Over the past decade a host of evangelical psychological clinics have sprung up. Though almost all of them claim to offer biblical counsel, most merely dispense secular psychology disguised in spiritual terminology.[3] Moreover, they are removing the counseling ministry from its proper arena in the church body and conditioning Christians to think of themselves as incompetent to counsel. Many pastors, feeling inadequate and perhaps afraid of possible malpractice litigation, are perfectly willing to let "professionals" take over what used to be seen as a vital pastoral responsibility.[4] Too many have bought the lie that a crucial realm of wisdom exists outside Scripture and one's relationship to Jesus Christ, and that some idea or technique from that extrabiblical realm holds the real key to helping people with their deep problems.[5]

True psychology (i.e., "the study of the soul") can be done only by Christians, since only Christians have the resources for understanding and transforming the soul. The secular discipline of psychology is based on godless assumptions[6] and evolutionary foundations and is capable of dealing with people only superficially and only on the temporal level. The Puritans, long before the arrival of godless psychology, identified their ministry with people as "soul work."

Scripture is the manual for all "soul work" and is so comprehensive in the diagnosis and treatment of every spiritual matter that, energized by the Holy Spirit in the believer, it leads to making one like Jesus Christ. This is the process of biblical sanctification.

It is reasonable for people to seek medical help for a broken leg, dysfunctional kidney, tooth cavity, or other physical malady. It is also sensible for those who are alcoholic, drug addicted, learning disabled, or traumatized by rape, incest, or severe battering to seek help in trying to cope with their trauma.

Certain techniques of human psychology can serve to lessen trauma or dependency and modify behavior in Christians or non-Christians equally. There may also be certain types of emotional illnesses where root causes are organic and where medication might be needed to stabilize an otherwise dangerous person. Such problems are relatively rare, however, and should not be used as examples to justify the indiscriminate use of secular psychological techniques for essentially spiritual problems. Dealing with the psychological and emotional issues of life in such ways is *not* sanctification.

"Christian psychology" as the expression is used today is an oxymoron. The word *psychology* no longer speaks of studying the soul. Instead it describes a diverse menagerie of therapies and theories that are fundamentally humanistic. The presuppositions and most of the doctrine of psychology cannot be successfully integrated with Christian truth.[7] In addition, the infusion of psychology into the teaching of the church has blurred the line between behavior modification and sanctification.

The path to wholeness is the path of spiritual sanctification. It is foolish to exchange the Wonderful Counselor, the spring of living water, for the sensual wisdom of earth and the stagnant water of behaviorism. The Lord Jesus reacted in a perfect and holy way to every temptation, trial, and trauma in life—the most severe ones that any human life could ever suffer. It should be clear that perfect victory over all life's troubles must be the result of being like Christ. No "soul worker" can lift another above the level of spiritual maturity he is on. So the supreme qualification for psychologists would be Christlikeness.

If one is a truly Christian psychologist, he must do soul work in the realm of the deep things of the Word and the Spirit and not be following around in the shallows of behavior modification. Why should a believer choose to do behavior modification when he has the tools for spiritual transformation? This would be like a surgeon wreaking havoc with a butter knife instead of using a scalpel. The most skilled counselor is the one who most carefully, prayerfully, and faithfully applies the divine spiritual resources to the process of sanctification, shaping another into the image of Jesus Christ.

The stampede to embrace the doctrines of secular psychology may be the most serious threat to the life of the church today. These doctrines are a mass of human ideas that Satan has placed in the church as though they were powerful life-changing truths from God. Most psychologists epitomize neo-gnosticism, claiming to have secret knowledge for solving people's real problems. Some of them even claim to perform a therapeutic technique they call "Christian counseling" when, in reality, they are using secular theory with biblical references tacked on to treat spiritual problems.[8]

The result is that pastors, biblical scholars, teachers of Scripture, and caring believers using the Word of God are disdained as naive, simplistic, and altogether inadequate counselors.[9] Bible reading and prayer are commonly belittled as "pat answers," incomplete solutions for persons struggling with depression or anxiety.[10] Scripture, the Holy Spirit, Christ, prayer, and grace are the traditional solutions Christian counselors have pointed people to. But the average Christian today has come to believe that none of them *really* offers the cure for people's woes.[11]

HOW SCIENTIFIC ARE THE
BEHAVIORAL SCIENCES?

Psychology is not a uniform body of scientific knowledge, like thermodynamics or organic chemistry. It rather refers to a complex menagerie of ideas and theories, many of which are contradictory. Psychology has not proven itself capable of dealing effectively with the human mind and with mental and emotional processes. Thus it can hardly be regarded as a science.

Many will object to classifying psychology as a pseudo-science,[12] but that is exactly what it is—the most recent of several human inventions designed to explain, diagnose, and treat behavioral problems without dealing with moral and spiritual issues. Little more than a century ago, the debate was over a different kind of "behavioral science" called phrenology. Phrenology held that personality characteristics were determined by the shape of someone's skull. The phrenologists' diagrams were maps of the head with specific areas labeled, showing which zone of the brain determined a particular emotion or characteristic. A phrenologist would feel people's skulls, diagnosing their problems by the location of bumps on their heads.[13]

If you think behavioral science has advanced greatly since then, ask yourself how reasonable it is to surround an adult in the fetal position with pillows so he can get back in touch with his prenatal anxieties.[14] Given the choice, someone poking around on one's head sounds preferable.

Modern psychologists use hundreds of counseling models and techniques based on a myriad of conflicting theories, so it is impossible to speak of psychotherapy as though it were a unified and consistent science.[15] However, the following views, popularized by psychology, have filtered down into the church from the assorted stuff in the psychological tank and are having a profound and disturbing effect on its approach to helping people:

- Human nature is basically good.
- People have the answers to their problems inside them.
- The key to understanding and correcting a person's attitudes and actions lies somewhere in his past.
- Individuals' problems are the results of what someone else has done to them.
- Human problems can be purely psychological in nature—unrelated to any spiritual or physical condition.
- Deep-seated problems can be solved only by professional counselors using therapy.

• Scripture, prayer, and the Holy Spirit are inadequate and simplistic resources for solving certain types of problems.

Ironically, even before the church became so infatuated with "behavioral science," those who know it best were beginning to question whether psychotherapy is a science at all. Eleven years ago, *Time* magazine ran a cover story called "Psychiatry on the Couch." It said,

> On every front, psychiatry seems to be on the defensive. . . . Many psychiatrists want to abandon treatment of ordinary, everyday neurotics ("the worried well") to psychologists and the amateur Pop therapists. After all, does it take a hard-won M.D. degree . . . to chat sympathetically and tell a patient you're-much-too-hard-on-yourself? And if psychiatry is a medical treatment, why can its practitioners not provide measurable scientific results like those obtained by other doctors?
>
> Psychiatrists themselves acknowledge that their profession often smacks of modern alchemy—full of jargon, obfuscation and mystification, but precious little real knowledge. . . .
>
> As always, psychiatrists are their own severest critics. Thomas Szasz, long the most outspoken gadfly of his profession, insisted that there is really no such thing as mental illness, only normal problems of living. E. Fuller Torrey, another antipsychiatry psychiatrist, is willing to concede that there are a few brain diseases, like schizophrenia, but says they can be treated with only a handful of drugs that could be administered by general practitioners or internists. . . . By contrast, the Scottish psychiatrist and poet R. D. Laing is sure that schizophrenia is real—and that it is good for you. Explains Laing: it is a kind of psychedelic epiphany, far superior to normal experience.
>
> Even mainline practitioners are uncertain that psychiatry can tell the insane from the sane.[16]

The article went on to chronicle the failures of psychiatry, noting that "of all patients, one-third are eventually 'cured,' one-third are helped somewhat, and one-third are not helped at all."[17] But, as the article further stated,

> The trouble is that most therapies, including some outlandish ones, also claim some improvement for two-thirds of their

patients. Critics argue that many patients go into analysis after a traumatic experience, such as divorce or a loved one's
death, and are bound to do better anyway when the shock
wears off. One study shows improvement for people merely
on a waiting list for psychoanalytic treatment; presumably
the simple decision to seek treatment is helpful.[18]

The article concludes with a pessimistic forecast by Ross Baldessarini,
a psychiatrist and biochemist at the Mailman Research Center. He told
Time, "We are not going to find the causes and cures of mental illness in
the foreseeable future."[19]

Several years later, a conference in Phoenix, Arizona, brought together
the world's leading experts on psychotherapy for what was billed as the
largest meeting ever on the subject. The conference, called "The Evolution of Psychotherapy," drew seven thousand mental-health experts from
all over the world. It was the largest such gathering in history, billed by
its organizer as the Woodstock of psychotherapy. Out of it came several
stunning revelations.

The *Los Angeles Times,* for example, quoted Laing, who "said that he
couldn't think of any fundamental insight into human relations that has
resulted from a century of psychotherapy. 'I don't think we've gone beyond Socrates, Shakespeare, Tolstoy, or even Flaubert by the age of 15,'
he said."[20] He added,

> "I don't think psychiatry is a science at all. It's not like chem-
> istry or physics where we build up a body of knowledge and
> progress."
> He said that in his current personal struggle with depres-
> sion, humming a favorite tune to himself (he favors one called
> "Keep Right on to the End of the Road") sometimes is of
> greater help than anything psychotherapy offers.[21]

Time magazine, reporting on the conference, noted that in a panel
discussion on schizophrenia, three out of four "experts" said there is no
such disease.[22]

> R. D. Laing, the favorite shrink of student rebels in the '60s,
> retains his romantic opinion of schizophrenics as brave vic-
> tims who are defying a cruel culture. He suggested that many
> people are diagnosed as schizophrenic simply because they
> sleep during the day and stay awake at night. Schizophrenia
> did not exist until the word was invented, he said. . . . At a

later panel, a woman in the audience asked Laing how he would deal with schizophrenics. Laing bobbed and weaved for 27 minutes and finally offered the only treatment possible for people he does not view as sick: "I treat them exactly the same way I treat anybody else. I conduct myself by the ordinary rules of courtesy and politeness."[23]

One clear truth emerged in the conference: among therapists there is little agreement. There is no unified "science" of psychotherapy, only a cacophony of clashing theories and therapies. Dr. Joseph Wolpe, a leading pioneer of behavioral therapy, characterized the Phoenix conference as "a babel of conflicting voices."[24]

Indeed it was. One specialist, Jay Haley, described what he called his "shaggy dog" technique. He evidently means his technique is like a fluffy animal that appears to be fat until it gets wet—there appears to be more substance than really exists. This is his approach to therapy:

> Get the patient to make an absolute commitment to change, then guarantee a cure but do not tell the patient what it is for several weeks. "Once you postpone, you never lose them as patients," he said. "They have to find out what the cure is." One bulimic who ate in binges and threw up five to 25 times a day was told she would be cured if she gave the therapist a penny the first time she vomited and doubled the sum each time she threw up. Says Haley: "They quickly figure out that it doubles so fast that they can owe the therapist hundreds of thousands of dollars in a few days, so they stop."[25]

Jeffrey Zeig, organizer of the conference, said as many as a hundred different theories may exist in the United States alone. Most of them, he said, are "doomed to fizzle."[26]

Not only do psychologists sell supposed cures for a high price, but they also invent diseases for which the cures are needed. Their marketing strategy has been effective. Invent problems or difficulties, harp on them until people think they are hopelessly afflicted, then peddle a remedy. Some of the supposed problems are pathetically trite. Self-image, looks, codependency, emotional abuse, midlife crisis, unfulfilled expectations—today's "infirmities" were once seen more accurately as the pains of selfishness. Egocentricity has become a major market strategy for psychotherapists. By fostering people's natural tendency toward self-indulgence, psychology has sold itself to an eager public. The church has witlessly jumped on the bandwagon.

Psychology is no more a science than the atheistic evolutionary theory upon which it is based. Like theistic evolution, Christian psychology is an attempt to harmonize two inherently contradictory systems of thought. Modern psychology and the Bible cannot be blended without serious compromise to or utter abandonment of the principle of Scripture's sufficiency.

Though it has become a profitable business, psychotherapy cannot solve anyone's spiritual problems. At best it can occasionally use human insight to superficially modify behavior. It succeeds or fails for Christians and non-Christians equally because it is only a temporal adjustment—a sort of mental chiropractic. Even experts admit it cannot change the human heart.

THE FAILURE OF "CHRISTIAN" PSYCHOLOGY

Meanwhile, however, the attitude within the church is to accept psychotherapy more than ever. If the Christian media serve as a barometer of the whole church, a dramatic shift is taking place. Christian radio, for instance, once a bastion of Bible teaching and Christian music, is overrun with talk shows, pop psychology, and phone-in psychotherapy. Preaching the Bible is passé. Psychologists and radio counselors are the new heroes of evangelicalism. Christian radio is the major advertising tool that has made psychology extremely lucrative.

The church is thereby ingesting heavy doses of dogma from psychology, adopting secular "wisdom" and attempting to sanctify it by calling it Christian, thereby redefining evangelicalism's most fundamental values. "Mental and emotional health" is a new buzzword. It is not a biblical concept, though many seem to equate it with spiritual wholeness. Sin is called sickness, so people think it requires therapy, not repentance. Habitual sin is called addictive or compulsive behavior, and many surmise its solution is medical care rather than moral correction.[27]

Human therapies are embraced most eagerly by the spiritually weak, those who are shallow or ignorant of biblical truth and who are unwilling to accept the path of suffering that leads to spiritual maturity and deeper communion with God. The unfortunate effect is that these people remain immature, held back by a self-imposed dependence on some pseudo-Christian method or psychoquackery that actually stifles real growth.

The more secular psychology influences the church, the further people move from a biblical perspective on problems and solutions. One-on-one therapists are replacing the Word, God's chief means of grace (1 Cor. 1:21; Heb. 4:12). The counsel these professionals dispense is often spiritually disastrous. Not long ago I listened aghast as a

Christian psychologist on live radio counseled a caller to express anger at his therapist by making an obscene gesture at him. "Go ahead!" he told the caller. "It's an honest expression of your feelings. Don't try to keep your anger inside."

"What about my friends?" the caller asked. "Should I react that way to all of them when I'm angry?"

"Why, sure!" this counselor said. "You can do it to anyone, whenever you feel like it. Except those who you think won't understand—they won't be good therapists for you." This is a paraphrase of the conversation, the broadcast of which is recorded on tape. Actually, the counselor suggested something much more explicit, but it is inappropriate to put it in print.

That same week, I heard another popular Christian broadcast that offers live counseling to callers nationwide. A woman called and said she has had a problem with compulsive fornication for years. She said she goes to bed with "anyone and everyone" and feels powerless to change her behavior.

The counselor suggested that her conduct is her way of striking back, a result of wounds inflicted by her passive father and overbearing mother. "There's no simple road to recovery," this radio therapist told her. "Your problem won't go away immediately—it's an addiction, and these things require extended counseling. You will need years of therapy to overcome your need for illicit sex." It was then suggested that the caller find a church that would be tolerant while she worked her way out of the "painful wounds" that were "making" her fornicate.

What kind of advice is that? First, the counselor in effect gave the woman permission to defer obedience to a clear command of Scripture, "Flee immorality" (1 Cor. 6:18; cf. also 1 Thess. 4:3). Second, he blamed her parents and justified her vengeance toward them. Third, he seemed to suggest she could taper off gradually from her sin—under therapy, of course.

Furthermore, he gave his nationwide audience the clear message that he has no real confidence in the Holy Spirit's power to transform a person's heart and behavior immediately. Worse, he encouraged churches to tolerate a person's sexual sin until therapy begins to work.

The profound simplicity of Galatians 5:16 is in contrast to both radio counselors' advice: "Walk by the Spirit, and you will not carry out the desire of the flesh." Is it possible that years of therapy could bring people to the point of walking by the Spirit? Certainly not if the therapist is someone who recommends obscene gestures, delayed repentance, and churches tolerant of chronic immorality! No biblical justification for such counsel exists. In fact, it flatly contradicts God's Word. The apostle Paul instructed the Corinthian church to turn an adulterer over to Satan, putting him out of the church fellowship (1 Corinthians 5).

Thanks is due to God for men and women in the church who depend on the Bible when counseling others, for godly counselors who urge troubled people to pray and who point them to Scripture, to God, and to the fullness of His resources to meet every need. There is no quarrel with those who use either common sense or social sciences as a helpful observer's platform to look at human conduct and develop tools to assist people in getting some external controls on their behavior. This may be useful as a first step for providing a real spiritual cure for them. But a wise counselor realizes that all behavioral therapy stops on the surface, far short of solutions to actual needs of the soul which can be resolved only in Christ.

On the other hand, those who exalt psychology above Scripture, intercession, and the perfect sufficiency of God should not be tolerated. People who mix psychology with divine resources and sell the mixture as a spiritual elixir should not be encouraged. Their methodology amounts to a tacit admission that what God has given in Christ is not adequate to meet the deepest needs of troubled lives.

God Himself does not think very highly of counselors who claim to represent Him, but rely instead on human wisdom. Job 12:17–20 says,

> He makes counselors walk barefoot [a sign of humiliation],
> He makes fools of judges.
> He loosens the bond of kings,
> And binds their loins with a girdle.
> He makes priests walk barefoot,
> And overthrows the secure ones.
> He deprives the trusted ones of speech,
> And takes away the discernment of the elders.

God's wisdom is so vastly superior to man's that the greatest human counselors are made into a spectacle. Verses 24–25 of Job 12 add,

> He deprives of intelligence the chiefs of the earth's people,
> And makes them wander in a pathless waste.
> They grope in darkness with no light,
> And He makes them stagger like a drunken man.

If anyone had to endure the folly of well-intentioned human counselors, it was Job. Their irrelevant, useless advice was as much a grief to him as the satanic afflictions he suffered.

The depth to which "sanctified" psychotherapy can sink is quite profound. A local newspaper recently featured an article about a thirty-four-bed clinic that has opened in Southern California to treat "Christian sex addicts."[28] (The article does not explain the reasons for beds in this kind of clinic.) According to the account, the clinic is affiliated with a large and well-known Protestant church in the area. Its staff comprises specialists described as "real pioneers in the area [of sexual addiction]. These are all legitimate, licensed psychotherapists who happen to have a strong Christian orientation to therapy," according to the director.[29]

Does their "Christian" orientation happen to be solid enough to allow these psychotherapists to admit that lasciviousness is sin? Evidently not. Interviews with several of them were in the article. They consistently used the terms *illness, problem, conflict, compulsive behavior, treatment,* and *therapy*. Words with moral overtones were carefully avoided. Sin and repentance were never mentioned.

Worse than this, these so-called experts scoffed at the power of God's Word to transform a heart and break the bondage of sexual sin. The article quoted the center's program director as he explained why he believes his treatment center specifically for Christians is essential: "There are some groups of Christians who believe the Bible is all you need."[30]

That statement is the echo of neo-gnosticism. Belittling those who believe the Bible is sufficient, these latter-day "clouds without water" (Jude 12) insist that they are privy to a higher, more sophisticated secret knowledge that holds the real answer to what troubles the human soul. Christians must not be intimidated by their false claims. No higher knowledge, no hidden truth, nothing besides the all-sufficient resources that are in Christ can change the human heart.

Any counselor who wants to honor God and be effective must see the goal of his efforts as leading a person to the sufficiency of Christ. The view that man is capable of solving his own problems, or that people can help one another by "therapy" or other merely human means, denies the doctrine of human depravity and man's need for God. It replaces the Spirit's transforming power with impotent human wisdom.

WONDERFUL COUNSELOR

It is significant that one of the biblical names of Christ is Wonderful Counselor (Isa. 9:6). He is the highest and ultimate One to whom Christians may turn for counsel, and His Word is the well from which they may draw divine wisdom. What could be more wonderful than that? In fact, one of the most glorious aspects of Christ's perfect sufficiency is the wonderful counsel and great wisdom He supplies in times of despair, confusion, fear, anxiety, and sorrow. He is the quintessential Counselor.

That is not to denigrate the importance of Christians counseling each other. A crucial need exists for biblically sound counseling ministries within the body of Christ. The important role of those who are spiritually gifted to offer encouragement, discernment, comfort, advice, compassion, and help to others is unquestionable. The truth is that one of the very problems leading to the current plague of bad counsel is the failure of churches to do as well as they could have in enabling people with those kinds of gifts to minister effectively. The complexities of the contemporary scene make it more difficult than ever to take the time necessary to listen well, serve others through compassionate personal involvement, and otherwise provide the close fellowship necessary for the church body to enjoy spiritual health and vitality.

Churches have looked to psychology to fill the gap, but it has not worked. Professional psychologists are not a substitute for spiritually gifted people, and the counsel psychology offers cannot replace biblical wisdom and divine power. Moreover, psychology tends to make people dependent on a therapist, whereas people with spiritual gifts always turn people back to an all-sufficient Savior and His all-sufficient Word.

King David was a person who occasionally sought advice from human counselors, but he always turned to God for answers in the end. As many of the psalms reveal, he was especially dependent on God alone when he struggled with personal problems or emotions. When hit with depression or inner turmoil, he turned to God and wrestled in prayer. When the problem was his own sin, he was repentant, broken, and contrite. He prayed, "Examine me, O LORD, and try me; test my mind and my heart" (Ps. 26:2). The spiritually mature always turn to God for help in times of anxiety, distress, confusion, or unrest in the soul, and they are assured of wise counsel and deliverance.

The reason for this assured deliverance is that every need of the human soul is ultimately spiritual. Such a thing as a "psychological problem" unrelated to spiritual or physical causes is nonexistent. God supplies divine resources sufficient to satisfy completely all the spiritual needs. David understood that. His writings reflect the depth of human experience, emotion, and spiritual insight of one who had fully experienced the extremities of life. He knew the exhilaration of going from shepherd to king. He wrote of everything from absolute triumph to bitter discouragement. He wrestled with pain so deep he could hardly bear to live. His own son Absalom tried to kill him and was then killed. He suffered from horrible guilt because of immorality and murder. His children brought him constant grief. He struggled to understand both the nature of God and his own heart. Of God he said, "Great is the LORD" (Ps. 145:3), while of himself he said, "Wash me thoroughly from my iniquity, And cleanse me from my sin" (Ps. 51:2). He told God what he felt and cried out for relief, though he admitted God had every right to punish him.

At the end of some of David's psalms he looked out a window of hope, and sometimes he did not. But David always went to God because he understood God's sovereignty and his own depravity.

Christians of this day and time, following David's example, should rest assured that their all-sufficient Savior alone has the answers to their needs and the power to apply those answers. They should stand convinced that those answers are to be found in the truth about God revealed in His Word, which is itself absolutely sufficient. The sufficient God has revealed Himself in His sufficient Word.

ENDNOTES

[1] This chapter is adapted from chapter 3 of John F. MacArthur Jr., *Our Sufficiency in Christ* (Waco, Tex.: Word, 1991), 55–77.

[2] Cf. Martin and Deidre Bobgan, *PsychoHeresy* (Santa Barbara, Calif.: EastGate, 1987), 53–54. The Bobgans list eight evidences of the "psychologizing of the church."

[3] "Nearly all recent counseling books for ministers, even conservative ones, are written from the Freudian perspective in the sense that they rest largely upon the presuppositions of the Freudian ethic of non-responsibility" (Jay E. Adams, *Competent to Counsel* [Grand Rapids: Baker, 1970], 17–18). Adam's extraordinarily accurate analysis of the state of counseling in evangelicalism is now more than twenty years old, but is more apropos than ever. He has given the church an indispensable corrective to several trends that are eating away at the church's spiritual vitality. Christian leaders would do well to heed his still-timely admonition.

[4] Jay E. Adams, *More Than Redemption* (Phillipsburg, N.J.: Presbyterian and Reformed, 1979), x–xi.

[5] E.g., Gary R. Collins, *Christian Counseling: A Comprehensive Guide* (Waco, Tex.: Word, 1980), 19. Collins believes the Bible "does not claim to be nor is it meant to be God's sole revelation about people-helping." He writes, "During the past century, God has permitted psychologists to develop careful research tools for studying human behavior and professional journals for sharing their findings. Perhaps hundreds of thousands of people have come for help and professional counselors have learned what makes people tick and how they can change."

[6] Cf. the comments of a psychological counselor cited in Bobgan, *PsychoHeresy*, 5–6.: "At the present time there is no acceptable Christian psychology that is markedly different from non-Christian psychology. It is difficult to imply that we function in a manner that is fundamentally distinct from our non-Christian colleagues."

[7] Ibid., 5–6.

[8] E.g., Frank B. Minirth, *Christian Psychiatry* (Old Tappan, N.J.: Revell, 1977), 186. Minirth advises counselors to "interject Scripture" with caution: "Proper timing and readiness are important. Once the counselee knows the counselor really cares, Scripture can usually be shared without any offense. The Scripture must meet the specific need of the individual, and a few verses are preferable to many."

[9] E.g., Larry Crabb recounts an anecdote where he challenged a friend committed to the utter sufficiency of Scripture to suggest how he would counsel an anorexic girl. Crabb writes, "It is difficult to come up with a biblical answer to a question that the Bible never seems to consider. My friend therefore changed the question from the one I (as well as the girl's parents) was asking to one that, in his mind, we *should* have been asking. . . .

"Two passages in the Bible (1 Cor. 3:16–17 and 2 Cor. 6:16) tell us that we are the temple of God; one passage indicates that our bodies are themselves temples of the Holy Spirit (1 Cor. 6:19). My friend turned to those verses and explained that anorexia can be understood as rebellion against our responsibility to care for the Spirit's temple. This so-called biblical counseling will focus on developing in the anorexic a respect for her body and exhorting her to treat her body accordingly. At best, the results of such counseling will be external conformity. The counselee will not be freed by truth to enter more deeply into loving relationship with God or others.

"When we limit the questions we are allowed to ask to those that the Bible specifically answers, the result will often be a nonthinking and simplistic understanding of life and its problems . . ." (Larry Crabb, *Understanding People* [Grand Rapids: Zondervan, 1987], 57–58).

[10] Ibid., 203.

[11] Crabb believes the church "promote[s] superficial adjustments while psychotherapists, with or without biblical foundations, . . . do a better job than the church of restoring troubled people to more effective func-

tioning" (ibid., 129). Later he adds, "Secularists sometimes seem to have a corner on honestly facing the disturbing complexity of life while Christians recite clichés that push away real questions of the heart. As a result, nonbelievers often help people with emotional problems more effectively than Christians" (ibid., 211).

[12] Most advocates of psychology assume rather than argue that psychology is truly scientific (cf. Collins, *Christian Counseling*, 19).

[13] Leo Steiner wrote, "Where will psychoanalysis be even 25 years from now? . . . I predict it will take its place along with phrenology and mesmerism" (Leo Steiner, "Are Psychoanalysis and Religious Counseling Compatible?" (paper read to the Society for Scientific Study of Religion, Harvard University, November 1958, cited by Adams, *Competent*, 18–19). Obviously Steiner's prediction failed to materialize, but his characterization of psychoanalysis was right on target.

[14] Primal therapy was popularized by Arthur Janov, *The Primal Scream* (New York: Dell, 1970). Daniel Casriel, *A Scream Away from Happiness* (New York: Grosset & Dunlap, 1972), expanded on Janov's ideas and formulated a group scream therapy, where group members hold hands and shriek at each other to work out their problems.

[15] Sigmund Koch, "Psychology Cannot Be a Coherent Science," *Psychology Today* (September 1969): 66.

[16] "Psychiatry on the Couch," *Time,* 2 April 1979, 74.

[17] Ibid., 79.

[18] Ibid.

[19] Ibid., 82.

[20] Ann Japenga, "Great Minds on the Mind Assemble for Conference," *Los Angeles Times,* 18 December 1985, p. 5, col. 1.

[21] Ibid., 17.

[22] "A Therapist in Every Corner," *Time,* 23 December 1985, 59.

[23] Ibid.

[24] Japenga, "Great Minds," 16.

[25] "Every Corner," 59.

[26] Japenga, "Great Minds," 16.

[27] Adams responds skillfully to this kind of thinking, citing O. Hobart Mowrer, *The Crisis in Psychiatry and Religion* (Adams, *Competent,* xvi–xvii).

[28] Nicole Brodeur, "Center Aids Christian Sex Addicts," *Orange County Register,* 13 February 1989, 1.

[29] Ibid.

[30] Ibid.

CHAPTER TWO

Modern-Day Prophecy

Fallible New Testament Prophecy/Prophets? A Critique of Wayne Grudem's Hypothesis

F. David Farnell

Spiritual gifts have long been a major topic of discussion in evangelicalism, but in recent years the focus has shifted somewhat from a discussion of gifts like tongues to the gift of prophecy. Wayne A. Grudem has proposed a novel definition of prophecy that he attempts to support from the NT. He traces part of his definition to cessationists and part to Charismatics in hopes of finding a middle ground acceptable to both. A central platform in Grudem's hypothesis is Ephesians 2:20, a verse whose interpretation he misrepresents because of a grammatical misunderstanding. Other weaknesses in his theory include his assumption of a strict discontinuity from OT to NT prophecy, a mistaken understanding of the prestige of the NT prophet, and a misapprehension of the need of continuous evaluation of NT prophecy.

* * * * *

SPIRITUAL GIFTS AS A CENTER OF CONTROVERSY

Controversy and crisis are no strangers to the Christian church. When Paul penned 1 Corinthians, this first-century church was already embroiled in turmoil over the nature and practice of spiritual gifts. Misconceptions and abuse of the gifts in Christian worship were rampant. A three-man delegation from the church (1 Cor. 7:1; 16:17) asked Paul for clarification on gifts such as prophecy, tongues, and knowledge (1 Cor. 13:8). The outcome of the turbulence in Corinth is unknown, but the second century saw the same confusion in the Montanist heresy. Now the tumult has reemerged in the twentieth century in the form of Pentecostalism, Neopentecostalism, and movements variously labelled as "Charismatic," "Vineyard," "Signs and Wonders," and "Third Wave."

The gift of tongues (cf. Acts 2:1–13; 1 Cor. 14:2ff.) has drawn a disproportionate amount of this debate until about the last fifteen years. Most recently, however, several books have dealt with the gift of prophecy. Since the nature and purpose of this gift had not been closely defined by either side of the controversy, this gift has provided a fertile topic as a new phase in the discussion of temporary and permanent spiritual gifts. Fundamental questions about the nature of this gift now threaten to become, if they have not done so already, a major storm center in NT theology and church worship. Recent works have challenged long-held views of what NT prophecy is. Among noncharismatics it has been relatively standard to regard the gift as foundational for the church and temporary in nature.[1] Charismatics who may be loosely labelled "noncessationists"—i.e., they deny that any of the spiritual gifts ceased after the first century—generally see prophecy as presently active as it was during the first seventy years after the church began.[2]

NEW CONTROVERSY OVER
THE GIFT OF PROPHECY

The recent surge of interest in the prophetic gift has witnessed a crossing of the traditional boundaries by some individuals in an apparent attempt to find a mediating position between the two perspectives. A prominent example of this is Wayne A. Grudem. Belonging to the Reformed tradition that is cessationist in background, Grudem has crossed traditional lines of understanding in proposing a compromise between the cessationist and noncessationist viewpoints regarding prophecy. In his recently published work on the subject, he writes,

> In this book I am suggesting an understanding of the gift of prophecy which would require a bit of modification in the views of each of these . . . groups. I am asking that the charismatics go on using the gift of prophecy, but that they stop calling it "a word from the Lord"—simply because that label makes it sound exactly like the Bible in authority, and leads to much misunderstanding. . . .
>
> On the other side, I am asking those in the cessationist camp to give serious thought to the possibility that prophecy in ordinary New Testament churches was not equal to

Scripture in authority, but was simply a very human—and sometimes partially mistaken—report of something the Holy Spirit brought to someone's mind. And I am asking that they think again about those arguments for the cessation of certain gifts. . . .

I should make it very clear at the beginning that I am not saying that the charismatic and cessationist views are mostly wrong. Rather, I think they are both mostly right (in the things they count essential), and I think that an adjustment in how they understand the nature of prophecy (especially its authority) has the potential for bringing about a resolution of this issue which would safeguard items that both sides see as crucial.[3]

By calling for a compromise between cessationists and noncessationists regarding the prophetic and other related gifts, Grudem has stirred up a "hornets' nest" of discussion on the gifts once again.[4]

He offers his own new definition of Christian prophecy, one that differs markedly from a traditional understanding: "prophecy in ordinary New Testament churches was not equal to Scripture in authority, but was simply a very human—and sometimes partially mistaken—report of something the Holy Spirit brought to someone's mind."[5] In other words, prophecy consists of "telling something God has spontaneously brought to mind."[6]

He traces his definition to both the cessationists and the charismatics. In common with the former he takes prophecy as noncompetitive with the authority of the canonical NT because of the close of the canon at the end of the apostolic era, but he concurs with the charismatic understanding that prophecy preserves "the spontaneous, powerful working of the Holy Spirit, giving 'edification, encouragement, and comfort' which speaks directly to the needs of the moment and causes people to realize that 'God is certainly among you' (1 Cor. 14:25)."[7] OT prophets are not comparable to NT prophets, but to NT apostles, according to his theory.[8]

Consequently, NT prophets were "simply reporting in their own words what God would bring to mind, and . . . these prophecies did not have the authority of the words of the Lord."[9] Grudem writes,

Much more commonly, prophet and prophecy were used of ordinary Christians who spoke not with absolute divine authority, but simply to report something God had laid on their hearts or brought to their minds. There are many indications in the New Testament that this ordinary gift of prophecy had authority less than that of the Bible, and even less than that of recognized Bible teaching in the early church.[10]

In other words, prophecy depended on a revelation from the Holy Spirit, but the prophet could either understand it imperfectly or report it inaccurately, or both.[11]

Only NT apostles spoke inspired words.[12] The very words of NT prophets were not inspired as were those of OT prophets.[13] This leaves Grudem with two forms of NT prophecy: nonauthoritative and authoritative (i.e., apostolic).

The crucial point of his thesis is that the apostles, not the NT prophets, were the true successors of the OT prophets and, like their earlier counterparts, spoke under the authority derived from the plenary verbal inspiration of their words.[14] This kind of gift is distinguished from that exercised at Corinth (cf. 1 Corinthians 12–14), Thessalonica (1 Thess. 5:19–21), Tyre (Acts 21:4), Ephesus (Acts 19:6), and other places (e.g., Agabus, Acts 11:28; 21:10–11). Only the general content of this secondary prophecy can be vouched for, with allowances made for its being partially mistaken.

It was therefore allegedly open to being disobeyed without blame (Acts 21:4), critical assessment by the whole congregation (1 Cor. 14:29), and outright rejection as subordinate to Paul's apostolic revelation (1 Cor. 14:37–38). According to Grudem, "these prophecies did not have the authority of the words of the Lord."

GRAMMATICALLY RELATED WEAKNESSES OF GRUDEM'S HYPOTHESIS

The newly proposed theory of a respected professor at Trinity Evangelical Divinity School has multiple weaknesses, only a few of which can be treated here. A discussion of these weaknesses affords an excellent opportunity to present by contrast a clearer picture of NT prophecy by focusing on characteristics that heretofore have been largely overlooked in discussions of this subject.

Misuse of Sharp's rule. Grudem's most significant argument stems from Ephesians 2:20 and an application of a grammatical rule dealing with two nouns connected by the Greek word for "and" and governed by only one article. This argument is seriously flawed as will be shown below.

Regarding Ephesians 2:20 he writes,

The absence of the second article in τῶν ἀποστόλων καὶ προφητῶν [tōn apostolōn kai prophētōn, "the apostles and prophets"] means that the writer views the apostles and prophets as a single group, and that we cannot immediately be sure whether that group has one or two components. But the grammatical structure clearly allows for the possibility that one group with one component is meant, for there are several instances in the New Testament where one definite article governs two or more nouns joined by καί and it is clear that one group with only one component (or one person) is implied. In Ephesians 4:11 it is noteworthy: ἔδωκεν τοὺς μὲν ἀποστόλους, τοὺς δὲ προφήτας, τοὺς δὲ εὐαγγελιστάς, τοὺς δὲ ποιμένας καὶ διδασκάλους [edōken tous men apostolous, tous de prophētas, tous de euaggelistas, tous de poimenas kai didaskalous, "He gave some as apostles, some as prophets, some as evangelists, some as pastors and teachers"]. The pastors and teachers are the same people but two different functions are named.[15]

At this point Grudem lists "most of the clear examples of this type of construction from the Pauline corpus, along with some scattered examples from elsewhere in the New Testament."[16] His list includes examples of the same person described with two or more titles (Rom. 16:7; Eph. 4:11; 6:21; Phil. 2:25; Col. 1:2; 4:7; Philem. 1; Heb. 3:1; 1 Peter 2:25; 2 Peter 3:18), of phrases in which God is named with a similar form (Rom. 15:6; 2 Cor. 1:3; 11:31; Gal. 1:4; Eph. 1:3; 5:20; Phil. 4:20; Col. 1:3; 3:17; 1 Thess. 1:3; 3:11 [2x]; [1 Tim., sic] 6:15; Titus 2:13; 2 Peter 1:1, 11), of nonpersonal objects occasionally referred to in this way (1 Thess. 3:7; Titus 2:13), and of participles and infinitives in this type of construction (1 Cor. 11:29; Gal. 1:7; 1 Thess. 5:12).[17] From these usages Grudem concludes,

> This does not imply that Ephesians 2:20 *must* mean "the apostles who are also prophets," for there are many other examples which could be listed where one group with two distinct components is named (cf. Acts 13:50). Nevertheless, it must be noted that I was unable to find in the Pauline corpus even one clear example analogous to Acts 13:50 or 15:2, where two distinct people or classes of people (as opposed to things) are joined by καί (kai, "and") and only one article is used. This may be more or less significant, depending in part on one's view of the authorship of Ephesians. But it should

not be overlooked that when Paul wants to distinguish two people or groups he does not hesitate to use a second article (1 Cor. 3:8; 8:6; etc.; cf. Eph. 3:10). And I have listed above over twenty Pauline examples where clearly one person or group is implied by this type of construction.

So Ephesians 2:20 views "the apostles and prophets" as one group. Grammatically, that group could have two components, but such an interpretation would not be exactly in accord with Pauline usage. If the author had meant to speak of a two-component group he certainly did not make this meaning very clear to his readers (as he could have done by adding another τῶν (tōn, "the") before προφητῶν (prophētōn, "prophets"). On the other hand, the large number of NT parallels shows that "the apostles who are also prophets" would have easily been understood by the readers if other factors in the context allowed for or favored this interpretation.[18]

From this reasoning he concludes that Ephesians 2:20 is speaking of apostle-prophets who are distinguished from those who are simply prophets described in such other passages as 1 Corinthians 12–14. Apostle-prophets, he says, were limited to the first-century church, but the other kind continues to the present day.

Though the case for this interpretation of Ephesians 2:20 may appear impressive, it is problematic for a number of reasons. Most basically, it rests on a fundamental error and a commonly misunderstood application of Sharp's rule.[19] The rule is as follows:

When the copulative καί (kai, "and") connects nouns of the same case [viz. nouns (either substantive or adjective, or participles) of personal description, respecting office, dignity, affinity, or connection, and attributes, properties, or qualities, good or ill,] if the article ὁ (ho, "the"), or any of its cases, precedes the first of the said nouns or participles, and is not repeated before the second noun or participle, the latter always relates to the same person that is expressed or described by the first noun or participle: i.e., it denotes a further description of the first named person. . . .[20]

Though challenged repeatedly, no one has succeeded in overturning or refuting it insofar as the NT is concerned.[21]

Yet four lesser known stipulations of Sharp's rule are often overlooked. These must be met if the two nouns in the construction are to be referred to the same person. The four are (1) both nouns must be personal; (2) both nouns must be common nouns, that is, not proper names; (3) both nouns must be in the same case; and (4) both nouns must be in the singular.[22] Sharp did not clearly delineate these stipulations in conjunction with his first rule, so most grammars are ambiguous in these areas.[23]

Most exegetes, including Grudem, reflect no awareness of the qualifications, and hence apply Sharp's first rule hastily and without proper refinements. For instance, though the fourth stipulation about the rule's limitation to singular nouns only was not *clearly* stated in the first rule, a perusal of Sharp's monograph reveals that he insisted that the rule applies absolutely to the singular only.[24] The limitation may be *inferred* via an argument from silence in his statement of the rule: "the latter always relates to the same person . . . i.e., it denotes a further description of the first-named person."[25] Later in the monograph he offers this clarification: "There is no exception or instance of the like mode of expression that I know of, which necessarily requires a construction be different from what is laid down, EXCEPT that the nouns be proper names, or in the plural number, in which there are numerous exceptions."[26] Again at another point he states that impersonal constructions are within the purview of the second, third, fifth, and sixth rules, but not the first or fourth.[27]

Middleton, whose early study on the Greek article is still highly respected,[28] was the first Greek grammarian to accept the validity of Sharp's rule. He notes many exceptions to Sharp's rule when plural nouns are involved:

> What reason can be alleged, why the practice in Plural Attributives should differ from that in Singular ones? The circumstances are evidently dissimilar. A *single* individual may stand in various relations and act in divers capacities. . . . But this does not happen in the same degree with respect to Plurals. Though *one* individual may act, and frequently does act, in several capacities, it is not likely that a *multitude* of individuals should all of them act in the *same* several capacities. . . .[29]

On the basis of an extensive analysis of plural nouns in comparable constructions in the NT, Wallace has confirmed that plural nouns are an exception to Sharp's rule. He has cited many passages where the members of a construction cannot be equated with each other and thus constitute clear exceptions (e.g., Matt. 3:7; 17:1; 27:56; Acts 17:12).[30] His conclusion is, "Granville Sharp applied his rule only to singular, nonproper, personal nouns of the same case."[31]

He has catalogued the abuse of Sharp's rule by several grammatical works considered standards in the field of NT grammar. Regarding this abuse he notes,

> But what about the *abuse* of the rule? Almost without exception, those who seem to be acquainted with Sharp's rule and agree with its validity misunderstand and abuse it. Virtually no one is exempt from this charge—grammarians, commentators, theologians alike are guilty. Typically, the rule is usually *perceived* to extend to plural and impersonal constructions—in spite of the fact that the evidence of the NT with reference to plural and impersonal nouns is contrary to this supposition.[32]

He cites several well known grammarians to illustrate his point.[33]

Wallace also focused specifically on the relevant passage in Ephesians 4:11 where Sharp's rule is often applied. His comment is,

> Although most commentaries consider the two terms to refer to one group, we must emphatically insist that such a view *has no grammatical basis,* even though the writers who maintain this view almost unanimously rest their case on the supposed semantics of the article-noun-καί-noun construction. Yet, as we have seen, there are no other examples in the NT of this construction with nouns in the plural, either clearly tagged or ambiguous, which allow for such a possibility. One would, therefore, be on rather shaky ground to insist on such a nuance here [Eph. 4:11]—especially if the main weapon in his arsenal is syntax![34]

Wallace affirms the validity of the rule for plural adjectives or participles, but indicates he has found no clear instances of the rule's applicability to plural nouns in the NT Koine, Papyri, Hellenistic, or Classical Greek.[35]

This refined application of Sharp's rule removes Grudem's major foundation for equating apostles and prophets, since the rule is not applicable to Ephesians 2:20. In this verse Paul designates two separate groups, apostles and prophets, without equating one to the other.[36] Since the passage labels prophecy in itself as a foundational gift, the inevitable conclusion is that NT prophecy has ceased along with the gift of apostleship.

Disregard for Ephesians 4:11. Another weakness in Grudem's reasoning regarding the equation of apostles and prophets in Ephesians 2:20

lies in his use of Ephesians 4:11 for support. Two aspects of Ephesians 4:11 can militate *against* his conclusion: (1) He argues, "When Paul wants to distinguish two people or groups he does not hesitate to use a second article. . . ."[37] On this basis he concludes that the single article with apostle and prophet dictates that Paul intended to equate the two to each other. Yet in Ephesians 4:11—a verse that he uses in another way as a supporting grammatical analogy—Paul uses two articles, one with "apostles" and one with "prophets": ἔδωκεν τοὺς μὲν ἀποστόλους, τοὺς δὲ προφήτας (*edōken tous men apostolous, tous de prophētas,* "on the one hand he gave apostles, and on the other, prophets"). It is cogent reasoning that since Paul thus distinguishes between apostles and prophets in 4:11, he must have intended the same distinction in 2:20. This belies Grudem's interpretation. (2) As noted above, the grammatical analogy that Grudem cites in Ephesians 4:11—i.e., the identification of "pastors" and "teachers"—provides no support for his theory, because the plural nouns forbid the pressing of Sharp's rule here, too.

Invalid cross-references. Furthermore, Grudem's cross-references cited to support an equation of apostles and prophets[38] are invalid, because every one of the examples is semantically unparallel. Not one is a clear example of an application of Sharp's rule to plural nouns as Grudem's position on Ephesians 2:20 would require. Many of the cross-references are singular nouns governed by a single article to which Sharp's rule *does* apply,[39] so long as the nouns are personal and not proper nouns or plural in number. These, however, are a quite different grammatical entity from the plural-noun construction in Ephesians 2:20 and do not support his view of this verse. Sharp's rule is applicable to a few plural adjectives (e.g., Rom. 16:7; Col. 1:2), but the same principle does not apply to plural-noun constructions. The same difference holds between plural participles (e.g., Gal. 1:7; 1 Thess. 5:12) and plural nouns. Grudem's use of impersonal nouns as a grammatical parallel is also inaccurate (e.g., 1 Thess. 3:7) because Sharp's rule requires personal nouns. Space forbids an exhaustive citation of all the alleged parallels, but every one of them is nonparallel for one of these reasons.

So none of the cross-references cited supports the case for identification of prophets with apostles in Ephesians 2:20. None presents an instance of analogous construction. It is wrong, therefore, to found such a conclusion on this verse.

Improper differentiation between Ephesians 2:20; 3:5; and 1 Corinthians 12–14. Besides the alleged grammatical reason, this proposed identification also rests on differentiating prophecy in 1 Corinthians 12–14 from prophecy in Ephesians 2:20 and 3:5, the latter being apostolic prophecy and the former congregational prophecy.[40] An inherent weakness in this distinction is reflected in a close scrutiny of technical terms used in both sections. The same "clusters" of revelational-type words occur in 1 Corinthians 12–14 as occur in the context of Ephesians 2–3. For example, προφήτης (*prophētēs*, "prophet") and προφητεύω (*prophēteuō*, "I prophesy") (cp. 1 Cor. 12:28; 13:9; 14:1–6, 24, 31–32, 37, 39 with Eph. 2:20; 3:5) are used in both. So are οἰκοδομή (*oikodomē*, "building") and οἰκοδομέω (*oikodomeō*, "I build up, edify") (cp. 1 Cor. 14:3–5, 12, 17, 26 with Eph. 2:20–22), μυστήριον (*mystērion*, "mystery") (cp. 1 Cor. 13:2; 14:2 with Eph. 3:3–4, 9), ἀποκάλυψις (*apokalypsis*, "revelation") and ἀποκαλύπτω (*apokalyptō*, "I reveal") (cp. 1 Cor. 14:6, 26, 30 with Eph. 3:3, 5), κρύπτω (*kryptō*, "I hide") and its cognates (cp. 1 Cor. 14:25 with Eph. 3:9), ἀπόστολος (*apostolos*, "apostle") (cp. 1 Cor. 12:28–29 with Eph. 2:20; 3:5), and σοφία (*sophia*, "wisdom") (cp. 1 Cor. 12:8 with Eph. 3:10). The grouping of such technical terminology in a single context signals a reference to direct divine communication to an authoritative prophetic instrument. The presence of this type of communication in Ephesians 2–3 is not in doubt, and no significant basis exists for questioning a reference to it in 1 Corinthians 12–14.[41] So the case for contrasting "congregational" prophecy with "apostolic" prophecy falters at another point.

EXEGETICALLY RELATED WEAKNESSES OF GRUDEM'S HYPOTHESIS

NT prophecy founded on OT prophecy. Grudem's case for an unauthoritative "congregational" prophecy in 1 Corinthians 12–14 and elsewhere in the NT also rests on positing a strong discontinuity between OT prophecy and NT prophecy. Unfortunately, he does injustice to the fact that NT prophecy is founded upon and has a significant continuity with the OT prophetic phenomenon and experience. An important passage in this regard is Acts 2:17–21 where Peter's Pentecostal sermon cites Joel 2:28–32.[42] The earlier part of Acts 2 has just described manifestations of the Holy Spirit (e.g., speaking in tongues, prophesying) witnessed by Jewish onlookers outside the circle of the 120 Christians who had been gathered for prayer (cf. Acts 2:1–11). Some outsiders were amazed, but others mocked and said the Christians were "full of sweet wine" (Acts 2:13). Empowered by the Spirit, Peter stood and offered an explanation by relating the charismatic phenomena being witnessed to the prophecy of Joel 2. It is highly significant that Peter linked this beginning of NT prophecy with prophetic phenomena of the OT. The same word for "prophecy" is used to depict NT prophecy as is used in the LXX translation of Joel: προφητεύω (*prophēteuō,* "I prophesy") (cp. Acts 2:17 with Joel 3:1 [LXX, 2:28 in English]).

A revival of the prophetic gift has been long expected in Israel, and Peter ties the prophecy experienced at Pentecost to that promised revival of OT prophecy. Gentry accurately assesses the situation:

> Thus, here we have prophecy of the Old Testament type . . . entering into the New Testament era. . . . And this is according to Peter's divinely inspired interpretation of Joel. . . .
>
> This establishes a fundamental continuity linking Old Testament and New Testament prophecy. . . . This divinely expected prophetic gift appears in numerous places in Acts, 1 Corinthians, and other New Testament books. . . .[43]

NT prophecy is fundamentally a development and continuation of OT prophecy.

The NT does not conceptualize any substantial differences in kind between prophetic expressions in the OT and those in the NT. The vocabulary and phraseology are the same.[44] Aune notes, "The early Christian application of the designation προφήτης to individual Christians, then, was originally determined by the prevalent conception of the prophetic role of the Old Testament."[45] The NT's application of the term *prophētēs* to its contemporary prophets (e.g., in 1 Corinthians 12–14) makes it evident that NT authors conceived of the existence of a fundamental continuity between these two eras of prophecy. Use of the term in fulfillment formulae in NT citations of the OT are indicative of this. OT prophets were seen as writing the very words of the Lord in regard to future happenings.[46]

This continuity of OT prophecy to NT prophecy is borne out elsewhere in the NT. The NT prophet Agabus modeled his prophetic style after the OT prophets. The historian Luke relates that Agabus "indicated by the Spirit" that a famine was about to occur in the world (Acts 11:28a).[47] He then records the occurrence of the famine in accord with Agabus's prediction (Acts 11:28b). Later Agabus introduces a prophecy with the words, "This is what the Holy Spirit says" (Acts 21:11), an expression that reflects a pattern similar to Matthew's fulfillment formulae when introducing OT prophecies (e.g., Matt. 2:15, 17; 3:3). It also parallels the OT prophetic formula, "Thus says the Lord."[48] It is significant also that no attempt is even made to distinguish between OT and NT prophetic expression in the vocabulary of introductions to NT prophecy. The cognates of *prophētēs* are used for NT prophecy as they are for OT prophecy.

Prestige of the NT prophet. Another weakness in Grudem's hypothesis is his failure to recognize the high degree of prestige enjoyed by NT prophets in the Christian community. As already shown from a correct understanding of Ephesians 2:20, they in association with the apostles held the honorable status of helping lay the foundation of the church. Their ranking in the list of gifted persons in 1 Corinthians 12:28 (cf. 1 Cor. 14:1) places them second only to the apostles in usefulness to the body of Christ.

Prophets also joined the apostles as recipients of special revelation regarding Gentile participation in the church (Eph. 3:5–10). The doctrine revealed through them in the context of Ephesians 3 concerned the mystery of the inclusion of Jews and Gentiles in one universal body of Christ. The presence of Gentiles in such a relationship was unrevealed before the NT era (cf. Eph. 3:5), but came to apostles and prophets as inspired utterances and writings such as the canonical epistle of Ephesians.

The reception and propagation of such revelations constituted the foundation of the church universal throughout the present age. Prophets were vehicles for these revelations and held a high profile among early Christians for this reason. Grudem's words do not match the high status of prophets upheld in the NT: "Prophecy in ordinary New Testament churches was not equal to Scripture in authority, but was simply a very human—and sometimes partially mistaken—report of something the Holy Spirit brought to someone's mind."[49] Such a relegation of prophecy to a lesser status raises the question of how the early church could have guarded itself against hopeless doctrinal confusion. If prophets at times were used to convey inspired revelations and at other times were nonauthoritative and mistaken, who could distinguish their authoritative accurate messages from the other kind?

Need for constant evaluation of NT prophecy. A primary argument for the existence of nonauthoritative congregational prophecy comes from the call for evaluation of prophetic utterances in 1 Corinthians 14:29–31.[50] The needed critical evaluation resulted from a changed status of believers under the new covenant. In accord with Joel 2:28–32 and Acts 2:17–21, the Holy Spirit was poured out on all believers. This did not mean that all Christians would be prophets, a possibility that Paul rejects in 1 Corinthians 12:29: "All are not prophets, are they?" It did, however, create the potential, according to the Joel and Acts passages, that the gift of prophecy would be much more widely disseminated than to a limited group of prophets like those who spoke for the Lord in the theocratic community under the old covenant. The expanded sphere of prophetic activity increased the need for greater care in discerning true prophecies from false prophecies.

This is the need that Paul attempted to meet in 1 Corinthians 14:29–31. The larger the group of prophets became, the more potential there was for the abuse of prophecy by those who were not NT prophets at all. This danger became a vivid reality in the latter part of the first century A.D. as evidenced by John's warning: "Beloved, do not believe every spirit, but test the spirits to see whether they are from God; because many false prophets have gone out into the world" (1 John 4:1; cf. 2 Peter 2:1–22; Jude 4, 11–16).

Grudem maintains that OT prophets were never challenged in this way because of the high regard in which they were held. For him, this signalled a great difference between OT and NT prophets, i.e., NT prophets were not so prestigious.[51] After evaluation and acceptance as a prophet, an OT prophet's words were never questioned, but each prophecy of a NT prophet had to be evaluated.[52] Herein lies a contrast, causing Grudem to conclude that the NT gift operated at a lower level of authority.[53]

Yet Grudem's picture of OT prophecy and its prestige is highly idealized and rather unrealistic. His idealized picture is obtained substantially from historical hindsight rather than from an examination of the actual state of affairs existing at the time of the OT prophets. A brief review reveals four relevant features of OT prophecy:

1. The Israelites frequently disobeyed OT prophets like Samuel, Elisha, and Jeremiah, to name only a few, even when their proclamations were authoritative as the very words of the Lord (e.g., 1 Sam. 13:8–14; Jer. 36:1–32), and put them to flight, threatening to kill them (e.g., 1 Kings 19:1–3). Also, Amos's preaching in Bethel aroused such opposition that he had to flee from Bethel for his life (Amos 7:10–17).

2. Some prophets enjoyed greater status and prestige than others who were less famous (e.g., an unknown prophet in 1 Kings 20:35–43; cf. also 1 Kings 19:10).

3. The people threatened and otherwise strongly opposed some prophets like Jeremiah because of their status as prophets of the Lord. Jeremiah could hardly have been said to have enjoyed much of an authoritative status in Israel at such times, because his hearers disobeyed him, despised him, rejected him, beat him, and imprisoned him because of his prophetic ministry (e.g., Jer. 11:18–23; 12:6; 18:18; 20:1–2; 26:1–24; 37:11–38:28).

4. According to Jewish tradition, some prophets like Isaiah were tortured and assassinated rather than given great honor (cf. 1 Kings 18:13).[54] Under some kind of duress, some prophets may even have lied or even apostatized (cf. 1 Kings 13:18).

Jesus recalled that Israel had consistently despised, rejected, and killed her prophets: "Jerusalem, Jerusalem, who kills the prophets and stones those who are sent to her!" (Matt. 23:37). Such a picture hardly conveys the impression of great respect afforded the OT prophets by their contemporaries. Nor does it suggest that their messages were never questioned or rejected (cf. Heb. 11:32–40).

Old Testament prophets became revered only by later generations of Jewish people. They had no such preeminence during their lifetimes. Only as later generations realized their ancestors had been disobedient idolaters who failed to recognize the prophets' advice (cf. Ezra 9:1–11) did the prophets ascend to a place of esteem in the eyes of the people. This elite group of OT spokesmen for the Lord experienced the anointing and influence of the Holy Spirit in a way that was not appreciated by their immediate listeners.[55]

The NT standard for evaluating prophets is comparable to relevant guidelines in the OT. The OT laid down certain rules in Deuteronomy 13 and 18 that were *always* taken as requirements for OT prophets. False prophets were frequently identified by an application of these rules. The rules were applicable even to established prophets like Isaiah and Samuel. In spite of their reputations, they still had to speak the truth. At the very least, the stated requirements served to reinforce the genuineness of the true prophet, because they stressed that a true prophet must accurately proclaim the truth.[56] So even though OT prophets were not evaluated formally or constantly as NT prophets were in Corinth, they were still subject to the background requirements of Deuteronomy 13 and 18. The NT furnishes no indication that NT-era Jews, particularly those who became apostles in the early church, considered the requirements for prophets in the OT to have been abrogated or substantially modified.

Identification of evaluators. This survey must content itself with noticing one final weakness in Grudem's theory regarding NT prophecy. It regards his method of handling 1 Corinthians 14:29 which reads, "Let two or three prophets speak, and let the others pass judgment." A critical question in this statement concerns the identity of those "passing judgment" or "discerning" the validity of alleged prophetic pronouncements. Grudem raises a psychological point:

> If we understand οἱ ἄλλοι [*hoi alloi,* "the others"] to be restricted to a special group of prophets, we have much difficulty picturing what the rest of the congregation would do during the prophecy and judging. Would they sit during the prophecy waiting for the prophecy to end and be judged

> before knowing whether to believe any part of it? . . . Especially hard to believe is the idea that the teachers, administrators, and other church leaders without special gifts of prophecy would sit passively awaiting the verdict of an elite group.[57]

Aside from the fact that this argumentation is nonexegetical in nature, it is weak in that reason and logic, to which he appeals, can also dictate that not everyone in the congregation would be in a position to evaluate the prophecy, especially in a public setting.[58] Admittedly, 1 John 4:1–3 urges a testing of spirits in a general sense by all Christians because of false prophecy and teaching, but Paul is very clear in this context at 1 Corinthians 12:10 regarding the "distinguishing of spirits" that everyone did not possess that special ability. The gift of doing so was dispensed to a limited number according to the sovereign will of the Holy Spirit (1 Cor. 12:11; cf. 1 Cor. 12:18). It is conspicuous that those possessing special ability in discerning were better equipped to pass judgment on congregational prophecies than the ones who did not possess the gift. This differentiation in valuative capabilities within the congregation raises a loud contextual objection to understanding that all members of the congregation were supposed to evaluate in 1 Corinthians 14:29.

In the immediate context of 14:29, the most natural grammatical and contextual antecedent of *hoi alloi* ("the others") is προφῆται (*prophētai,* "prophets") in the first half of verse 29. Paul's use of *allos* ("another of the same kind") instead of ἕτερος (*heteros,* "another of a different kind") indicates his intention to designate the same category of persons as those prophets referred to just before. Referring "the others" to other prophets is further confirmed by the use of ἄλλῳ (*allō,* "to another") immediately afterward in verse 30 where it is an evident reference to "another" prophet. This repetition of the same adjective, "other" or "another," shows that Paul still had prophets in mind when he used *hoi alloi* in verse 29. In this statement, then, where interpretation is tedious, the contextual probabilities rest on the side of identifying those who evaluate prophetic utterances of others as being the prophets who apparently possessed the gift of the discerning of spirits along with their prophetic gift.

They were to pass judgment on what other prophets said to ascertain whether their utterance came from the Holy Spirit or not. Just as ἑρμηνεία (*hermēneia,* "interpretation") was needed in conjunction with the exercise of γλωσσῶν (*glōssōn,* "tongues") (1 Cor. 12:10c), διακρίσεις (*diakriseis,* "discernings") needed to accompany προφῆται (*prophētai,* "prophesies") (1 Cor. 12:10b).[59] Inspired spokesmen were in the best position to judge spontaneously whether a new utterance agreed with Paul's teachings (cf. Gal. 1:8–9; 2 Thess. 2:1–3) and generally accepted beliefs of the Christian community (1 Cor. 12:1–3).

The context surrounding 1 Corinthians 12:3 sheds light on the situation addressed in 1 Corinthians 14:29. Apparently false prophets had preached that Jesus was "accursed" (12:3) even though they professed to be true prophets. The person making such a startling statement must have been a professing Christian. Otherwise, his statement would not have been tolerated in a Christian assembly and would not have been attributed to the Holy Spirit, as he apparently claimed. In the face of such starkly erroneous prophesying, Paul warned the congregation to evaluate each prophecy carefully to ensure that a genuine prophet was speaking a genuine prophecy. Some recognized voice was needed to declare that the Spirit was not the source of such a statement and that the person voicing it showed himself to be a false prophet. First Corinthians 14:29 does not necessarily mean established prophets had to be verified continually.

Yet it does set down the general principle that any potential prophet needed to be scrutinized by other potential prophets. This principle invalidates Grudem's conclusion that a genuine prophet's message contained a mixture of truth and error. The guideline established merely enforces the need for careful analysis of any prophet who claimed to speak by the Spirit of God to determine the source of his message. Once his source was identified as God, further examination was most likely unnecessary. Yet, according to 2 Corinthians 11:13–15, even false prophets had potential to feign a true prophecy, so Paul encouraged a continued vigil. The regular ministry of prophets was to ensure the genuineness of prophets and prophecies as a safeguard against doctrinal heresies.

The fact that a prophecy could be interrupted (1 Cor. 14:30–32) does not contradict this picture of prophecy and discernment. The permissible interruption did not mark the prophecy as nonauthoritative or fallible, i.e., as not from God. The apparent thrust of verse 32 is that if a revelation is from God, the prophet will remain in conscious control of his mind and will. In other words, a true prophecy from God can wait to be given in an orderly manner.

In summary, judging a prophecy does not imply that the gift could result in errant pronouncements.[60] The responsibility of NT prophets to weigh the prophecies of others does not imply that *true* prophets were capable of giving false prophecies, but that *false* prophets could disguise their falsity by occasional true utterances.

Grudem observes that Paul rates the authority of Christian prophets below his own in 1 Corinthians 14:37–38. He uses this to support his view that NT prophetic authority was inferior to that of the apostles and hence the OT prophets also.[61] This understanding of Paul's words is not probable, because Paul is here more likely asserting that if a Christian prophet is truly from God, his prophecies will concur with apostolic truths (cf. Gal. 1:8–9). False prophets and teachers consistently challenged apostolic authority and doctrine (e.g., Gal. 2:4–5; 2 Tim. 2:18; cf. Jude 3–4). In light of his own apostolic office, Paul's comparison between the Corinthian claims of authority and his own is best understood to teach that true prophets and their prophecies would be consistent with apostolic truth and would recognize Paul's words and commandments as coming directly from the Lord Jesus Christ. Any alleged prophet opposing apostolic standards and elevating himself to the role of God's only spokesman (1 Cor. 14:36) was to be recognized as false, and his authority rejected (1 Cor. 14:38).

A CONCLUDING WORD ABOUT GRUDEM'S HYPOTHESIS

The above discussion of Grudem's theory about NT prophecy, both the detailed criticisms and the summary observations, shows the idea of a bifurcation of the prophetic gift to be suspect at many points. His central thesis that the NT apostle be equated with the OT prophet in terms of prophetic activity and that a second kind of prophetic gift consisting of "speaking merely human words to report something God brings to mind" be recognized is extremely weak and therefore unconvincing. His grammatical basis for equating NT apostle with NT prophet in Ephesians 2:20 is flawed, and in relevant passages, particularly 1 Corinthians 12–14, his evidence crumbles in comparison with interpretations that provide explanations with more exegetical coherence. His basic conclusion regarding the nature of NT prophecy, therefore, cannot be endorsed.

ENDNOTES

[1] Exemplifying standard noncharismatics, Ryrie writes, "The gift of prophecy included receiving a message directly from God through special revelation, being guided in declaring it to people, and having it authenticated in some way by God Himself. The content of that message may have included telling the future (which was what we normally think of as prophesying), but it also included revelation from God concerning the present. This too was a gift limited in its need and use, for it was needed during the writing of the New Testament and its usefulness ceased when the books were completed. God's message then was contained in written form, and no new revelation was given in addition to the written

record" (Charles C. Ryrie, *The Holy Spirit* [Chicago: Moody, 1965], 86). Other prominent dispensational noncharismatic works are John F. Walvoord, *The Holy Spirit at Work Today* (Chicago: Moody, 1965); Robert G. Gromacki, *The Modern Tongues Movement* (Philadelphia: Presbyterian and Reformed, 1967); Robert L. Thomas, *Understanding Spiritual Gifts* (Chicago: Moody, 1978); Merrill F. Unger, *The Baptism and Gifts of the Holy Spirit* (Chicago: Moody, 1974); John F. MacArthur Jr., *The Charismatics* (Grand Rapids: Zondervan, 1978); Charles R. Smith, *Tongues in Biblical Perspective* (Winona Lake, Ind.: BMH, 1972). Works by noncharismatics who are Reformed and covenant theologians are B. B. Warfield, *Counterfeit Miracles* (Carlisle, Pa.: Banner of Truth, 1918); Anthony Hoekema, *What About Tongues-Speaking?* (Grand Rapids: Eerdmans, 1966); J. I. Packer, *God Has Spoken* (London: Hodder and Stoughton, 1958).

[2] Kirby, a noncessationist, laments that the cessationists, especially those of the dispensational persuasion, have hindered the present usefulness of spiritual gifts: "Early on, I had a hunch that more had been lost to humanistic enlightenment, dispensationalism, liberal or extential theology, and fear of the loony fringe than we had guessed" (Jeff Kirby, "The Recovery of the Healing Gifts," in *Those Controversial Gifts,* ed. George Mallone [Downers Grove, Ill.: InterVarsity, 1983], 102). By erroneously linking the cessationist beliefs of some dispensationalists with those of existentialism, liberalism, and humanism and with fear of the "loony fringe," he illustrates the sharp cleavage that exists between the cessationist and noncessationist camps. He also reflects a basic misunderstanding of broader theological issues, because cessationism is not a dispensational issue, i.e., many noncessationists are dispensational, and many cessationists are nondispensational.

[3] Wayne A. Grudem, *The Gift of Prophecy in the New Testament and Today* (Westchester, Ill.: Crossway, 1988), 14–15.

[4] Other recent writers who have helped bring the prophecy issue to the forefront of discussion include H. A. Guy, David E. Aune, David Hill, Theodore M. Crone, Eduard Cothenet, and Gerhard Friedrich. These more notable ones serve as examples of a number of others. Guy is usually cited as responsible for the most recent round of scholarly debate regarding prophecy (H. A. Guy, *New Testament Prophecy: Its Origin and Significance* [London: Epworth, 1947], but his work has now been largely superseded by more recent research). Crone has been praised for his useful, scholarly, and thorough research in the field (Theodore M.

Crone, "Early Christian Prophecy: A Study of Its Origin and Function" [Ph.D. dissertation, Tübingen University, 1973]). Other significant works include David E. Aune, *Prophecy in Early Christianity and the Ancient Mediterranean World* (Grand Rapids: Eerdmans, 1983); David Hill, *New Testament Prophecy* (Atlanta: Knox, 1979); Eduard M. Cothenet, *"Prophétisme dans le Nouveau Testament,"* in *Dictionnaire de la Bible,* 8:1222–337; Helmut Krämer, Rolf Rendtorff, Rudolf Meyer, and Gerhard Friedrich, "προφήτης," *Theological Dictionary of the New Testament* (Grand Rapids: Eerdmans, 1968), 6:781–861. The last of these works is not as recent as the others, but it is still one of the most basic and best treatments on the subject. Another recent work by Grudem is "Why Christians Can Still Prophesy: Scripture Encourages Us to Seek the Gift Yet Today," *Christianity Today* 32, no. 13 (September 16, 1988): 29–35.

[5] Grudem, *Prophecy in the New Testament,* 14.

[6] Grudem, "Still Prophesy," 29.

[7] Grudem, *Prophecy in the New Testament,* 15.

[8] Wayne A. Grudem, *The Gift of Prophecy in 1 Corinthians* (Washington: University Press, 1982), 71.

[9] Accordingly, the NT prophets at Corinth were "speaking merely human words to report something God brings to mind" (Grudem, *Prophecy in the New Testament,* 67). That is, sometimes the prophet was accurate and sometimes not. In some circumstances, the prophet could be "mistaken" (ibid., 96).

[10] Grudem, "Still Prophesy," 30.

[11] Ibid.

[12] Ibid., 40–41.

[13] Grudem, *Prophecy in 1 Corinthians,* 69–70. Grudem draws upon 1 Corinthians 12–14 as his principal source regarding "secondary" (i.e., nonapostolic) prophecy.

[14] Ibid., 7–113.

[15] Ibid., 97 [transliterations and translations added].

[16] Ibid., 97–98.

[17] Ibid., 98–100.

[18] Ibid., 100–101; transliterations and translations added.

[19] Grudem does not specifically mention the name "Granville Sharp," the person whose formulation of this grammatical phenomenon is widely recognized, but he appears to base his interpretation on principles derived from that rule.

[20] Granville Sharp, *Remarks on the Definitive Article in the Greek Text of the New Testament: Containing Many New Proofs of the Divinity of Christ, from Passages Which Are Wrongly Translated in the Common English Version,* 1st American ed. (Philadelphia: B. B. Hopkins, 1807), 3 [transliteration and translation added]. This is the first of six rules articulated by Sharp whose feeling was that the other five merely confirmed his first.

[21] The best modern defense of the rule is in a seven-part series by C. Kuehne that appeared in the *Journal of Theology*: "The Greek Article and the Doctrine of Christ's Deity." The seven parts appeared in the following numbers: 13 (September 1973): 12–28; 13 (December 1973): 14–30; 14 (March 1974): 11–20; 14 (June 1974): 16–25; 14 (September 1974): 21–34; 14 (December 1974): 8–19; 15 (March 1975): 8–22. See also the excellent article by Daniel B. Wallace, "The Semantic Range of the Article-Noun-καί-Noun Plural Construction in the New Testament," *Grace Theological Journal* 4 (1983): 59–84.

[22] Wallace, "Semantic Range," 62. The present discussion is limited to the issue of the singular number of the nouns (i.e., qualification "4" in the listed stipulations). For further discussion of the other three qualifications, see ibid., 62–63, and idem, "The Validity of Granville Sharp's First Rule with Implications for the Deity of Christ" (unpublished paper presented to Southwestern Section of the Evangelical Theological Society, March 4, 1988), 15–31.

[23] Wallace, "Semantic Range," 62.

[24] Ibid., 63.

[25] Sharp, *Remarks,* 3.

²⁶ Ibid., 5–6.

²⁷ Ibid., 120. For an excellent discussion of these important qualifications regarding Sharp's rule, see Wallace, "Validity," 4–5.

²⁸ Wallace, "Validity," 7; cf. C. F. D. Moule, *An Idiom-Book of New Testament Greek,* 2d ed. (Cambridge: University Press, 1959), 94, 109 (n. 3), 113 (n. 2), 114–117.

²⁹ Thomas F. Middleton, *Doctrine of the Greek Article,* ed. H. J. Rose (1841), 20. Wallace, "Validity," 8, cites this quotation from the "new edition" of a work originally published in 1808.

³⁰ Wallace summarizes, "There are no clear instances of the plural construction involving *nouns* which speak of identity, while plural constructions involving *participles,* where the sense could be determined, always had identical referents" (Wallace, "Validity," 10).

³¹ Ibid.

³² Ibid., 12.

³³ For examples of applications of Sharp's rule that are insufficiently precise, see A. T. Robertson, *A Grammar of the Greek New Testament in the Light of Historical Research* (Nashville: Broadman, 1934), 785–89; H. E. Dana and J. R. Mantey, *A Manual Grammar of the Greek New Testament* (New York: Macmillan, 1955), 147.

³⁴ Wallace, "Semantic Range," 83.

³⁵ Wallace, "Validity," 15–31.

³⁶ Had Paul wished to equate the two, he could have done so clearly with the insertion of a participial phrase (e.g., τῶν ὄντων [*tōn ontōn,* "those who are"]) or through a relative clause (e.g., "apostles who are also prophets"). This would have removed any doubt about the two groups being equivalent (cf. Dan McCartney, "Review of Wayne Grudem's, *The Gift of Prophecy in 1 Corinthians,*" *Westminster Theological Journal* 45 [spring 1983]: 196).

³⁷ Grudem, *Prophecy in 1 Corinthians,* 101.

[38] Ibid., 98–100.

[39] Cf. Ephesians 6:21; Philippians 2:25; Colossians 4:7; Philemon 1; Hebrews 3:1; 1 Peter 2:25; 2 Peter 3:18.

[40] Grudem, *Prophecy in the New Testament,* 64.

[41] Robert L. Thomas, "The Spiritual Gift of Prophecy in Revelation 22:18," *Journal of the Evangelical Theological Society* 32, no. 2 (June 1989): 205 n. 30.

[42] In the Masoretic Text and the LXX, Joel 2:28–32 in English translations corresponds to Joel 3:1–5a.

[43] Kenneth L. Gentry Jr., *The Charismatic Gift of Prophecy* (Memphis, Tenn.: Footstool, 1989), 8.

[44] This continuity does not rule out minor differences. It only excludes any differences substantial or crucial enough to warrant a distinction between two kinds of prophetic gifts or expressions that were operable in the OT or the NT.

[45] Aune, *Prophecy in Early Christianity,* 195.

[46] Two examples are sufficient to illustrate this point: ἵνα πληρωθῇ τὸ ῥυθὲν ὑπὸ κυρίου διὰ τοῦ προφήτου λέγοντος (*hina plērōthē to rhēthen hypo kyriou dia tou prophētou legontos,* "in order that the word spoken by the Lord through the prophet should be fulfilled," (Matt. 1:22), a reference to Isaiah, and γεγραμμένον ἐν τοῖς προφήταις (*gegrammenon en tois prophētais,* "having been written in the prophets," John 6:45), a reference to the prophets as a group.

[47] Luke uses a fulfillment formula, "by the Spirit," similar to the one describing Agabus's prophesying in Acts 21:11.

[48] William Neil, "Acts," *New Century Bible* (Grand Rapids: Eerdmans, 1973), 217. See also G. H. W. Lampe, "Acts," in *Peake's Commentary,* ed. Matthew Black (London: Thomas Nelson, 1962), 919.

[49] Grudem, *Prophecy in the New Testament,* 14.

[50] Ibid., 70–79.

[51] Grudem, *Prophecy in the New Testament,* 17–23; idem, *Prophecy in 1 Corinthians,* 82–105.

[52] Grudem, *Prophecy in 1 Corinthians,* 58–66.

[53] D. A. Carson supports Grudem regarding two levels of authority (D. A. Carson, *Showing the Spirit* [Grand Rapids: Baker, 1987], 98).

[54] Cp. Hebrews 11:37–40 with Isaiah 6:9–10. Rabbinic tradition includes Isaiah among the persecuted heroes of faith alluded to by the writer of Hebrews in the passage cited (cf. *Yebam.* 49b; *Sanh.* 103b).

[55] David, Moses, and other leaders experienced the anointing of the Spirit too, but not in the special way of the true prophets of the Lord, both the canonical ones like Isaiah and the noncanonical ones like Nathan and Gad.

[56] Cf. 1 Samuel 3:19. The mere fact that the writer of 1 Samuel could assert that Yahweh did not let Samuel's words fail indicates that some form of evaluation of Samuel by the people had been going on to provide for such a reply. This may be in some form of hindsight, looking back over Samuel's life.

[57] Grudem, *Prophecy in 1 Corinthians,* 60–62 [transliteration and translation added].

[58] In addition, Aune notes, "The observation in verse 31 that 'you can all prophesy one by one' cannot mean everybody present, but 'all upon whom the spirit of prophecy comes'" (Aune, *Prophecy in Early Christianity,* 133).

[59] This correlation is not explicit in 1 Corinthians 14, but it is strongly implicit by virtue of the contextual flow of chapters 12–14 and the use of cognate words in 12:10 and 14:29 to depict the gift of discernings and the exercise of discerning (cf. A. T. Robertson and Alfred Plummer, *First Corinthians,* International Critical Commentary [Edinburgh: T & T Clark, 1914], 267, 321–22).

[60] Contra Grudem, *Prophecy in 1 Corinthians,* 67–70, 115–36, 242.

[61] Grudem, *Prophecy in the New Testament,* 85–86.

CHAPTER THREE

Dispensationalism

Who Is Wrong?
A Review of John Gerstner's
Wrongly Dividing the Word
of Truth[1]

Richard L. Mayhue

Dr. John H. Gerstner, a recognized scholar with impressive credentials, has issued a call for dispensationalists to admit the glaring gaps between their system and orthodox Christianity. However, his presentation of dispensationalism contains shortcomings that necessitate this special review article to point out some of these and to challenge dispensationalists to publicize a greater clarification of their position. Many of the assumptions that undergird Dr. Gerstner's case against dispensationalism are in error. These faults are magnified by a number of major weaknesses in his argument. A review of the book shows how the author's treatment of his subject deteriorates even more through ten representative theological misstatements. The work is of such a misleading nature that a retraction of some kind seems to be in order.

* * * * *

General Anthony C. McAuliffe, commanding officer of the 101st Airborne Division at Bastogne, found his troops surrounded by the Germans early in the famous World War II Battle of the Bulge (December 1944). The opposing Nazi general, sensing quick victory, sent word to surrender immediately. McAuliffe replied with what is now one of the most famous one-word responses in military history, "Nuts!" In love, that also is our response to Dr. Gerstner's call for the surrender of "dispensationalism."

This strong retort, borrowed from WW II, answers R. C. Sproul's (President of Ligonier Ministries and a disciple of Dr. Gerstner) initial comments in the Foreword (p. ix).

This bomb—unlike missiles that suffer from dubious guidance systems and are liable to land on civilian populations wreaking havoc indiscriminately—is delivered with pinpoint accuracy into the laps of dispensational scholars.

According to Sproul,

Gerstner would prefer torture or death to intentionally distorting or misrepresenting anyone's position. . . . If Gerstner is inaccurate—if he has failed to understand dispensational theology correctly—then he owes many a profound apology. But first he must be shown where and how he is in error. This is the challenge of the book. If Gerstner is accurate, then Dispensationalism should be discarded as being a serious deviation from Biblical Christianity. (p. xi)

Dr. Gerstner delivers his "Surrender!" demand in the Introduction and elsewhere in the book:

Dispensationalism today, as yesterday, is spurious Calvinism and dubious evangelicalism. If it does not refute my charges and the charges of many others, it cannot long continue to be considered an essentially Christian movement. (p. 2)

Dispensationalism . . . is in constant deviation from essential historical Christianity. . . . (p. 68)

Since Gerstner believes so strongly that soteriology determines eschatology, one could expect that the President of The Master's Seminary, John F. MacArthur Jr., would be the first to wave a white flag. Gerstner affirmingly quotes him (without documentation or obvious connection to his point) as saying, "There is no salvation except Lordship Salvation" (p. 2). Gerstner finds this strongly reformed view of salvation incompatible with his understanding of dispensationalism. This convincingly illustrates the most obvious *non sequitur* in the book, i.e., Dr. Gerstner's assertion throughout his book that Reformed soteriology necessarily eliminates dispensational ecclesiology and eschatology. He labors for more than half the book—chapters 7–13—to prove that dispensationalism should surrender because it is unbiblical (pp. 105–263).

He seems to debate from the following basic syllogism, though he never states it so succinctly as this:

Premise 1:   Calvinism is central to all true theology.
Premise 2:   Dispensationalism does not embrace Calvinism.
Conclusion: Dispensationalism is a "spurious" and "dubious" expression of true theology (p. 2).

Thus, he strongly calls for dispensationalism's quick surrender.

ABOUT THE AUTHOR AND HIS WORK

Dr. Gerstner, Professor Emeritus of Pittsburgh Theological Seminary, is Associate Pastor of Trinity (PCA) Church in Johnstown, Pennsylvania, and currently serves as theologian-at-large at Ligonier Ministries. He also lectures on the Bible at Geneva College. Gerstner has been a Visiting Professor at Trinity Evangelical Divinity School since 1966 and is Adjunct Professor of Theology at both Reformed Theological Seminary and Knox Theological Seminary. He holds a B.A. from Westminster College, an M.Div. and Th.M. from Westminster Theological Seminary, and a Ph.D. in Philosophy of Religion from Harvard University.

Dr. Gerstner has published many books, audio and video tapes, plus numerous articles in theological journals and magazines. He was a pastor for ten years and a professor of church history at Pittsburgh Theological Seminary for thirty years (1950–80). He is best known for his lectures and writings on Jonathan Edwards.

In describing the author, R. C. Sproul writes glowingly about his mentor (p. ix):

> As a world-class historian, Gerstner has done his homework. The book is a result of years of careful and painstaking research. Gerstner has examined in the minutest detail the works of the most important historic dispensational theologians. He has canvassed scholarly journals and Ph.D. dissertations. He has been in repeated dialogue and debate with contemporary dispensational scholars. The current publication is the crystalized essence of over one thousand typescript pages of Gerstner's research and conclusions.

J. I. Packer declares that this volume clarifies "the issues more precisely than any previous book has done."[2] The publisher suggests that "Dr. Gerstner . . . presents the most extensive and systematic study of Dispensational theology ever published."[3]

SYNOPSIS OF DR. GERSTNER'S THINKING

Dr. Gerstner divides his volume into three sections:

1. Historical Sketch of Dispensationalism (pp. 7–72).
2. Philosophy and Hermeneutics of Dispensationalism (pp. 73–101).
3. Theology of Dispensationalism (pp. 103–263).

Dispensationalism Historically

The author's sketch of history looks back to the early church, the middle ages, the Reformation, and post-Reformation periods (pp. 7–20). The dispensationalism of nineteenth-century England receives attention (pp. 21–36) with special mention of John Nelson Darby (pp. 23–27). Next, he reviews American dispensationalism ranging from C. I. Scofield to E. W. Bullinger (pp. 37–56). Finally, he looks at dispensationalism in relation to American Reformed churches of the late nineteenth and early-to-middle twentieth centuries (pp. 57–72).

He notes in his brief historical survey of twenty centuries (66 pages) that dispensationalism "has a new theology, anthropology, soteriology, ecclesiology, eschatology, and a new systematic arrangement of all of these as well" (p. 18).

> Dispensationalism is a theology of persons holding to a deviation from the Christian religion. Just as truly as a proper premillennialist would resent being called a Jehovah's Witness because Jehovah's Witnesses also are premillennialists, or a Mormon because Mormons also are premillennialists, so also, a premillennialist should resent being called a dispensationalist because dispensationalists also are "premillennialists" (though I do not infer for a moment that Jehovah's Witnesses and Mormons are orthodox trinitarians at the heart as are *all* dispensationalists). (p. 69)

Dispensationalism Philosophically and Hermeneutically

Gerstner first looks at the philosophy, epistemology, and apologetical method of dispensationalism (pp. 75–81). Then he turns to dispensational hermeneutics (pp. 83–101). He concludes that dispensationalism is essentially anti-philosophical and without a proper philosophy (p. 75), devoid of an articulated epistemology (p. 78), but generally adhering to Gerstner's own "classical" approach to apologetics associated with the theology of Old Princeton. However, he asserts that dispensationalists hold a "weakened form" of this method (p. 79).

Regarding hermeneutics, Gerstner writes that ". . . almost all dispensationalists maintain that their mode of Biblical interpretation is more fundamental than their theology" (p. 83). Yet he concludes that ". . . far from determining dispensational theology, the dispensational literal hermeneutic (with all its inconsistencies), is in fact the direct result of that theology" (p. 101).

Dispensationalism Theologically

Gerstner first states and then attempts to prove that dispensationalism significantly deviates from all five points relating to the nature of man, sin, and salvation as articulated by the Synod of Dort (1619). These are commonly called the five points of Calvinism (pp. 105–47, esp. p. 105). Next, he accuses dispensationalists of teaching more than one way of salvation (pp. 149–69, esp. p. 149). "If Dispensationalism has actually departed from the only way of salvation which the Christian religion teaches, then we must say it has departed from Christianity" (p. 150).

Gerstner discusses the issue of Christ's kingdom preaching (pp. 171–79). He variously calls the dispensational position "appalling" and "novel" (p. 172). The dispensational view on Christ making a bona fide kingdom offer to the Jews, according to the author, ". . . is a direct affront to the righteousness of God, involving as it does the implication that God can and did lie" (p. 179).

Only one chapter discusses eschatology proper (chap. 10, pp. 181–208). Gerstner approaches the issue of Israel's relationship to the church with the view that "from the earliest period of Christian theology onward, the essential continuity of Israel and the church has been maintained" (p. 186). "Nevertheless, this scriptural unity of Israel and the church is directly challenged by Dispensationalism, wrongly dividing asunder what God's Word has joined together" (p. 187). He concludes, "The dispensational distinction between Israel and the church implicitly repudiates the Christian way of salvation" (p. 206):

> The root of the problem is the Israel/church distinction which assumes that Israel is an entirely temporal matter and the church an entirely spiritual affair. As a result, dispensationalists retreat into a hyper-spiritual Gnosticism which spurns the structures of the visible church which God has graciously given to His people. (p. 208)

Returning to the issue of soteriology, Gerstner then discusses sanctification (chaps. 11–12, pp. 209–50). He attempts to ". . . show that all traditional dispensationalists teach that converted Christian persons *can* (not may) live in sin throughout their post-conversion lives with no thought to their eternal destiny" (p. 209). "To depart from it (antinomianism) is to depart from dispensationalism" (p. 231). He perceives in the conclusion to this discussion that "there is no question that dispensationalism has been relatively indifferent to strict morality and usually indifferent to reform activities" (p. 250).

A brief discussion of the Lordship Salvation issue concludes Gerstner's case against dispensationalism (pp. 251–59). "We have shown throughout this volume that Dispensationalism teaches another gospel" (p. 251). ". . . Dispensationalism is another gospel" (p. 259).

He draws his argument to an ultimate conclusion (pp. 261–63) by stating first,

> We have now examined the Dispensationalism of yesterday and today. We have found that Dispensationalism is virtually the same today as yesterday. There have been some variations, of course, but none are essential. There are many varieties (to use an expression from natural science), but no new species. (p. 261)

He then abstracts the allegations enumerated in chapters 7–13 (pp. 261–62). Finally, Dr. Gerstner issues the following appeal:

> My plea to all dispensationalists is this—show me the fundamental error in what I teach or admit your own fundamental error. We cannot both be right. One of us is wrong—seriously wrong. If you are wrong (in your doctrine, as I here charge), you are preaching nothing less than a false gospel. This calls for genuine repentance and fruits worthy of it before the Lord Jesus Christ whom we both profess to love and serve. (p. 263)

An appendix summarizing and evaluating Charles Lincoln's 1943 article on covenants from a dispensational perspective caps off the book (pp. 265–72).[4] Because Gerstner believes that he successfully refutes all sixteen of Lincoln's points, he reasons, ". . . Covenant theology ought, . . . to be vindicated in the minds of dispensationalists" (p. 266).

WHY A REVIEW ARTICLE?

When someone with Dr. Gerstner's credentials, with such extensive teaching and writing experience, addresses a subject so significant as "dispensationalism," he cannot go unnoticed or unread. Out of respect for the author's reputation and in response to his invitation for interaction (p. 263), this review is undertaken.

To ignore this work, which has been heralded by some as possibly providing an epochal contribution to the theological debate between covenantalists and dispensationalists, would be an insult to the author and the position he represents. Furthermore, silence would imply that his facts are correct, his logic impeccable, his conclusions formidable, and his call to "surrender" as unavoidable to one who truly has a passion to be biblical in all areas of theology.

If one assumes that Dr. Gerstner has his facts straight, always represents dispensationalism accurately, has studied both the older classic dispensational works and is familiar with the current dialogue among dispensationalists, correctly understands the theological issues, and is exegetically valid in his approach to the subject, then he will tend to conclude that dispensationalism must indeed surrender. At face value and upon first reading, the majority of people (especially those who have not studied the issues for themselves) will be convinced that Gerstner is right in his conclusions.

This review is not an unabridged analysis of Gerstner's arguments and conclusions. Nor would this reviewer suggest that, if Gerstner can be shown to be mistaken theologically, dispensationalism is vindicated. Rather, the purpose of this review is twofold. First, it intends to demonstrate that what Dr. Gerstner delivers in the book falls well short of what he repeatedly claims to have accomplished throughout the book and what the testimonials of his friends and publishers urge the readers to believe are his contributions to this debate.

Second, it hopefully challenges in a small way the dispensational community to publish decisive clarification of the significant issues of dispensationalism in terms of its history, its essential identifying elements, the features that most or all dispensationalists currently embrace, the textual interpretations and theological conclusions of older dispensationalists that the current generation has questioned, the current debate over the exegesis of particular biblical texts, the current articulation of dispensational conclusions, and the decisive issues that distinctly set dispensationalists apart from covenantalists. Dispensationalists must seize the present opportunity to state what is and what is not essential to dispensationalism, upon whom current dispensational theology is dependent, and how dispensationalism of the 1990s differs from that of past decades.

EXAMINING THE AUTHOR'S ASSUMPTIONS

Presuppositions and assumptions undergird all reasoned thought. At times they are enumerated explicitly in the introduction to a subject while in other cases, such as this book, assumptions make their appearance somewhat randomly throughout the discussion, either in implicit or explicit fashion. This review suggests that at least ten of Dr. Gerstner's major assumptions are in error and thus seriously damage the validity of his conclusions.

1. Dr. Gerstner is perceived to assume that he is right and thus speaks on this subject *ex cathedra*.[5] One only needs to ponder the book's title, *Wrongly Dividing the Word of Truth* to sense the author's confidence. Implicitly, one gains the idea throughout the book that the author believes he stands in the theological gap at the eleventh hour as the champion of covenantalism and thus the destroyer of dispensationalism.

2. Dr. Gerstner seems to assume that he is factually, logically, and theologically decisive. Both R. C. Sproul's mild acknowledgment that Dr. Gerstner could be wrong (p. xi) and the author's own challenge to be corrected (p. 263) are more like a challenge than a humble invitation to other brothers in Christ "to come let us reason together" (cf. Isa. 1:18).

3. When Dr. Gerstner writes, ". . . that Calvinism is just another name for Christianity" (p. 107), one senses that he presumes to be the spokesman for all Calvinists. His own discussion of the atonement, which highlights varying approaches to the subject in the Reformed community, evidences that this is not altogether true (pp. 127–28).

4. One gets the distinct impression that Dr. Gerstner's view on soteriology, as expressed by the Synod of Dort (1619), serves as the canon by which other people's doctrine is judged as true or heretical (p. 105). Yet, much later in the book he writes, "The standard of judgment is fidelity to God's inerrant Word" (p. 262). A noticeable lack of biblical discussion throughout the book, plus the obvious appeal to a "dogmatic" approach in his own theology, leads the reviewer to suggest that the author frequently seems to espouse the latter (Scripture) but employ the former (Dortian doctrine) to authenticate truth.

5. Dr. Gerstner further narrows the field of those who understand and hold to Scripture correctly regarding the atonement by limiting this group to the Protestant Reformed Church (p. 128). This reviewer challenges this assumption and so do some of his covenantal brethren. In a letter dated September 12, 1991, the Elders of Trinity Baptist Church in Montville, New Jersey, pastored by Al Martin, himself a staunch proclaimer of Reformed doctrine, disavow Dr. Gerstner's teaching on the atonement beginning on p. 118 and continuing through p. 131. They write that, "Dr. Gerstner strays from the mainstream of historic calvinistic teaching regarding the free offer of the Gospel." This disclaimer letter comes with every copy of Dr. Gerstner's book that they distribute. A review of Dr. Gerstner's work by *Reformation Today* seriously questions his discussion of total depravity, election, and irresistible grace as it relates to his analysis of dispensational thought.[6]

6. Throughout the volume one receives the strong impression that Dr. Gerstner believes that Dallas Theological Seminary speaks representatively for all dispensationalists. He refers to "Dallas Dispensationalism" (p. 47). While this reviewer would not want to take away from DTS's contributions to furthering dispensational thought, dispensational thinking extends significantly beyond Dallas, especially in its theological formation. While Grace Theological Seminary, Capital Bible Seminary, and Western Conservative Baptist Seminary are mentioned (p. 52), numerous other schools such as Grand Rapids Baptist Seminary, The Master's Seminary, Talbot School of Theology, and a host of Christian colleges, not to mention scholars and pastors who do not teach at dispensationally oriented schools, swell the ranks of institutions and individuals who claim to be "dispensational" in their ecclesiology and eschatology.

7. Dr. Gerstner identifies dispensationalism with a certain view of soteriology. ". . . Dispensationalism is another gospel" (p. 259). "When Dispensationalism does truly give up mere nominalistic faith for a working faith, Dispensationalism will be Dispensationalism no more" (p. 272 n. 9). R. C. Sproul says of the author's view, "For Gerstner, when a dispensationalist eschews Antinomianism,

he is, in effect, eschewing Dispensationalism" (p. x). Nothing could be further from reality or better illustrate the meaning of *non sequitur*. Both Zane Hodges and John MacArthur consider themselves dispensationally oriented in their ecclesiology and eschatology, and yet see a great gulf fixed between their views on soteriology.[7] One could be both "a five-point Calvinist" and dispensational without being biblically inconsistent. D. G. Hart has recently written about the Westminster Seminary faculty of Machen's day being explicitly Reformed, yet having dispensationalist Allan A. MacRae as Professor of Old Testament.[8]

8. Dr. Gerstner assumes that dispensationalism is in a theological rut and has brought no essential change to its thinking: "A pressing question today is whether Dispensationalism has changed in any significant ways in recent years. I think not" (p. 72). "In spite of numerous contemporary fringe changes, Dispensationalism in America is still essentially Scofieldian . . ." (pp. 252–53). He does not acknowledge the Dispensational Study Group that has been meeting since 1985 just prior to the Evangelical Theological Society's Annual Meeting.[9] Nor does he interact with several recent, major works such as *Continuity and Discontinuity* (Wheaton, Ill.: Crossway, 1988) where John Feinberg, the editor, brings together both sides of the debate on key issues.[10] Robert Saucy has recently contributed several important articles: "The Crucial Issue Between Dispensational and Non-Dispensational Systems," *Criswell Theological Review* 1, no. 1 (fall 1986): 149–65; "Contemporary Dispensational Thought," *TSF Bulletin* (March–April 1984): 10–11; "The Presence of the Kingdom and the Life of the Church," *Bibliotheca Sacra* 145, no. 577 (January–March 1988): 30–46. Dr. Saucy is now completing a full-length volume tentatively entitled *The Interface Between Dispensational and Covenantal Theology* to be published by Zondervan in 1992.[11] In all these, dispensational spokesmen have moved rapidly and significantly beyond Scofield, Chafer, and Ryrie.[12]

9. Dr. Gerstner assumes that dispensationalism is a theological system much like the Calvinistic system. He refers to the "dispensational theological system" (pp. 105, 158).

Then he erroneously tries to equate dispensational thinking with the Arminian system of theology (p. 103). Earl
D. Radmacher makes the point that dispensational
thought comes more from a hermeneutical approach to
Scripture than from any theological system.[13]

10. Dr. Gerstner continually assumes that because he thinks
he has proven dispensationalism wrong, therefore
covenantalism is demonstrated to be a correct expression of truth. Nowhere does the author adequately demonstrate the biblical correctness of his own beliefs. Until
he does so, his brand of covenantalism is just as suspect
as the dispensationalism he sets out to discredit. And, let
this reviewer and all his dispensational friends be alert
to remember the need to do the same in the debate with
covenantalists.

NOTING MAJOR WEAKNESSES

In addition to unwarranted assumptions, Dr. Gerstner's book contains
a number of flaws that greatly lessen its credibility as a significant critique of dispensationalism. The following list briefly discusses some of
the more serious deficiencies:

1. Dr. Gerstner's volume does not generally reflect the writings of dispensationalists since 1980, as illustrated above.
Therefore, it could not possibly represent or interact with
current dispensational thinking as it purports to do (p. 72).[14]

2. Dr. Gerstner frequently cites certain men as representative
of dispensational thought. To current dispensationalists, most
of these men represent anachronistic referencing and/or a
giant caricature of dispensational spokesmen. Examples
include Jim Bakker (p. 54), Harold Barker (p. 223), M. R.
DeHaan (pp. 54, 88), Jerry Falwell (p. 54), Norm Geisler
(p. 75), Billy Graham (pp. 54, 137, 174), Zane Hodges
(pp. 225–30), W. W. Howard (p. 224), Rex Humbard (p. 54),
Hal Lindsey (pp. 175, 221), James Robison (p. 54), Jimmy
Swaggart (p. 54), R. B. Thieme (p. 225), and A. W. Tozer
(p. 139). Throughout this volume Dr. Gerstner has presented "strawman" arguments, among which this is his
masterpiece.

3. Dr. Gerstner resorts in places to a "guilt by association" form of argumentation. R. C. Sproul (p. x) in the

Foreword associates dispensationalists with Joseph Fletcher, father of modern "situational ethics." Gerstner puts dispensationalists alongside cults like Mormonism and Jehovah's Witnesses (p. 69). Dispensational thought is equated with Arminian theology (p. 103). Gerstner calls John Nelson Darby the "major theologian" of dispensationalists (p. 84). Trivialization and dispensationalism are equated (pp. 69–70). He even implies that dispensationalism is more deceptive than liberalism and the occult (p. 2).

4. Dr. Gerstner frequently resorts, out of character with a carefully reasoned scholastic exchange, to pejorative language and sarcasm.[15] One wonders why one needs inflammatory rhetoric—e.g., cult (p. 150), pantheism (pp. 136, 143), and "departed from Christianity" (p. 150)— to disprove such a supposedly lame theological opponent as "dispensationalism."

5. Dr. Gerstner shows familiarity with the writings of Darby, Scofield, Chafer, and Ryrie, citing them frequently. However, the author shows little or no familiarity with other older dispensational works that are classics. These include Alva J. McClain, *The Greatness of the Kingdom* (Chicago: Moody, 1968) and George N. H. Peters, *The Theocratic Kingdom,* 3 vols. (1978 reprint, Grand Rapids: Kregel, n.d.). Besides a brief quote from German dispensationalist Eric Sauer (p. 183 n. 8), Gerstner attributes no significance to his classic trilogy which includes *The Dawn of World Redemption: A Survey of the History of Salvation in the Old Testament* (Grand Rapids: Eerdmans, 1951), *The Triumph of the Crucified: A Survey of the History of Salvation in the New Testament* (Grand Rapids: Eerdmans, 1951), and *From Eternity to Eternity* (Exeter: Paternoster, 1954). A volume making the promise of being "the most extensive and systematic study of Dispensational theology ever published" would surely interact with these indispensable works. Yet Dr. Gerstner has in essence ignored them. This reviewer does not affirm all that is taught in these classics. However, a comprehensive critique of dispensationalism should certainly recognize and comment on them.

6. Dr. Gerstner has not paid the kind of attention to historical, factual, and bibliographic details that one would

expect. Examples of such discrepancies have been catalogued by Dr. John A. Witmer, archivist at Dallas Theological Seminary.[16]

7. Dr. Gerstner would have served his readers far better in
his discussion of sanctification (pp. 209–50) by quoting
from John F. Walvoord, "The Augustinian-Dispensational
Perspective," in *Five Views on Sanctification* (Grand
Rapids: Zondervan, 1987), 197–226. Here is a recent
and focused expression on sanctification by a noted Dallas dispensationalist. While this reviewer does not agree
with all that Dr. Walvoord writes there,[17] the doctrine
that he articulates is far different in many respects than
the dismal picture painted by Gerstner (esp. pp. 231–39).
It should be noted that one's view with regard to sanctification does not necessarily identify a person as dispensational or nondispensational, contrary to the author's
conclusion.

8. Dispensationalists would generally say that their consistently applied, normal hermeneutic leads them to their
views on the church and its relationship to national Israel.
These conclusions would then set them distinctly apart
from covenantalists.[18] Dr. Gerstner has chosen to major
on the *non sequitur* that one's soteriology determines his
ecclesiology and eschatology by devoting at least six full
chapters to its discussion (chaps. 7–9, 11–13). In contrast,
he minors (only chap. 10) on what dispensationalists would
consider to be one of their major distinctives—eschatology.
Thus his discussion of dispensationalism is notably out
of proportion with the real issues distinguishing
dispensationalism from covenantalism.

9. Nowhere does Gerstner distort the facts more than with
his stereotypical chart on p. 147. The right-hand column,
inaccurately labeled "dispensationalism," should be more
accurately titled "modified Arminianism." In so doing,
he has led his readers to equate dispensationalism with
Arminianism. This reviewer does not deny that some
dispensationalists subscribe to an Arminian soteriology,
but asserts rather that an Arminian soteriology is not synonymous with dispensationalism.

Sadly, Dr. Gerstner's volume does not live up to its advanced billing
and hints of irrefutable argumentation. Numerous books and booklets

have been written in the recent past with the purpose of analyzing dispensational thinking.[19] Of them all, Dr. Gerstner's most resembles the maiden voyage of the Titanic. This supposedly "unsinkable" book seems to have sustained severe damage below the water line at the hands of its own self-imposed icebergs of specious reasoning, fallacious assumptions, incomplete and outdated research, inaccurate data, distorted characterizations, and a seemingly premature celebration of victory.

ASSESSING THEOLOGICAL VALIDITY

In this reviewer's opinion, dispensational thought entered a new era somewhere in the late '70s or early '80s. Because no one person or single institution speaks for all dispensationalists and because it is not a theological system like Calvinism (but rather tends to result from a consistent hermeneutic applied with exegetical skill to particular texts whose individual conclusions comprise a macro-summation of a biblical truth), no designated person speaks for the movement. Scores of individual scholars and schools are involved in formulating dispensational thought.

Unfortunately, Dr. Gerstner has not accurately identified the current makeup or movement of dispensationalism. Thus, the almost unrecognizable image he paints of current dispensationalism results from several errors of fact and/or omission. First, he looks at the Darby/Scofield era and then the Chafer/Walvoord/Ryrie era as the bases for his conclusions, rather than being current with the new era of dispensational thought in the '80s–'90s whose leading spokesmen might well include Robert L. Saucy and John F. MacArthur Jr. The former deals more with eschatology and the latter soteriology/ecclesiology. The author limits his research primarily to earlier Dallas Theological Seminary expressions of dispensationalism that do not comprehensively reflect the whole of dispensational thought, past or present.

The Master's Seminary could agree with much of what Dr. Gerstner affirms as biblical truth about salvation and sanctification.[20] However, it strongly opposes the wrong equation of a soteriological position with the distinctive feature of dispensationalism. Further, it disavows what Dr. Gerstner pictures as the current consensus of dispensational thinking. The Master's Seminary, in opposing easy believism for salvation,[21] does not deny its dispensational roots, but rather works hard to sink them deeper into the good soil of solid biblical exegesis with the result of proper theological conclusions.

"Covenantalism" and opposition to easy believism are not synonymous. Conversely, dispensationalism and antinomianism are not necessarily synonymous either. One may be a five-point Calvinist and still be a consistent dispensationalist with regard to one's view of Israel in relationship to the NT church and one's expectation regarding events on God's prophetic calendar. The Achilles' heel in Dr. Gerstner's entire argument is the assumption that Calvinism, or Reformed theology, stands as the antithesis of dispensationalism, thus making one's soteriology determine whether he is a dispensationalist or not.[22] On the other hand, this reviewer affirms that dispensationalism does stand in notable contrast to covenantalism.

Now, in order to limit this review article to a reasonable length, brief note will be taken of a series of selected theological misstatements by Dr. Gerstner in his discussions of philosophy, hermeneutics, apologetics, and theology.[23]

1. In his brief discourse on dispensationalists and philosophy, Dr. Gerstner charges, " . . . It [dispensationalism] is almost impatient in its desire to get to Holy Scripture" (p. 75). Dispensationalists consider this a great compliment consistent with their high view of Scripture's sufficiency as outlined in such classic passages as Psalm 19, Psalm 119, and 2 Timothy 3:14–17.[24] Therefore, to dispensationalists, logic and philosophy are secondary to Scripture and serve as a means to an end, not the end itself.

2. Dr. Gerstner, an avowed advocate of the "classical" approach to apologetics, states, "Dispensationalists are not disposed to conscious fideism" (p. 79). This reviewer is amazed that Dr. Gerstner personally finds the "classical" approach in common with most dispensationalists (p. 79). Gerstner is surprised that more dispensationalists do not embrace the presuppositional approach to apologetics, since it is in the vanguard of contemporary, conservative thinking (p. 81). This reviewer is even more surprised since the author asserts, ". . . All presuppositionalists are thoroughgoing Calvinists and they do not think that Dispensationalism is an authentic form of Calvinism" (p. 81). Those dispensationalists who are presuppositionalists are so because they believe it is taught in Scripture, not because they believe it is Calvinistic.[25] There is no necessary connection, other than consistent biblical thought and conclusion, between dispensational theology and presuppositional apologetics.

3. The discussion of hermeneutics deserves at least a whole volume rather than just a chapter (pp. 83–101). However, given the reality of limitations in a review article and in Dr. Gerstner's book, in kindness it is proposed that his discussion contributes more heat than light as it relates to understanding dispensationalism. His eclectic discussion of older and/or "pop" dispensationalists such as Darby, M. R. DeHaan, Feinberg, Scofield, and Lindsey is, at best, inadequate. His discussion of "spoof-texting" or throwing "massive citations" at an issue (pp. 99–100) is certainly an unfair caricature of dispensationalists who have a legitimate desire to allow Scripture to interpret Scripture. Many dispensationalists hold in high regard the Reformed approach of interpreting the Bible by the Bible with the principle of *analogia Scriptura*.[26]

4. Dr. Gerstner has strong words against anyone who tampers with the Reformed view of "the eternal sonship of Christ" (pp. 33–34). In discussing this issue, he attempts to discredit dispensationalists historically by associating them with F. E. Raven, a Brethren figure of the late 19th century, who, according to Gerstner, denied full humanity to Christ. One's view of Christ's eternal sonship, so long as it does not deny or diminish His eternality, deity, and full humanity in His incarnation, does not affect whether one is a dispensationalist or a covenantalist. As such, it serves no logical purpose in Dr. Gerstner's discussion, other than trying to portray dispensationalists as guilty of the same heresy.[27]

5. Concerning unconditional election, Dr. Gerstner writes, "A predestination of some corpses to life and foreordination of some corpses to remain dead is what is meant by the Bible doctrine but dispensationalists refuse to accept that" (p. 113). Dr. Gerstner's assertion is generally true of dispensationalists with regard to the reprobative corollary of unconditional election, but it is not a defining distinctive of dispensationalism. One can believe in the doctrine of double predestination as articulated by sane Calvinists and still be a dispensationalist.[28]

6. Dr. Gerstner questions the orthodoxy of dispensationalists concerning the full humanity of Jesus Christ. He asserts that, regardless of whether it comes more from a lack of theological care than heterodoxy, dispensationalists have

an unusual conception of Christ's full humanity (pp. 116–17). The author's discussion is altogether too brief for such a major charge, being limited to Darby, Chafer, and C. H. Mackintosh. Regarding Christ's humanity, covenantalists and dispensationalists agree that it remained without sin throughout His earthly life (2 Cor. 5:21). The theological discussion still goes on as to whether the impeccability of Christ's human nature meant that He was susceptible to temptation like humanity, yet without sin, or whether He could not be tempted at all. After everything is said and written, the issue at hand is not really germane to the discussion of dispensationalism.

7. Dr. Gerstner's own view that one must be regenerated before becoming an object of God's call to salvation is stated but never defended biblically (p. 119). How then can he accuse dispensationalists of being unorthodox until he proves the point scripturally? Furthermore, his own view is seriously questioned by others who, like Gerstner, are strong Calvinists.[29]

8. Throughout the book, but especially in chapter eight, "Dubious Evangelism: The Dispensational Understanding of 'Dispensation' Denies the Gospel" (pp. 149–69), Dr. Gerstner repeatedly charges that dispensationalists teach multiple ways of salvation. Since the author acknowledges the existence of the book *Continuity and Discontinuity* (p. 151 n. 4), this reviewer cannot understand why Dr. Gerstner does not inform his readers of and then interact with one of its contributors, Allen P. Ross, "The Biblical Method of Salvation: A Case for Discontinuity," 161–78. To do so would have pushed the debate from the 1960s almost to the 1990s. Dr. Gerstner's charge that current dispensationalists teach multiple ways of salvation is defenseless.[30]

9. In chapter 11 (p. 209), the author writes, ". . . I will show that all traditional dispensationalists teach that converted Christian persons *can* (not may) live in sin throughout their post-conversion lives with no threat to their eternal destiny." Then he points out a contradictory exception on p. 216: "Harry Ironside is especially interesting, for surely no classical dispensationalist has tried more strenuously to avoid Antinomianism (unless it be John MaeArthur [*sic*], who succeeded)." It seems to have escaped

Dr. Gerstner's attention that not only has John MacArthur succeeded, but also every dispensationalist who believes as MacArthur does. Therefore, Gerstner subsequently disproves what he originally set out to prove.

10. "There is no question that Dispensationalism has been relatively indifferent to strict morality and usually indifferent to reform activities" (p. 250). Here Dr. Gerstner libels dispensationalists by making a universal statement about them without any documentation or real substance (documented or otherwise). The statement is false and damaging to dispensationalism's reputation. This defamatory caricature alone brings Dr. Gerstner's objectivity in his critique of dispensational teaching into serious question.

A CLOSING WORD[31]

This review article did not set out to prove Dr. Gerstner altogether theologically wrong or to affirm dispensationalism as theologically correct. But in response to the book's invitation to be evaluated, this reviewer has attempted to comply with that wish. Here are the conclusions.

Dr. John Gerstner has sincerely attempted to the best of his scholastic skills, intellect, theological prowess, and debate technique to critique dispensationalism. The work appears to be a culmination of his lifelong study of dispensationalism. This review concludes, however, that (1) Dr. Gerstner's claim to comprehensive research falls seriously short of its boast, (2) his penchant for factuality and accurate representation of dispensationalism has failed, (3) he demonstrates his apparent unwillingness to discuss major theological issues without uncalled-for and repeated diatribe, and (4) his *non sequitur* argumentation disqualifies much of this book as a positive or helpful contribution to the growing rapprochement between covenantalists and dispensationalists. If anything, it has attitudinally and informationally hurt the dialogue.

This review might not satisfy Dr. Gerstner's challenge to ". . . show me the fundamental error in what I teach" (p. 263). However, it should be more than enough to respond to R. C. Sproul's conditional offer of Dr. Gerstner's apology when substantial reason can be shown: "If Gerstner is inaccurate—if he has failed to understand dispensational theology correctly—then he owes many a profound apology" (p. xi). At best, one could hope that this title would be withdrawn from circulation as unworthy of the author's reputation for accuracy and fairness. But at the very least, R. C. Sproul's promise on the author's behalf should be kept.

In private correspondence received from Dr. Gerstner soon after this essay first appeared and well before his recent homegoing, he vigorously expressed a desire to write a rejoinder rather than an apology.

ENDNOTES

1 John H. Gerstner, *Wrongly Dividing the Word of Truth: A Critique of Dispensationalism* (Brentwood, Tenn.: Wolgemuth and Hyatt, Publishers, Inc., 1991). This volume greatly expands on Dr. Gerstner's previous brief presentation of these issues in his booklet *A Primer on Dispensationalism* (Phillipsburg, N.J.: Presbyterian and Reformed, 1982).

2 Endorsement on the outside back of the dust cover.

3 Inside front of the dust cover.

4 Charles Fred Lincoln, "The Development of the Covenant Theory," *Bibliotheca Sacra* 100, no. 397 (January–March 1943): 134–63. Gerstner remarks, "His work on the covenants is the best dispensational presentation of the subject I have seen" (p. 266). This reviewer suggests that Dr. Gerstner consider Renald E. Showers, *There Really Is a Difference: A Comparison of Covenant and Dispensational Theology* (Bellmawr, N.J.: The Friends of Israel Gospel Ministry, 1990), 1–111, as more current and representative material to evaluate.

5 John Witmer will note this tendency in his "A Review of *Wrongly Dividing the Word of Truth,* Part 2," *Bibliotheca Sacra* 149, no. 595 (July–September 1992).

6 Tom Wells, "*Wrongly Dividing the Word of Truth: A Critique of Dispensationalism*: A Review," *Reformation Today* (January–February 1992): 25–32.

7 Dr. Gerstner takes great issue with Zane C. Hodges, *Absolutely Free* (Grand Rapids: Zondervan, 1989), but so does John F. MacArthur Jr., *The Gospel According to Jesus* (Grand Rapids: Zondervan, 1988). Yet Hodges and MacArthur both remain dispensationalists. Why? Because one's soteriology does not necessarily dictate the essence of his ecclesiology and eschatology.

8 D. G. Hart, "The Legacy of J. Gresham Machen and the Identity of the

Orthodox Presbyterian Church," *Westminster Theological Journal* 53 (1991): 213.

[9] Craig Blaising, who teaches theology at Dallas Theological Seminary, presented a major paper to the 1986 meeting of the Dispensational Study Group (DSG), which was subsequently published as two articles. "Doctrinal Development in Orthodoxy," *Bibliotheca Sacra* 145, no. 578 (April–June 1988): 133–40, and "Development of Dispensationalism by Contemporary Dispensationalists," *Bibliotheca Sacra* 145, no. 579 (July–September 1988): 254–80. Dr. Gerstner acknowledged this latter article on p. 159 n. 19. For a short history of the DSG see Ronald T. Clutter, "Dispensational Study Group: An Introduction," *Grace Theological Journal [GTJ]* 10, no. 2 (fall 1989): 123–24. This same issue of *GTJ* also contains the papers presented at the 1989 DSG by Vern S. Poythress, Paul S. Karleen, and Robert L. Saucy.

[10] Gerstner hardly acknowledges this significant work, *Continuity and Discontinuity,* including only a two-sentence reference to it on p. 151 n. 4.

[11] Also expected in 1992 are Craig Blaising and Darrell Bock, eds., *Israel and the Church* (Grand Rapids: Zondervan, 1992) and D. Campbell and J. Townsend, eds., *Premillennialism* (Chicago: Moody, 1992). The recent publishing of Larry V. Crutchfield, *The Origins of Dispensationalism: The Darby Factor* (Lanham, Md.: University Press of America, 1992) is also significant. In this he strongly refutes Dr. Gerstner's charge that Darby is ". . . to this day the chief influence" (p. 24).

[12] Covenantalist Vern S. Poythress, *Understanding Dispensationalists* (Grand Rapids: Zondervan, 1987), 12, agrees that "many dispensational scholars have now modified considerably the classic form of D-theology. . . ."

[13] Earl D. Radmacher, "The Current State of Dispensationalism and Its Eschatology," in *Perspectives on Evangelical Theology* (Grand Rapids: Baker, 1979), 163–76. Compare Paul D. Feinberg, "Hermeneutics of Discontinuity," in *Continuity and Discontinuity,* 109–28. See also Darrell L. Bock, "Evangelicals and the Use of the Old Testament in the New, Part 1," *Bibliotheca Sacra* 142, no. 567 (July–September 1985): 209–23 and "Part 2," *Bibliotheca Sacra* 142, no. 568 (October–December 1985): 306–19.

[14] In addition to the literature cited above, Dr. Gerstner does not acknowledge such notable pieces as Kenneth L. Barker, "False Dichotomies Between the Testaments," *Journal of the Evangelical Theological Society* 25, no. 1 (March 1982): 3–16, or David L. Turner, "The Continuity of Scripture and Eschatology: Key Hermeneutical Issues," *Grace Theological Journal* 6, no. 2 (fall 1985): 275–87.

[15] This charge has more than adequately been documented by both John Witmer, "A Review of *Wrongly Dividing the Word of Truth,* Part 1," *Bibliotheca Sacra* 149, no. 594 (April–June 1992): 132–33, and Thomas Ice, "How Trinitarian Thinking Supports A Dispensational Rationale," *Dispensational Distinctives* 1, no. 5 (September–October 1991): 1. Therefore, I will not duplicate their observations.

[16] Witmer, "A Review, Part 1," 133–36.

[17] This reviewer found Reformed theologian Anthony A. Hoekema to be fair but forthright in his critique of Walvoord in *Five Views* (230–32), in contrast to the "worst-case scenario" approach of Dr. Gerstner.

[18] Consult Parts 1 and 2 of Willem A. Van Gemeren, "Israel as the Hermeneutical Crux in the Interpretation of Prophecy," *Westminster Theological Journal [WTJ]* 45 (1983): 132–44, and *WTJ* 46 (1984): 254–97, for a thorough survey of Reformed thinking about Israel, beginning with Calvin, who had "no clearly defined position on Israel" and extending to the publication dates of these articles.

[19] For example, Oswald T. Allis, *Prophecy and the Church* (1977; reprint, Nutley, N.J.: Presbyterian and Reformed, n.d.); Greg L. Bahnsen and Kenneth L. Gentry Jr., *House Divided: The Breakup of Dispensational Theology* (Tyler, Tex.: Institute for Christian Economics, 1989); Clarence B. Bass, *Backgrounds to Dispensationalism* (Grand Rapids: Baker, 1977); William E. Cox, *An Examination of Dispensationalism* (Phillipsburg, N.J.: Presbyterian and Reformed, 1980); Poythress, *Understanding Dispensationalists;* Jon Zens, *Dispensationalism: A Reformed Inquiry into Its Leading Figures and Features* (Phillipsburg, N.J.: Presbyterian and Reformed, 1980).

[20] As evidenced by MacArthur, *Gospel According to Jesus*. Note also the affirming review by dispensationalist Homer A. Kent Jr., "*The Gospel According to Jesus*: A Review Article," *Grace Theological Journal* 10, no. 1 (spring 1989): 67–77. Darrell Bock of Dallas Theological Seminary

does not fully commend all of Dr. MacArthur's book, but he gives it affirmation beyond what one would expect based on Gerstner's discussions (p. 253) ("A Review of *The Gospel According to Jesus,*" *Bibliotheca Sacra* 146, no. 581 [January–March, 1989]: 21–40).

[21] "Opposition to easy believism" more accurately defines the issue under discussion than the expression "lordship salvation," because the latter implies a false addition to faith as the sole condition for salvation (cf. MacArthur, *Gospel According to Jesus,* xiii–xiv, 28–29 n. 20).

[22] Gerstner writes "The Bible teaches Dispensationalism or Calvinism. It cannot teach both and be the infallibly true Word of God" (2 n. 1). This statement, as it stands, is erroneous and/or potentially very misleading. First, it could be true that the Bible teaches something other than these two schools of thought. The burden rests with him to prove his point biblically. Second, his reasoning would make dispensationalism the antithesis to Calvinism. If by Calvinism, Dr. Gerstner means Calvinistic soteriology, then he errs because dispensational thought does not essentially involve soteriology and is not formulated from a certain creedal soteriology. If by dispensationalism he means to include ecclesiology and eschatology, then he errs because the antithesis would be with "covenantalism" rather than "Calvinism." For a reasonable clarification of terms to allow a comparison of "apples with apples," see Michael Harbin, "The Hermeneutics of Covenant Theology," *Bibliotheca Sacra* 143, no. 571 (July–September 1986): 246–59, from a dispensationalist's perspective, and Morton H. Smith, "The Church and Covenant Theology," *Journal of the Evangelical Theological Society* 21, no. 1 (March 1978): 47–65, for a covenantalist's view.

[23] In a soon-to-appear article John A. Witmer, "A Review, Part 2" *Bibliotheca Sacra* 149, no. 595 (July–September 1992) will biblically challenge and attempt to correct Dr. Gerstner's attack on varying aspects of dispensationalism as taught in the past or as currently being taught by some at Dallas Theological Seminary.

[24] McClain, *Greatness of the Kingdom,* 527–31, lets some air out of Dr. Gerstner's overinflated charge that dispensationalism is "almost anti-philosophical" (p. 75) with his chapter 28, "A Premillennial Philosophy of History."

[25] Dr. Gerstner does recognize John C. Whitcomb as a dispensationalist who is also a presuppositionalist (80 n. 14). However, he fails to mention

The Master's Seminary which embraces presuppositionalism. See TMS Professor of Theology, George J. Zemek, "Review Article: *Classical Apologetics: A Rational Defense,*" *Grace Theological Journal* 7, no. 1 (spring 1986): 111–23, where he evaluates the discussion of apologetical method by R. C. Sproul, John Gerstner, and Arthur Lindsey.

[26] Dispensationalist Elliott E. Johnson has recently provided a comprehensive discussion of hermeneutics in general in *Expository Hermeneutics: An Introduction* (Grand Rapids: Zondervan, 1990). In contrast to Gerstner, Vern Poythress, *Understanding Dispensationalists,* 78–96, presents a covenantalist's perspective on this issue in a more informative and irenic fashion.

[27] See John MacArthur, *The Sonship of Christ* (Grandville, Mich.: IFCA Press, 1991), for a discussion of the incarnational approach to Christ's sonship.

[28] Cp. dispensationalist Emery H. Bancroft, *Christian Theology,* 2d rev. ed. (Grand Rapids: Zondervan, 1976), 241, whose discussion of reprobation in its conclusion is essentially indistinguishable from that of R. C. Sproul, "Double Predestination," in *Soli Deo Gloria* (Phillipsburg, N.J.: Presbyterian and Reformed, 1976), 63–72.

[29] E.g., the elders of Trinity Baptist Church in Montville, N.J., mentioned above (p. 81). Why, then, attempt to hold dispensationalists responsible for error in this point when even fellow Calvinists do not agree?

[30] For another excellent refutation of Dr. Gerstner's charge, see John S. Feinberg, "Salvation in the Old Testament," in *Tradition and Testament,* eds. John S. Feinberg and Paul D. Feinberg (Chicago: Moody, 1981), 39–77.

[31] It is beyond the scope of this review, but a subsequent article is needed to interact with and evaluate Dr. Gerstner's exegesis of key passages that dispensationalists use to show a distinction between Israel and the church (cf. pp. 187–200).

CHAPTER FOUR

Theonomy

Theonomy and
the Dating of Revelation

Robert L. Thomas

In 1989, a well-known spokesman for the theonomist camp, Kenneth L. Gentry, published a work devoted to proving that John the apostle wrote Revelation during the sixties of the first century A.D. Basing his position heavily on Revelation 17:9–11 and 11:1–13, he used internal evidence within the book as his principal argument for the early date. His clever methods of persuasion partially shield his basic motive for his interpretive conclusions, which is a desire for an undiluted rationale to support Christian social and political involvement leading to long-term Christian cultural progress and dominion. If the prophecies of Revelation are yet to be fulfilled, no such progress will develop—a prospect the author cannot accept. Inconsistency marks Gentry's hermeneutical pattern. Predisposition keeps him from seeing the book's theme verse as a reference to Christ's second coming. His explanation of Revelation 17:9–11 is fraught with weaknesses, as is his discussion of 11:1–2. Two major flaws mar Gentry's discussion of John's temporal expectation in writing the book. Besides these problems, five major questions regarding Gentry's position remain unanswered.

* * * * *

Theonomist[1] Kenneth L. Gentry Jr., makes evidence derived from exegetical data within the Apocalypse his major focus in building a case for dating the book prior to the destruction of Jerusalem in A.D. 70.[2] Though acknowledging that other advocates of either a Neronic (i.e., in the 60s) or Domitianic date (i.e., in the 90s) for Revelation's composition find no such direct evidence within the book, he proceeds to find "inherently suggestive and positively compelling historical time-frame indicators in Revelation."[3] He uses the contemporary reign of the sixth king in 17:9–11 and the integrity of the temple and Jerusalem in 11:1–13 to exemplify arguments that are "virtually certain" proof of a date some time in the sixties.[4]

Before a look at his exegesis of these two passages and several others, however, Gentry's general methodology deserves attention.

METHOD OF PRESENTATION

His first tactic is to create an environment of what may be called "virtual reality." This phenomenon is becoming very popular in this day of computer-generated illusionary data. I call Gentry's use of it an experience in "back-to-the-future" manipulation.

A few years ago, I went with one of my sons and two of my grandsons on what was then the new "Back to the Future" experience on the lot of Universal Studios in Burbank. I call it an "experience" for the lack of a better term. It was not a "ride" such as most attractions at Six Flags or Disneyland, because we never left a small room in which we originally sat down. We were in an automobile-type enclosure with a very complicated dashboard. We were enclosed on three sides in the dark room with only a three-dimensional screen in front of us. When our back-to-the-future experience began, all we could see was the screen with its images portraying our "movement" through time and near collisions with all kinds of objects including dinosaurs, cliffs, large buildings, vehicles, and the like. To enforce this, our auto-like enclosure was bumping around, pitching up and down, rolling side-to-side, and leaning in synchronization with what we saw on the screen. It was a very realistic experience, but it was not real. All the apparent movement made my son sick at his stomach. I attribute this to his right-brain orientation. It did not bother me at all, however, because I rested in the reality that I was still in a small room enclosed in a larger building and had never left that room. In fact, I experienced the attraction again later in the day, but this time at the request of and in the company of my two grandsons only.

Gentry like others of the reconstructionist movement is a master in using words to take his readers back to the future, i.e., in creating virtual reality that many will not distinguish from reality itself. He does this by stating his "correct" view first,[5] then often following it up with a long list of writers to support that view.[6] This has the effect of blinding the reader on three sides so that he can see only what Gentry wants him to see in front of him. Only after the reader's exposure to the positive evidence for his view does the author turn to evaluate some of the weaknesses of that viewpoint.[7] By this time, the merits of other viewpoints have become lost in the shuffle.

Behind this exegetical methodology lies a preunderstanding that controls the whole process. In about the last thirty years it has become increasingly fashionable among some evangelicals to factor the step of preunderstanding or hermeneutical self-consciousness into the interpretive process,[8] but to others, such as myself, to do so confuses the picture by making what has traditionally been known as application partially determinative of one's understanding of the historical-grammatical meaning of Scripture. Gentry tries to shield his preunderstanding from view most of the time, but it shows itself once early in the book and then in the book's concluding remarks.[9] After quoting Ryrie's words about the inevitable misery that the future holds for the world, he writes, "If such is the case, why get involved?"[10] He associates cultural defeatism and retreatist pietism with assigning a late date to Revelation and wants to date the book before A.D. 70 so as to have biblical support for the implementation of long-term Christian cultural progress and dominion.[11]

This probably reflects his basic motivation for the early dating of Revelation: a desire for an undiluted rationale to support Christian social and political involvement. He is looking for an escape from the tension between the cultural mandate given to Christians and a realization that the prophecy of Revelation dictates that the culture will inevitably go downhill despite the best efforts of God's people to reverse the trend. No one can deny that Christians are to be good citizens by doing everything they can to make this world a better place, but the fact remains that evil will eventually prevail until the end of history when Christ returns. This is apparently a paradox with which Gentry cannot live, so his exegetical methodology moves in a direction that finds Revelation's prophecies of a decaying society fulfilled in the era up to and including the fall of Jerusalem in A.D. 70.

HERMENEUTICAL PATTERN

As Gentry weaves his case for Revelation's early date, the absence of a consistent set of hermeneutical principles is evident. It is most conspicuous in a number of inconsistencies that emerge in different parts of the treatment. He does not interpret the same passage in the same way from place to place, or within the same discussion differing principles take him in different directions regarding his mode of interpretation.

For instance, he accepts the principle of the symbolic use of numbers, but only for large, rounded numbers such as 1,000, 144,000, and 200,000,000. Smaller numbers, such as seven, are quite literal.[12]

Again, he rejects the equation of "kings = kingdoms" in 17:10,[13] but in a later discussion of the *Nero Redivivus* myth in 17:11, he identifies one of the kings or heads of the beast in 17:10 as the Roman Empire revived under Vespasian.[14] The latter is part of his strained attempt to explain the healing of the beast's death-wound.

When discussing the 144,000, Gentry is uncertain at one point whether they represent the saved of Jewish lineage or the church as a whole.[15] Yet just ten pages later they are definitely Christians of Jewish extraction, because he needs evidence to tie the fulfillment of Revelation to the land of Judea.[16] This provides another example of his lack of objective hermeneutical principles to guide interpretation.

The forty-two months of 11:2 is the period of the Roman siege of Jerusalem from early spring 67 till September 70, according to Gentry.[17] A bit earlier he finds John, even while he is writing the book, already enmeshed in the great tribulation (1:9; 2:22), a period of equal length and apparently simultaneous with the Roman siege.[18] In a discussion of 13:5–7, however, he separates the Neronic persecution of Christians which constituted "the great tribulation" (13:5–7) from the Roman siege of Jerusalem in both time and place, dating it from 64 to 68 and locating it in the Roman province of Asia.[19] So which is it? Is John writing during "the great tribulation" of 64–68 or the one of 67–70? Later still, he assigns 65 or early 66 as the date of writing,[20] so John predicted a forty-two month period of persecution (13:5) that was already partially past when he wrote. This is indeed a puzzling picture.

Another puzzling discussion concerns the raising of the beast from his death-wound. At one point Gentry identifies Galba as the seventh king of 17:10, in strict compliance with the consecutive reigns of Roman emperors.[21] But suddenly he skips Otho and Vitellius to get to Vespasian who is the eighth and shifts from counting kings with his identification of the healing of the beast's death-wound as Rome's survival from its civil war in the late sixties.[22] This is enough to dash in pieces any effort to decipher a consistent pattern of hermeneutics, because such is nonexistent.

So much for preliminaries and generalities. The attention of the remainder of this chapter will be on individual passages, with special attention to Gentry still, but with a few side glances at other reconstructionists.

INDIVIDUAL PASSAGES

The Theme Verse

All, including Gentry and Chilton,[23] agree that the theme verse of Revelation is Revelation 1:7: "Behold, He is coming with clouds, and every eye will see Him, even those who pierced Him, and all the families of the earth will mourn over Him." But these two theonomists do not refer this to the second coming of Christ. Rather they see it as referring to the coming of Christ in judgment upon Israel, so as to make the church the new kingdom.[24] To reach this conclusion, they must implement special proposals regarding "those who pierced Him," "the tribes of the earth," and "the land."

"Those who pierced Him." Blame for the piercing of Jesus falls squarely and solely on the shoulders of the Jews, according to Gentry.[25] He cites a number of passages in the gospels, Acts, and Paul to prove this responsibility, but conspicuously omits from his list John 19:31 and Acts 4:27 which involve the Romans and Gentiles in this horrible act.[26] This determines for him that the book's theme is the coming of God's wrath against the Jews.[27]

By limiting the blame for Christ's crucifixion to the Jews, Gentry excludes from the scope of the theme verse any reference to the Romans whom he elsewhere acknowledges to be the chief persecutors of Christians.[28] He also includes the Romans elsewhere as objects of this "cloud coming" of Christ,[29] and yet does not give the Romans a place in the theme verse of the book.

"The tribes of the earth." Without evaluating any other possibility, Gentry assigns φυλή *(phylē)* the meaning of "tribe" and sees in it a reference to the tribes of Israel.[30] This interpretation has merit because that is the meaning of the term in the source passage, Zechariah 12:10ff., and in a parallel NT passage, John 19:37.[31] The problem with the way Gentry construes it, however, is that if this refers to Israel, it is a mourning of repentance, as in Zechariah, not a mourning of despair as he makes it.

For this to be a mourning of despair as the context of Revelation requires (cf. 9:20–21; 16:9, 11, 21), *phylē* must be taken in the sense of "family" and must refer to peoples of all nations as it does so often in the Apocalypse (cf. 5:9; 7:9; 11:9; 13:7; 14:6).[32] This is the only way to do justice to the worldwide scope of the book as required by such verses as 3:10, which even Gentry admits refers to the whole Roman world.[33] The sense of a mourning of despair throughout the whole earth is the sense Jesus attaches to the words in His use of the Zechariah 12:10ff. passage in Matthew 24:30.[34]

"The land." The reconstructionists actually take "the tribes of the *earth"* to be "the tribes of the *land,"* i.e., the land of Palestine.[35] It is true that γῆ *(gē)* can carry such a restricted meaning, but special support in its context of usage is necessary for it to mean this. The acknowledged

worldwide scope of Revelation already cited rules out this localized meaning of the term in 1:7.

So in the theme verse of Revelation, Gentry strikes out on the three pitches that he himself has chosen. He also leaves other unanswered questions regarding this alleged "cloud coming" in the sixties. He identifies the cloud coming against the Jews as the judgment against Judea in 67–70.[36] Against the church, that coming was the persecution by the Romans from 64 to 68.[37] The cloud coming for Rome was her internal strife in 68–69.[38] But nowhere does he tell what the promised deliverance of the church is (e.g., 3:11). It appears to be a question without a clear-cut answer as to how this "cloud coming" could be a promise of imminent deliverance for God's people. All he can see in it is judgment against them and the "privilege" of being clearly distinguished from Judaism forever. He finds covenantal and redemptive import for Christianity in the collapse of the Jewish order,[39] but this falls short of a personal appearance of Christ to take the faithful away from their persecution.

The Sixth King

As mentioned above, one of the two internal indicators that make the early date "virtually certain" is the identity of the sixth king in 17:9–11.[40] Gentry first uses the "seven hills" of 17:9 to indicate that Rome or the Roman Empire is in view.[41] Then he concludes that the seven kings of 17:9 (Greek text; 17:10 in English) are seven consecutive Roman emperors.[42] He lists ten kings, beginning with Julius Caesar (49–44 B.C.) and continuing with Augustus (31 B.C.–A.D. 14), Tiberius (14–37), Gaius or Caligula (37–41), Claudius (41–54), Nero (54–68), Galba (68–69), Otho (69), Vitelius (69), Vespasian (69–79).[43] The sixth in this series is Nero, so because 17:10 says "one is," he concludes that John must have written the book during Nero's reign.[44]

Gentry faces four objections to his theory that the sixth king is Nero,[45] but except for the fourth one, to which this discussion will return shortly, bypasses the exegetical crux of the issue. Regarding the seven hills, he assumes without consideration of any contrary evidence that they tie the beast to the city of Rome, but is this a valid assumption? The formula introducing this explanation, "Here is the mind which has wisdom" (17:9a; cf. 13:18a), indicates a need for special theological and symbolic discernment to comprehend it. Gentry's proposal requires only a basic knowledge of geography and numbers, not a special God-given wisdom.[46] Further, it is hard to see any connection between the topography of Rome and seven of its emperors.[47] Verses 9–10 refer to the scope and nature of the beast's power, not to the physical layout of a city.[48] No single historical city, particularly Rome, can meet all the characteristics John speaks of in

Revelation 17–18.[49] The added expression, "They are seven kings," seems to require that an identification of the mountains or hills be of a political rather than a geographical nature. Strangest of all, though, is Gentry's unfulfilled obligation to explain what a reference to Rome is doing in the midst of a chapter dealing with Babylon, which he takes to represent Jerusalem.[50] The best he can do is theorize that the harlot's riding on the beast is an alliance between Jerusalem and Rome against Christianity.[51] To support the existence of such an alleged alliance, he cites Matthew 23:37ff.; John 19:16; Acts 17:7, none of which support his theory.[52] Rome's prolonged siege and destruction of Jerusalem from the late 60s to 70 hardly gives the impression of any alliance.

The harlot sits upon or beside the seven mountains (17:9), just as she sits upon or beside "many waters" (17:1). Since the "many waters" are a symbol explained in 17:15, analogy would dictate that the seven mountains are also symbolic and not literal hills.[53] The very next clause in 17:9 explains the symbolism of the seven mountains: they are seven kings or kingdoms. As noted above, Gentry as part of his answer to the fourth objection to the Neronian identification rejects the equating of kings with the kingdoms they rule, but later he incorporates such an equation into his explanation of the identity of the eighth head.[54]

Besides the tenuous nature of Gentry's use of the seven hills, his conclusion that Nero is the sixth or "the one [who] is" also faces serious obstacles. The greatest obstacle is his need to begin counting "kings" with Julius Caesar. He tries to defend this by citing several ancient sources,[55] but the fact is that Rome was a Republic, ruled by the First Triumvirate, in the days of Julius Caesar and became a Principate under Augustus and the emperors that followed him.[56] Neither does Gentry attempt to explain the thirteen-year gap between Julius Caesar's death and the beginning of Augustus' reign. They were not consecutive rulers as he makes them out to be. The exclusion of Julius Caesar makes Nero the fifth instead of the sixth "king." Another good reason for not making Nero the sixth is that it eliminates the necessity of making Galba the seventh and seeing the eighth as the revived Roman Empire rather than an individual king. This scheme is fraught with hermeneutical difficulties.

Gentry's further use of 666 to prove that the first beast of chapter 13 is Nero, he admits, is only corroborative and cannot stand alone,[57] so the efficient course is to turn now to his second major item of internal evidence to prove an early date of writing.

The Contemporary Integrity of the Temple
Gentry finds indisputable evidence in Revelation 11:1–2 that the temple was still standing and that the destruction of Jerusalem was still

future when John wrote the book.[58] He goes to great lengths to prove that it was the Herodian temple of Jesus' day by locating it in Jerusalem, and to show that it does not serve as a symbolic representation of the church.[59] Yet he gives no attention to the possibility that this may be a future literal temple.

He is quite defensive of his hermeneutical methodology in handling these two verses, a method that involves a mixture of figurative-symbolic and literal-historical.[60] He takes the measuring to represent the preservation of the innermost aspects—including the ναός (*naos, "temple"*), altar, and worshipers—and the casting out (ἔκβαλε *[ekbale]*) as indicative of the destruction of the external court of the temple complex. The former or inner spiritual idea speaks of the preservation of God's new temple, the church, while the latter or material temple of the old covenant era will come to destruction. In other words, v. 1 is figurative and v. 2 literal. In yet other terms, the τὸν ναὸν τοῦ θεοῦ (*ton naon tou theou*, "the temple of God") and τὸ θυσιαστήριον (*to thysiastērion*, "the altar") are symbolic and τὴν αὐλὴν τὴν ἔξωθεν τοῦ ναοῦ (*tēn aulēn tēn exōthen tou naou*, "the court outside the temple") is literal.

Gentry justifies the radical switch in hermeneutical approaches by appealing to Walvoord and Mounce, whom he says combine literal and figurative in this passage also.[61] He cites Walvoord's silence regarding John's literally climbing the walls of the temple to get his measurements and Mounce's reference to the necessity of a symbolic mixture in interpreting the passage. What Gentry does is drastically different from these two, however. He wants a figurative and literal meaning for essentially the same terminology. For example, he assigns the term *naos* both a literal and a symbolic meaning in consecutive verses. In fact, he refers the temple and the altar to literal structures earlier[62] and to the spiritual temple of the church a few pages later.[63] This compares to changing the rules in the middle of the game. Any interpretation can win that way.

His response to objections to his interpretation of 11:1–2 includes an assigning of a pre-70 date to Clement of Rome's epistle to the Corinthians, though its accepted dating is in the 90s. He does this because Clement speaks as though the temple were still standing. Then Gentry has a lengthy discussion of the silence of the rest of the NT regarding the destruction of Jerusalem,[64] during which he apparently accepts dates prior to 70 for all four Gospels, including the gospel of John, and the rest of the NT canon.[65] This theory creates further problems for his case, with which he does not deal and so this discussion will not either.

Gentry does not venture an explanation of how John, isolated on the Island of Patmos so many miles from Jerusalem, can visit the literal city to carry out his symbolical task of measuring the temple. He seems oblivious to John's being in a prophetic trance (4:2) to receive this and other revelations in this visional portion of the book. His task in 11:1–2 is the first of his assigned duties to perform following his recommissioning at the end of chapter 10 (10:11). So he is not to transport himself physically across the Mediterranean Sea to Judea, but "in spirit" he is already there.

One cannot quarrel with the conclusion that John's visional responsibility of measuring points in its fulfillment to a literal temple, but it is not the Herodian temple of Jesus' day. It is a future temple to be rebuilt just before Christ's second advent (cf. Dan. 9:27; 12:11; Matt. 24:15; 2 Thess. 2:4). It indeed will be a literal temple, but without symbolic meaning such as Gentry assigns. His idea that the temple and the altar of v. 1 represent the church leaves no room to identify the worshipers in the same verse. His approach to symbolism is inconsistent and self-contradictory. This aspect of the description as well as v. 2 shows that the entire description is on Jewish ground and is not part Jewish and part Christian.[66]

John's measuring of the temple is clearly not for the purpose of obtaining dimensions, but for the sake of acquiring information necessary for his new prophetic task. That information comes in the sequel to the command to measure and cast out, in the description of the two witnesses in 11:3–14.[67] The two witnesses in association with the sanctuary, the altar, and the worshipers enjoy God's favor (11:5–6, 11–12), but their Gentile foes who oppose and kill them eventually experience a devastating earthquake because of God's disfavor (11:13). So the measuring is an object lesson of how entities favored by and opposed to God will fare during the period of Gentile oppression of Jerusalem that lies ahead during the period covered by the remainder of John's prophecies.

Temporal Expectation of the Author

One other temporal feature that Gentry magnifies is the emphasis of Revelation on the nearness of Christ's coming (Rev. 1:1, 3, 19; 22:6–7, 12, 20). He faults those who refer this to Christ's second advent, noting that the "shortly" or "soon" that characterizes the coming is hardly a suitable way to speak of the already nineteen-hundred-year interval that separates that coming from the writing of Revelation.[68] His solution is to refer the book to the imminence of the events to come upon the Jews, the church, and the Roman Empire during the decade of the sixties, culminating in the destruction of Jerusalem in A.D. 70.[69]

At least two flaws mar his theory. The first is that his placement of the coming of Christ to the church precedes his date for the writing of the book. The coming of Christ for the church, he says, is the Neronic persecution of A.D. 64–68,[70] but John did not write the book until 65 or early 66.[71] This "coming" was not imminent; it was already in progress.

The other flaw is that of setting time limitations on how long "soon" must be. If the NT makes anything clear, it is that no one knows the day or hour of Christ's coming (e.g., Matt. 24:42, 44; 25:13; Mark 13:32). That coming will be like a thief in the night (Rev. 3:3) so as to catch everyone by surprise, but according to Gentry's scheme, it was quite predictable. Jesus' teaching about His coming occurring in "this generation" (Matt. 24:34) is no exception to this rule,[72] because He made that statement in the same context of confessing ignorance as to the time of His own coming.

The teaching of Christ's imminent return is not about setting a time limit on when He will come. It is about teaching an attitude of expectancy that provides motivation for a godly lifestyle. Paul expected Christ's return during his lifetime (1 Cor. 15:51; 1 Thess. 4:15, 17) and this was proper. Yet Paul did not lay down strict guidelines that Christ had to come before he died.

For Gentry, "soon" means already (i.e., Christ's coming for the church), in two years (i.e., Christ's coming for the Jews), and in four years (i.e., Christ's coming for the Roman Empire). If this were correct, in itself it illustrates that "soon" is a relative term with a good bit of elasticity. The Apocalypse computes time either relatively to the divine apprehension as here and in 22:10 or absolutely in itself as long or short (8:1; 20:2). God is not limited by the time constraints that are so binding on man (2 Peter 3:8), so man cannot be impatient in limiting the time span covered by "soon."[73]

A GENERAL OVERVIEW OF THE ISSUE

Gentry's book itemizes a number of other supposed supports for the early date, but admits in most cases that these are only corroborative of his main proofs and have no independent value.[74] Throughout most of the work he gives the impression that he uses two criteria of independent value in dating the book, Nero as the sixth king of 17:10 and the existence of the temple and Jerusalem contemporary to the writing of the book. Yet when he arrives near the end he speaks of the "wealth of internal considerations for an early date."[75] His wealth of considerations consists of only two, both of which are useless in demonstrating his case, as pointed out above.

This discussion of internal criteria for dating the book of Revelation would not be complete without posing some questions that Gentry does not answer satisfactorily in his book.

1. How is it that the "cloud-coming" of A.D. 70 involves no personal coming of Christ (Matt. 24:30; 26:64; Rev. 1:7; 2:5, 16, 25; 3:3, 11, 20; 16:15; 22:7, 12, 20), but the "cloud-coming" at the end of history does (Acts 1:11; 1 Thess. 4:13ff.)?[76] In the first place, where did Christ distinguish between two such comings, and in the second place, where did He say that He would personally appear at one and not at the other? The answer to both questions is "nowhere." Such a distinguishing between two future comings is the product of a dominion-theological distortion of NT teaching, not of sound exegetical practice.

2. How could John dwell on the prosperity of the church in Laodicea when the city had been completely destroyed by an earthquake only five years earlier? Gentry responds to this problem by suggesting that Laodicea's wealth was spiritual and not material, by supposing the possibility of a quick rebuilding, and by theorizing that the earthquake did not impact the sector of the city where the Christians were.[77] A careful exegesis of 3:17, however, shows that Christians in the city thought their material prosperity was equivalent to spiritual prosperity, not that they were spiritually rich while materially poor. The possibility of a quick rebuilding contradicts the facts. The rebuilding effort was still in progress as late as 79 when a gymnasium that was part of the rebuilding effort was completed.[78] Also an abrupt numismatic poverty marks this period in all the cities of the Lycus district of which Laodicea was a part. This too illustrates the prolonged effect of the destructive earthquake.[79] As for Gentry's theory that part of the city was spared the devastation that affected the whole district, this is pure speculation that belies the available facts.

3. Did the ministry of John overlap that of Paul in the churches of Asia? Gentry's reconstruction of the chronology of the period would require this. If John wrote in 65 or early 66, he must have been in Asia for at least five years prior to that to have unseated Paul as the authoritative apostle for the region and to have gained the respect of Christians throughout the whole province. It would have been necessary for him to have been there long enough to become a problem for Nero too, resulting in his exile to Patmos some time after 64. Paul visited Ephesus at least once after this (A.D. 65), following his release from his first Roman imprisonment (1 Tim. 1:3). Yet after leaving the city, he left Timothy in charge of the church and made no reference to the presence of John the apostle and his influence on the church. If John had been there and had taken charge, why would Paul return to Asia? The answer is that he would not have, but he did—so John had not yet arrived in Asia.

4. When did John arrive in Asia? According to the best tradition, John was part of a migration of Christians from Palestine to the province of Asia just before the outbreak of the Jewish rebellion in A.D. 66, so he did

not arrive there before the late sixties.[80] A Neronic dating of the book would hardly have allowed time for him to settle in Asia, replace Paul as the respected leader of the Asian churches, and be exiled to Patmos before Nero's death in 68. Gentry does not respond to this problem, but his dating of the book in 65 or 66 renders its apostolic authorship impossible.

5. What was the condition of the churches of Asia during the sixties, that portrayed in Paul's epistles to Ephesians (A.D. 61), Colossians (A.D. 61), and Timothy (A.D. 65 and 67) or that in John's seven messages of Revelation 2–3? Recognizing true apostles and prophets had become a problem in the latter (e.g., 2:2, 20), but the former epistles give no inkling of this kind of a problem. In Paul's epistles to this area, false teaching regarding the person of Christ was a crucial issue (e.g., Col. 1:13–20), but not so in John's seven messages. A need in Paul's epistles was strong emphasis on Christian family roles (e.g., Eph. 5:22–6:9; Col. 3:18–4:1; 1 Tim. 6:1–2), but John's messages do not touch this subject at all. A prominent danger in John's messages is the Nicolaitan heresy (2:6, 15), but Paul's epistles say nothing about it. Differences of this type are almost limitless, the simple reason being that Paul's four epistles and John's seven messages belong to decades separated by twenty years. Gentry responds to this problem only superficially,[81] and therefore ineffectively.

A FINAL REVIEW

It has been impossible to deal with all the peculiar interpretations of dominion theology in the Apocalypse, because the proposed topic has been the internal evidence for dating the book. Probably when Gentry completes his forthcoming commentary, *The Divorce of Israel: A Commentary on Revelation,*[82] further works of refutation will have to deal with Babylon a symbolic title for Jerusalem,[83] why the seven last plagues are not final,[84] why 19:11–16 is not the second coming of Christ to earth,[85] why the state pictured in 21:9–22:5 is the church age and not the future eternal state,[86] and the like. This recently revived postmillennial movement is very aggressive and will continue its efforts to win converts from among both premillennialists and amillennialists.

Meeting its challenge will call for patient exegesis of the separate texts, the kind that requires much time. Yet it is vital to spend this time in the text if the truth of the Word of God is to prevail over propagated error. May this be a call to all to handle the Scriptures carefully in the face of this and many other threats that tend to disfigure the face of Christian doctrine here at the end of the twentieth century. Though human efforts are feeble, may God help His servants to do a good job in what He has put them here to do.

ENDNOTES

[1] Theonomy—also known as "dominion theology" and "Christian reconstructionism"—is a worldview that foresees a progressive domination of world government and society by Christianity until God's kingdom on earth becomes a reality. Its eschatology is essentially that of the postmillennialism so popular around the beginning of the twentieth century.

[2] Kenneth L. Gentry Jr., *Before Jerusalem Fell: Dating the Book of Revelation* (Tyler, Tex.: Institute for Christian Economics, 1989), 113, 116.

[3] Ibid., 119.

[4] Ibid., 118–19.

[5] E.g., ibid., 153–54.

[6] E.g., ibid., 30–38, 168, 200, 296 n. 50. Many citations in these lists are not from primary sources.

[7] E.g., ibid., 203–12.

[8] E.g., Craig A. Blaising, "Dispensationalism: The Search for Definition," in *Dispensationalism, Israel, and the Church,* ed. Craig A. Blaising and Darrell L. Bock (Grand Rapids: Zondervan, 1992), 30.

[9] Gentry, *Before Jerusalem Fell,* 5 n. 12, 336–37.

[10] Ibid., 5 n. 12.

[11] Ibid., 336–37.

[12] Ibid., 162–63.

[13] Ibid., 163–64.

[14] Ibid., 310–16.

[15] Ibid., 223–24.

[16] Ibid., 233.

[17] Ibid., 250–53.

[18] Ibid., 234.

[19] Ibid., 254–55.

[20] Ibid., 336.

[21] Ibid., 158, 208.

[22] Ibid., 310–16.

[23] Ibid., 121–23; David Chilton, *The Days of Vengeance* (Fort Worth, Tex.: Dominion, 1987), 64.·

[24] Chilton, *Days of Vengeance,* 64; Gentry, *Before Jerusalem Fell,* 131–32.

[25] Gentry, *Before Jerusalem Fell,* 123–27.

[26] Robert L. Thomas, *Revelation 1–7: An Exegetical Commentary* (Chicago: Moody, 1992), 77–78. Even Chilton allows a reference to Gentiles here (*Days of Vengeance,* 66).

[27] Gentry, *Before Jerusalem Fell,* 127.

[28] Ibid., 144.

[29] Ibid., 143–144.

[30] Ibid., 127–28.

[31] William Lee, "The Revelation of St. John," in *The Holy Bible,* ed. F. C. Cook (London: John Murray, 1881), 4:502; J. P. M. Sweet, *Revelation* (Philadelphia: Westminster, Pelican, 1979), 67; G. V. Caird, "A Commentary on the Revelation of St. John the Divine," in *Harper New Testament Commentaries* (New York: Harper and Row, 1966), 18; James Moffatt, "The Revelation of St. John the Divine," in *The Expositor's Greek Testament,* ed. W. Robertson Nicoll (Grand Rapids: Eerdmans, n.d.), 5:339–40; J. B. Smith, *A Revelation of Jesus Christ* (Scottdale, Pa.: Herald, 1961), 44.

[32] Alan F. Johnson, "Revelation," in *Expositor's Bible Commentary,* ed. Frank E. Gaebelein (Grand Rapids: Zondervan, 1981), 12:423.

[33] Gentry, *Before Jerusalem Fell,* 143 n. 27.

[34] For a fuller discussion of this issue, see Thomas, *Revelation 1–7,* 78–79.

[35] Gentry, *Before Jerusalem Fell,* 128–29; Chilton, *Days of Vengeance,* 66.

[36] Gentry, *Before Jerusalem Fell,* 143.

[37] Ibid., 144.

[38] Ibid., 144–45.

[39] Ibid., 144.

[40] Ibid., 146.

[41] Ibid., 149–51.

[42] Ibid., 151–52.

[43] Ibid., 152–59.

[44] Ibid., 158.

[45] Ibid., 159–64.

[46] Lee, "Revelation," 4:744; Johnson, "Revelation," 12:558.

[47] George E. Ladd, *A Commentary on the Revelation of John* (Grand Rapids: Eerdmans, 1972), 227.

[48] Martin Kiddle, *The Revelation of St. John* (New York: Harper, 1940), 349.

[49] Ladd, *Revelation,* 228.

[50] Gentry, *Before Jerusalem Fell,* 240–41 n. 26.

[51] Ibid.

[52] Ibid.

[53] Lee, "Revelation," 4:744.

[54] Gentry, *Before Jerusalem Fell,* 163–64, 310–16.

[55] Ibid., 154–58.

[56] *Collier's Encyclopedia,* 20:180, 190.

[57] Gentry, *Before Jerusalem Fell,* 198. "Fanciful" is the best description of some of Gentry's hermeneutical methodology to prove that 666 refers to Nero. He concludes that the beast who is Nero, like Satan himself, is a serpent because in English and in Greek (χξσ *[chxs]*) pronunciation of the number "sounds hauntingly like a serpent's chilling hiss" (215). He adds that the middle number-letter even has the appearance of a writhing serpent: ξ *(x)* (ibid.). Another means of identifying Nero as the beast is his red beard that matches the color of the beast (17:3) (217).

[58] Ibid., 165–69.

[59] Ibid., 169–74.

[60] Ibid., 174–75.

[61] Ibid.

[62] Ibid., 169–70.

[63] Ibid., 174.

[64] Ibid., 181–92.

[65] Ibid., 182–83.

[66] J. A. Seiss, *The Apocalypse,* 3 vols. (New York: Charles C. Cook, 1909), 2:159; Ladd, *Revelation,* 152.

[67] Henry Alford, *The Greek Testament,* 4 vols. (London: Longmans, Green, 1903), 4:657.

[68] Gentry, *Before Jerusalem Fell,* 133–37.

[69] Ibid., 142–43.

[70] Ibid., 144.

[71] Ibid., 336.

[72] Contra ibid., 131.

[73] Cf. Thomas, *Revelation 1–7,* 54–56.

[74] E.g., Gentry, *Before Jerusalem Fell,* 220–21, 246 n. 44.

[75] Ibid., 329.

[76] Cf. ibid., 122–23.

[77] Ibid., 319–22.

[78] Colin J. Hemer, *The Letters to the Seven Churches of Asia in Their Local Setting, Journal for the Study of the New Testament,* Sup 11 (Sheffield: U. of Sheffield, 1986), 194.

[79] Ibid.

[80] Thomas, *Revelation 1–7,* 22.

[81] Gentry, *Before Jerusalem Fell,* 327–29.

[82] Cf. ibid., 241 n. 26.

[83] Cf. Joseph R. Balyeat, *Babylon: The Great City of Revelation* (Sevierville, Tenn.: Onward, 1991), 49–142.

[84] Cf. Chilton, *Days of Vengeance,* 383–84.

[85] Cf. ibid., 481–89.

[86] Cf. ibid., 535–73.

CHAPTER FIVE

The Holy Spirit

Who Surprised Whom?
The Holy Spirit or Jack Deere?[1]

Richard L. Mayhue

Dr. Jack Deere, a former professor at Dallas Theological Seminary and a highly visible convert from the cessationist to the noncessationist position regarding miraculous acts of God through men, recounts his journey in Surprised by the Power of the Spirit. *He reasons that cessationists have argued more from silence than from Scripture, have twisted Scripture, and have no one single Scripture passage that proves their point. In this brief analysis of his work, it is apparent that Deere, not cessationists, has made these interpretive errors in coming to his biblically unfounded conclusion that the miraculous acts of God have continued beyond the apostolic age—but with lesser quality and frequency.*

* * * * *

In three places in his volume *Surprised by the Power of the Spirit,*[2] Dr. Jack Deere sets forth something like the following hypothetical scenario. What is your reaction to it?

> If you take a new convert, who prior to his conversion knew nothing about the history of Christianity or the New Testament, and you lock him in a room with a Bible for a week, he will come out believing that he is a member of a body that is passionately in love with the Lord Jesus Christ and a body that consistently experiences miracles. It would take a clever theologian with no experience of the miraculous to convince this convert differently.[3]

At first glance and without much thought, one might agree. But for this reviewer another look at the statement quickly causes it to become an *agree/disagree* situation. He *agrees* that a new convert who is totally unknowledgeable of history, who has no experience interpreting the Bible, and who has no study tools might conclude that the church today experiences miracles like the first-century church.

But he totally *disagrees,* along with you too probably, that the new convert would be correct. Since when is a new convert with nothing but a Bible an authority on the correct theological analysis of a subject so complex as miracles? Further, why would the theologian have to be "experienced" in the miraculous to be credible if the Scriptures are sufficient, without recourse to experience, to articulate clear doctrine (2 Tim. 3:16–17)?

This raises an even bigger question about Deere and those like him: Why do some trained theologians, who do have a knowledge of history and who do have the capabilities to use good Bible-study tools, come up with the same immature conclusion as a new believer who knows nothing? Could it be that they have used a combination of experience and a redetermined[4] theology to override otherwise reasonable conclusions?

Not so according to several men whom the author and/or publisher solicited for endorsements. Wayne Grudem, professor of Biblical and Systematic Theology at Trinity Evangelical Divinity School, writes, "This is the most persuasive answer I have ever read to the objections of people who say that miraculous gifts like healing and prophesy are not for today."[5] Since Grudem holds the highest of scholastic credentials, one can reasonably assume that he has read all the best volumes on this subject and finds Dr. Deere's book making the superlative contribution to this subject.

Other well-known men have offered equally glowing comments. "It is truly a landmark book!"[6] C. Peter Wagner of Fuller Theological Seminary has written. R. T. Kendall, minister of Westminster Chapel in London, has enthusiastically suggested, "Simply written, brilliantly argued, Dr. Deere's thesis is, in my opinion, irrefutable."[7]

Given Deere's well-publicized conversion to noncessationism and his highly visible relationship with John Wimber and Paul Cain, plus these exceptional recommendations, one who takes the ministry of the Holy Spirit seriously must read Deere's book, using the "Berean approach" of examining the Scriptures to see whether these things are so (Acts 17:11).[8] Does Deere's word correspond to God's Word?

AUTHOR'S BACKGROUND

Deere holds several degrees: an A.B. from Texas Christian University and a Th.M. and a Th.D. from Dallas Theological Seminary. He taught at Dallas Theological Seminary from 1976 until 1987 when the institution dismissed him because of his noncessationist views (37–38).

According to the author, he originally held strong cessationist views in line with his training and teaching experience at Dallas Theological Seminary. After a year's study leave in Germany (1984–85), he returned to DTS for the 1985–86 school year (15). While inviting Dr. John White, a British psychiatrist, to preach at a church conference, Deere had his life-changing, twenty-minute phone conversation with White in January 1986 (13, 22).

White had been worshiping at the Vineyard Fellowship of Anaheim—pastored by John Wimber—since mid-1985 (33). White came to Fort Worth in April 1986, to hold the conference Deere writes about in chapter 2 (25–32). Several weeks later Deere attended a Wimber[9] meeting in Fort Worth (33). As a result, Deere and Wimber became good friends; Deere visited the Anaheim Vineyard Fellowship on several occasions during 1986–87 (37).

After departing from DTS in fall of 1987, Deere also became acquainted with the Kansas City Fellowship pastored by Mike Bickle (38). He then made plans to move to Anaheim and become a full-time associate of John Wimber (38).

Deere remained with Wimber into the early 1990s, when he returned to the Dallas-Fort Worth area. According to the dust jacket, Deere now writes and lectures worldwide on the gifts of the Holy Spirit.

By Deere's own testimony, John Wimber, British psychiatrist John White, and Paul Cain have had a major influence on him (33–41). In addition, four months of intense Scripture study—January to April 1986 (22)—and his experiences (13–41) have combined to convince him that miraculous gifts still operate in the church as they did in the first century.

SYNOPSIS

Deere divides his presentation into three distinct sections with three appendixes:

1. Shocked and Surprised (13–41).
2. Shattered Misconceptions (45–159).
3. Seeking the Gifts and the Giver (163–215).
The appendixes address,

A. Other Reasons Why God Heals and Works Miracles (219–27).
B. Did Miraculous Gifts Cease with the Apostles? (229–52).
C. Were There Only Three Periods of Miracles? (253–66).

In addition, he includes a helpful Scripture Index.[10]

Shocked and Surprised

Deere begins with a three-chapter, twenty-nine page confession of how, in January 1986, his best cessationists arguments, accumulated over numerous years of pastoring, doctoral study, and postgraduate theological seminary experience did not hold up in a twenty-minute conversation with psychiatrist John White (16–22). Over the next four months of studying Scriptures, Deere became a noncessationist who believes that God heals today and speaks today (23). At some undesignated time in the past, Deere's wife, Lessa, had embraced the noncessationist position (15) and had been praying frequently for his conversion (15–16).

Chapter two recounts White's conference at Deere's church in Fort Worth (25–32). As a result of White's ministry and introduction of Deere to Wimber's ministry, Deere visited a Wimber meeting in Texas (33). As a result of the meeting, Deere became a close friend of Wimber (37) and subsequently met Paul Cain, then a Wimber associate (cf. 167).

This section, which autobiographically recounts Deere's odyssey, closes with a clearly stated purpose (41):

> In the following pages I want to share with you some of the things I have learned over the last few years, both in the Scriptures and in practical experience, that may help you to learn how to pursue and experience the reality of the gifts of the Spirit without all the hype and abuses that have plagued others who have attempted to minister in the power of the Spirit. I also want to share with you the biblical and theological objections that I had to the present-day, supernatural ministry of the Holy Spirit, and the answers that removed those objections for me. Finally, I want to discuss the fears and the hindrances I experienced in trying to minister in the power of the Holy Spirit, and how these have been and are being removed.

Shattered Misconceptions

Deere continues with his autobiographical narration through chapter 4—"The Myth of Pure Biblical Objectivity" (45–56)—when he concludes, "No cessationist writer that I am aware of tries to make his case on Scripture alone" (55).

Chapters 5–6 recount his three major reasons why Bible-believing Christians do not believe in the miraculous gifts of the Holy Spirit today:

1. They have not seen them (55, 57–71).
2. They cannot find New Testament-quality miracles in the history of the church (71–76).
3. They are confused by the misuse, or the perceived misuse, of the gifts in contemporary churches and healing movements (77–86).

Chapter 7, "Scared to Death by the Holy Ghost," argues from (1) the Azusa Street ministry, (2) John Wimber and Jonathan Edwards, (3) selected Scriptures, and (4) personal experience in an attempt to validate the theory that God is giving physical manifestations today.

The crux of Deere's case comes in chapters 8–10, "Were Miracles Meant to be Temporary?" "Why Does God Heal?" and "Why God Gives Miraculous Gifts?" Deere concludes, "Nor can we say that God did miracles to authenticate the Apostles, or to prove the authority of Scripture" (114). He adds, "In James 5:14–16, God commissioned the whole church to heal. . . ." (129). Further he says, "1 Corinthians 12–14 gives us six reasons that apply just as much today as they did in the first century . . ." (142).

In chapter 11—"Why God Doesn't Heal"—Deere stops short of denying that some good can come from sickness (155–57). He concludes that (1) apostasy, (2) legalism, (3) lukewarm faith, and (4) unbelief thwart God's plan to heal (147–55). He ends by appealing to 2 Chronicles 7:14 as a promise that he believes is valid for today (159).

Seeking the Gifts and the Giver

The final chapters deal with a Christian's passion and love for Christ. The section in which Deere warns against splitting churches over the issue of gifts (174–77) is commendable. Chapter 13, "A Passion for God," recounts Deere's lack of passion as a cessationist (184, 186–87) and how he regained his passion as a noncessationist (189–93). The final chapter—"Developing Passion and Power"—reasons that (1) passionate love for God is the key to power (201–2) and (2) cessationists have no power; therefore cessationists have no passionate love for God (184). He attempts to prove his point with a five-page illustration he received second hand (203–6). One wonders, then, why John the Baptist whom Jesus said was the greatest born of women (Luke 7:28) did no miracles in his ministry (John 10:41)?

In his epilogue—"Hearing God Speak Today" (209–15)—Deere defers this discussion to a later book. Those who want to know what and why the author believes in continuous revelation from God will have to wait for his sequel, *Surprised by the Voice of God* (Grand Rapids: Zondervan, 1994).

In the three appendixes, Deere argues against Benjamin B. Warfield,[11] John MacArthur, and Peter Masters, all of whom have written from a cessationist perspective. He reasons that supernatural gifts seen in the Gospels and Acts were not limited to just a few (230–41) and that an apostleship of lesser quality than the original apostles still exists today (241–52). In appendix C—"Were There Only Three Periods of Miracles?"—Deere takes issue with John MacArthur's understanding of miracles (253–66).

HERMENEUTICS AND EXPERIENCE

By selective reading, one might perceive that Deere has reached his noncessationist conclusions primarily through a careful survey of Scripture (22–23, 75, 99, 101). Deere testifies, "This shift in my thinking was not the result of an experience with any kind of supernatural phenomenon. *It was the result of a patient and intense study of the Scriptures*" (23).

Yet, his own discussions cast serious doubt on the accuracy of this perception. For instance, in describing his conversion from a cessationist to a noncessationist position (13–41), he lists ten major experiences to bolster his testimony:

1. phone conversation with Dr. White (13–23)
2. his cessationist history (13–15)
3. his charismatic wife who prayed for him (15–16)
4. Dr. White's conference (25–30)
5. a demon possessed Christian (26–30)
6. a woman healed of an aneurysm (31–32)
7. his John Wimber relationship (33–37)
8. a woman healed of back problems (35–37)
9. his Paul Cain relationship (38–41)
10. the healing of Linda Tidwell (39–41).

In this twenty-nine page description of one experience after another, he does not discuss or explain a single Scripture passage. At best, he cites only eight texts:

1. Phil. 2:25–27 (19)
2. 1 Tim. 5:23 (19)
3. 2 Tim. 4:20 (19)

4. Matt. 18:3–4 (29)
5. Luke 8:26 (30)
6. James 5:14–16 (30)
7. 1 Cor. 14:24–26 (35)
8. 1 Cor. 14 (37).

He sets forth three premises in the section after this (45–86), in which he reasons that if cessationists meet these conditions, they will convert as he did:

1. If they see the authentic miraculous in real experience (55, 57–71).
2. If they find New Testament-quality miracles in church history (56, 71–76).
3. If they find a sane use of miraculous gifts in the church (56, 77–86).

Let the reviewer return to the hypothetical situation mentioned at the beginning of this article. Deere argues, "If you were to lock a brand new Christian in a room with a Bible and tell him to study what Scripture has to say about healing and miracles, he would never come out of the room a cessationist" (54). He follows in the very next sentence, "I know this from my own *experience*." That is shocking! The very thing he denies— experience influencing his theology (22–23)—he here admits. This is a very serious contradiction. Even more amazing, this was not originally "his experience." He testifies in the same paragraph that from the time of becoming a Christian at age seventeen until his conversion, he re- mained a cessationist. Later he refers to "a clever theologian with no *experience* of the miraculous to convince this young convert differently" (114). He makes his unintended point quite well: Jack Deere believes that without experience one will not be a noncessationist. He writes, "My *experience* has brought me to the opposite conclusion than that of MacArthur and his researchers" (274).

Consider this conclusion in the very widely distributed review of Deere's work:

> Certainly Deere's view of the role of the prophet and the "ap- ostolic dimensions" of ministry (especially as manifested by Paul Cain) prompts significant questions about his reading of the New Testament: In laying aside Scofield's grid, has Deere replaced it with another that is equally or more manipulative in its use of God's Word?

Deere suggests that when experience and argument con-
verge, people open themselves to a life of infinite surprises in
engagement with the Holy Spirit. And his personal experiences punctuate each chapter. Indeed, there is almost a sense
in which the book affirms that the power of the Spirit is real
primarily because Deere experienced and saw it. He comes
precariously close to using experience as a form of expanded
translation of the biblical text.

Ultimately, *Surprised by the Power of the Spirit* is another contribution to a growing body of literature that unites
the power of personal testimony with a hermeneutic that
offers dispensational fundamentalists a fresh way of approaching the biblical text. But, although Deere offers a
welcomed alternative to the Scofieldian reading of Scripture, he unfortunately leaves the reader with the impression
that it is the religious experience itself that validates what
he argues.[12]

Although for reasons outlined in the next section it is difficult to know
with certainty, it is possible that Deere has *unintentionally* fallen into
two major hermeneutical errors. The first is that of generalizing, i.e.,
believing the occurrence of a miracle in the past means that nothing
prevents it from happening again, and therefore expecting its recurrence.
The second is experientializing, i.e., accepting someone's claims to have
a miraculous experience today of the kind that appeared in biblical history, then letting that experience prove that God is presently working the
same kind of miracles. The first involves a biblically unwarranted hermeneutic that reasons, unless Scripture denies the continuance of an experience, that experience has continued and will do so. The second reads
experience into Scripture so that experience validates Scripture rather
than the reverse.

Deere never deals with the counterfeit miracles that have existed
throughout church history. He does not deal with those who claimed to
do great miracles but were rejected by Christ (Matt. 7:21–23). Perhaps
this is why he does not openly confront the obviously false teachers of
noncessationist persuasion like Kenneth Hagin and Benny Hinn.

After reading the first five chapters, this reviewer concluded that Deere
converted to a noncessationist position because of the logic of a British
psychiatrist, the healings of John Wimber, and the prophecies of Paul
Cain. Despite his pleas otherwise and because of his own carefully
scripted testimony, it seems likely that Scripture took a back seat in the
process of his change.

EXEGESIS AND EXPOSITION

If the above analysis relating to "Hermeneutics and Experience" is remotely correct, then as its corollary, Deere excels at selective prooftexting, but has done too little solid exegesis and exposition of key biblical texts. That is a serious charge neither reached hastily nor to be treated lightly. An illustration is in order.

A purpose of a significant part of Deere's work is to deal with healing.[13] The subtitle of the book, "A Former Dallas Seminary Professor Discovers That God Speaks and Heals Today," gives the impression that the author intends to deal definitively with healing.

Anyone, new converts included, who desires to understand fully God's involvement in healing *must* interact with two major biblical texts—Isaiah 53 and James 5. Not to do so is unimaginable. So the lack of attention to Isaiah 53 is a great surprise to this reviewer. Only one paragraph in 299 pages mentions Isaiah 53. Nowhere does Deere attempt to explain this most significant text. Associated texts—Matthew 8:14–17 and 1 Peter 2:24—likewise suffer from neglect.

Deere acknowledges James 5:13–20 more than he does Isaiah 53, but his approximately seven references do little more than cite the passage—he never explains James 5. He recounts how the elders of his church called for the sick, supposedly in obedience to James 5 (30). Yet James 5 says, "Is anyone among you sick? Let him call for the elders of the church . . ." (v. 14). That is just the opposite of Deere's practice. Further, Deere claims that in James 5:14–16 God commissioned the whole church to heal (129). Though 5:16 does involve "praying for one another," more as a preventative measure than a corrective one, the major point of the passage focuses on elders, *not* the congregation.

A work on healing cannot ignore James 5. However, it must not merely recognize the passage and then conform it to one's predetermined theology and/or experiences, as Deere has apparently done. Nowhere does the author attempt to deal with the text in order to answer probing questions such as, "Is the passage limited to the first century or is it applicable today? Does it apply to all humanity or just Christians? Does it extend to all Christians or just some? Is its purpose to prepare people to die or to restore people to quality living? Does it refer to physical, emotional, or spiritual problems? Is the practice to be done in a public service or privately? Does the intent involve medicinal or symbolic anointing? Is the healing miraculous or providential? Is the promise absolute or conditional?"

Deere uses obscure texts such as those found in Jeremiah 32:20 or Galatians 3:5 to establish his own thesis and to discredit those with whom he disagrees. For instance, he cites Galatians 3:5 on at least eight occasions to support the idea that miraculous gifts of healing were given to the church as a continuing ministry up to the present. Yet nowhere does he inform the reader of interpretations of this passage that are at least equally credible (and possibly more so) and that do not involve the miraculous. Nor does he ever tell his readers that the word translated "miracle" can just as easily be translated "power" and refer to the power of God in salvation (Rom. 1:16; 1 Cor. 1:18; 2 Cor. 6:7; 1 Thess. 1:5; 2 Tim. 1:8).

He cites Jeremiah 32:20 to prove that miracles extended through Jeremiah's day. But he does not tell the reader that those skilled in the Hebrew language and specialists in OT studies do not agree on the correct interpretation of the passage.[14] The same characteristic applies to his comments on 2 Corinthians 12:7 (288) and Mark 16:9–20 (277).

Deere suggests that Romans 11:29—"For the gifts and the calling of God are irrevocable"—teaches that the miraculous gifts of the Spirit did not cease with the apostles, but continue on to this very day because they are irrevocable (289). However, the context of Romans 11 requires that the subject matter refer to Israel and her spiritual heritage, not to spiritual gifts in the church. The *charismata* ("gifts") of Romans 11:29 look back to God's grace gifts for Israel, recited in Romans 9:4–5. This is the clearest example of his inaccurate prooftexting.

In summary, Deere's treatment of Scripture leaves something to be desired. For example, he does not interpret major texts such as Isaiah 53 and James 5. He makes much out of passages that contribute little because their interpretation has several legitimate, nonmiraculous alternatives—e.g., Jeremiah 32:20 and Galatians 3:5—and resorts at times to inappropriate prooftexting. He majors on passages that are obscure and minors on passages that are definitive of the issue, while giving neither category the kind of detailed attention he gives to experiences.

ON HEALING

Deere looks to 1 Corinthians 12 as a major biblical text to explain healing for today (64–68). He reasons that since (1) the apostles were the most gifted of all people in the church, (2) spiritual gifts range in strength and intensity, and (3) miraculous gifts were not limited to the apostles but distributed throughout the church, then (1) there is a distinction between signs/wonders and "gifts of healings," and (2) it is wrong to insist that apostolic miracles set the standard by which to measure today's healings. He concludes (1) that healings today will not be as spectacular as Paul's or Peter's, (2) that healings might not be as abundant as in the apostolic era, and (3) that this allows for some failure in attempted healings.[15]

The reviewer's response is that Deere has developed a theory more from what Scripture *does not* say than from what it *clearly* says. His theory fails for several reasons:

1. The phrase "gifts of healings" is so ambiguous in its context that no one can really know for sure what it means (1 Cor. 12:9, 28, 30). Certainly something as important as a theology of physical healing should not rest on such a treacherous foundation.

2. His theory does not explain the decline in quality and quantity of even the apostolic healings as the apostolic age drew to a conclusion.

3. His theory does not adequately account for "gifts of healings" appearing only in the 1 Corinthians 12 gift list.

4. His theory does not anticipate the total lack of instruction in the epistles on the matter of healing, with the exception of what is found in James 5. The reviewer's suggestion is that James 5 and 1 Corinthians 12 have no connection in their contexts through exegesis or by logic.

5. His theory assumes throughout that if Scripture does not prohibit healing or does not speak directly about a cessation of apostolic healing, then implicitly the Scriptures teach healing for today (18–19, 99–115). Since it is impossible to interpret the white spaces of the Bible, this is inadmissible in the discussion.

6. He seems to contradict his own theory when he writes, "I believe that God is doing New Testament-quality miracles in the church today, and I believe He has done them throughout the history of the church" (58). The only quality of miracles we know of from Acts are those of the quality of the ones done by the apostles. Yet Deere later theorizes that the miracles of the church were substandard compared to those of the apostles (66–67). Both cannot be true.

7. Given the well-documented biblical history of miracles in Scripture, Deere never explains why "lesser" periods did not come after Moses, Elijah, or Christ. He just asserts that a continuing, substandard period of miracles follows the apostles and continues to this day. His argument from silence falls short of good interpretation and makes him the perpetrator of the exegetical fallacy of which he accuses cessationists (19).

ON MIRACLES

In general, Deere's discussion of major theological themes lacks a logical, systematic, and categorical quality. Take miracles for instance. About one-half of his discussion comes in the appendixes, which by definition involve "subsidiary matters at the end of a book." But let the reader decide whether discussions of the following questions are primary or subsidiary in regard to miracles: "Did Miraculous Gifts Cease with the Apostles?" and "Were There Only Three Periods of Miracles?" Discussion of both issues is in the appendixes. In contrast, chapter 5—where Deere gives his opinion about "The Real Reason Christians Do Not Believe in the Miraculous Gifts"—is clearly a subsidiary issue that should have been an appendix.

Deere states this about cessationists' major tenet that miracles ceased with the conclusion of the apostolic age:

> Yet here they faced not only a formidable obstacle but an insurmountable obstacle, for they could not produce one specific text of Scripture that taught that miracles or the spiritual gifts were confined to the New Testament period. Nor has anyone else since then been able to do that. (101)

In light of the above assertion, one would assume that Deere is about to produce one or more specific texts of Scripture to teach that miracles and spiritual gifts were to continue throughout the church age in the same manner as seen in Acts. However, Deere *cannot* produce that verse because it does not exist. Neither side wins or loses the cessationist/noncessationist debate based on a single passage, but on deductive conclusions from numerous passages. By using Deere's logic with the doctrine of God's triunity, blasphemous conclusions regarding that doctrine could result that Deere would not tolerate. This reviewer will not tolerate his conclusion regarding miracles because of his skewed logic.

Deere claims, "No cessationist writer that I am aware of tries to make his case on Scripture alone" (55). In fact, just the opposite is true. Deere builds his case for current-day miracles primarily on experience (13–41). Cessationists are willing to build their case and stand on it with Scripture alone. The appeal to history is not to establish their theology, but rather to test it.[16]

This reviewer would have expected to see Deere thoroughly interact with the well-known work, *Perspective on Pentecost,* by Richard Gaffin, especially chapter 5, "The Question of Cessation" (89–116). However, Deere makes no significant comment on Gaffin's reasoning.

He does interact with John MacArthur's *Charismatic Chaos* in appendix C (253–66). He begins with this observation: "John MacArthur is a modern-day proponent of the view that there were only three periods of miracles in the biblical record" (253). Later he derisively writes, "But most ludicrous of all, on MacArthur's view we could not call the resurrection of Jesus Christ a miracle" (263).

Earlier in the book Deere tells of leading a doctoral-program applicant through questioning about miracles, which Deere would have the reader believe characterizes the supposed sophomoric logic of cessationists (47–52). In appendix C, he charts seven pages of miracles in the OT (255–61) in an attempt to prove that MacArthur has seriously underestimated the miraculous element of the OT.

Several brief comments on Deere's discussion are in order:

1. MacArthur would affirm every supernatural event cited by Deere and so would all other conservative cessationist Bible teachers.
2. Deere mistakenly accuses MacArthur of saying that all miracles in the Bible were limited to three periods (253). Amazingly, Deere undermines his own charge by correctly quoting MacArthur as saying, "*Most* biblical miracles . . ." (253).
3. What MacArthur and other cessationists want to establish is the biblical fact that God's supernatural work, mediated through men, occurred primarily, not exclusively, in three periods. Deere even admits this (263).[17]
4. Deere can quibble over definitions related to the supernatural and the miraculous (263); nonetheless, everyone recognizes the difference between the supernatural enacted directly by God and the supernatural mediated by God through men, which is the element of the supernatural that Deere tries to establish as normative.
5. Deere writes, "MacArthur does not want to accept as normative any of the supernatural events from the previous table" (264). One might ask Deere the same question, "Do you want to accept creation, the flood and Babel as normative? Do you want to accept the destruction of Sodom and Gomorrah as normal? Do you want to accept the plagues of Egypt as normative?" Certainly not! Just because a specific act occurred once, does not necessarily demand that God must repeat it.

6. Deere asserts that "*you cannot find any period in Israel's history* when supernatural events were not common among the people of God" (263). To correct this statement, during at least two periods supernatural events were uncommon: (1) the almost 300-year gap between Genesis 50:26 and Exodus 2:1 and (2) the over 400-year gap between Malachi 4:6 and Matthew 1:1 in which one finds no evidence of God working supernaturally. This is not to mention the thousands of years that Genesis 1–12 represents, most of which the record does not cover.

ATTITUDES AND MISREPRESENTATIONS

Seemingly, Deere structured his work to sound and flow more like an emotionally charged testimony or debate than a well-reasoned, biblically based discussion of miracles.

Attitudes
Sprinkled throughout the book are overdone, self-deprecating remarks made by the noncessationist Jack Deere about the former cessationist Jack Deere. He implies that what he once was, all cessationists still remain. Here's a sample:

1. ignorantly prejudiced against charismatics and Pentecostals (267)
2. arrogant (28, 46)
3. damaging the church (28)
4. deceiving, manipulating, playing at church (29)
5. deceived into thinking his theology is exceptionally good, even flawless (15, 35)
6. spiritually anemic (184)
7. rationalistic (184)

Yet Deere would have the reader believe that after he converted to the noncessationist position, he had a dramatic turn around in attitude and approach to Scripture. He suddenly became an open-minded, patient, and intent student of Scripture (22–23, 47, 75). The apparent implication is that Deere had not been this way as a cessationist nor can any other cessationist.

He criticizes cessationist scholars for not being able to read the original, historical writings of the church fathers in Greek and Latin (273). Is he suggesting that most noncessationists can? If they could, would it help their exegesis/exposition of the biblical text? When he predicts that in his own lifetime a majority of the church is going to believe in and practice the miraculous gift of the Spirit, does he expect people to believe this on his word alone (173)?

He would have the reader believe that to the sincere, open-minded seeker of truth, Scripture, history, and experience all point to a noncessationist position (56). His assertions, however strongly made or frequently repeated, do not prove the point. Perhaps he reflects his attitude toward the whole issue when he compares the cessationist's case to the noncessationist's position as having the strength of a sparrow in a hurricane (102).

Misrepresentations

Former cessationist Jack Deere, now a leading spokesman for the noncessationist side, portrays the cessationist more in caricature fashion than accurately. The following points illustrate this:

1. Deere would intimate that all cessationists believe that spiritual gifts are not operating today (135).
2. Deere would paint cessationists as so spiritually anemic that they are quite vulnerable to gross sexual improprieties such as pornography (80–81, 133, 184) and homosexuality (82).
3. Deere would contend that cessationist seminary professors are close-minded and arrogant (22–23, 45–46). Thus their students, even those approaching the doctoral level of study, are bumbling and backwards when it comes to good theological thinking (47–52).

A FINAL QUESTION

If Deere, as he admits, was so prejudiced, so close-minded, so arrogant, so spiritually anemic, and so theologically off-base as a cessationist, what reason is there to believe that he is now humble, unprejudiced, open-minded, spiritually dynamic, and theologically correct? Is it because he now embraces a noncessationist theology? Does he give such compelling evidence of a real, dramatic turnaround that everyone else should abandon what they believe the Scriptures teach, to embrace the conclusions that Deere found at the end of his spiritual odyssey?

Is it because he relies on Scripture rather than experience to develop his beliefs? Is it because he fairly and accurately represents those who differ with him? Is it because he displays exemplary hermeneutical style and exegetical skills in coming to biblical conclusions? Is it because he does not engage in debate technique to make his point, but rather relies on well-reasoned dialogue with full disclosure of the facts? Is it because his case is biblically convincing?

As have others, this reviewer believes that Jack Deere's work, in the main, is theologically defective. Rather than resembling a careful study by an open-minded, trained theologian, it is more like the product of an immature new convert who, after reading the Gospels and Acts for the first time, concludes that what took place in the first century will continue throughout the church age.

So I ask, "Who surprised whom?" Did the Holy Spirit surprise Jack Deere, or was it vice versa?

ENDNOTES

[1] Jack Deere, *Surprised by the Power of the Spirit* (Grand Rapids: Zondervan, 1993). A subsequent volume, *Surprised by the Voice of God* (Grand Rapids: Zondervan, 1994) should be released in late fall 1994, according to *Surprised by the Power,* "Epilogue: Hearing God Speak Today," 209–15. The goal of this review is not to be unabridged, but rather to comment representatively on major features of Deere's work. Concluding that Deere's position is biblically indefensible does not logically mean that the cessationist position is thereby *vindicated*. It too must rise or fall on what the Scriptures teach.

[2] Ibid., 54, 99, 114.

[3] Ibid., 114.

[4] I have purposely used "redetermined" in contrast to "predetermined." When one changes his theology as radically as Deere has (from a cessationist to a noncessationist persuasion), it does not free him altogether from predetermination; but he also bears the additional weight of a less than objective approach (by reaction) that fuels "redetermination." At best, he is now equally as subjective as he was as a cessationist, and at worst, more—not less—vulnerable to possible error.

[5] Jack Deere, *Surprised by the Power,* endorsement page prior to page 1.

[6] Ibid.

[7] Ibid., back dust cover.

[8] Others who have reviewed Deere's work include Robert A. Pyne, *Bibliotheca Sacra* 151, no. 602 (April–June, 1994): 233–34; Larry L. Walker, *Mid-America Theological Journal* 18 (1994): 126–27; R. Fowler White, "'For the Sparrow in the Hurricane,' A Review of Jack Deere's *Surprised by the Power of the Spirit*" (unpublished paper presented at the 1994 ETS Eastern Regional Meeting).

[9] To see what Deere has been exposed to in his relationship with John Wimber, read John Wimber and Kevin Springer, *Power Evangelism,* 2d ed. (San Francisco: Harper and Row, 1992), and John Wimber and Kevin Springer, *Power Healing* (San Francisco: Harper and Row, 1987). In this reviewer's opinion, the most substantial defense of John Wimber's thinking has come from Gary S. Greig and Kevin N. Springer, eds., *The Kingdom and the Power* (Ventura, Calif.: Regal, 1993).

[10] For correcting future reprints, the publisher should note that all references from Mark 9:40 to the end of Mark (16:20 in Deere's opinion) have been omitted (296). Citations from Luke 10:9 through 24:49 stand erroneously in their place.

[11] This reviewer will not attempt to defend Warfield against Deere's charges, other than to say that Deere does not adequately represent Warfield's position. Those interested may read Warfield in *Counterfeit Miracles* (reprint, London: Banner of Truth, 1972), especially chapter 1, "The Cessation of the Charismata" (3–31).

[12] Edith L. Blumhofer, "Dispensing with Scofield," *Christianity Today* 38, no. 1 (January 10, 1994): 57. Let the record show that dispensationalism is not a determining issue in this discussion. Many dispensationalists and nondispensationalists strongly affirm a cessationist view of the miraculous gifts.

[13] See the reviewer's recent release, *The Healing Promise* (Eugene, Oreg.: Harvest House, 1994), for a thorough discussion of what the Bible says about physical healing.

[14] Compare C. F. Keil, *Commentary on the Old Testament* (reprint, Grand Rapids: Eerdmans, n.d.), 8:54, who supports Deere's treatment of

Jeremiah 32:20, with Charles L. Feinberg, *Jeremiah* (Grand Rapids: Zondervan, 1982), 228, and J. A. Thompson, *The Book of Jeremiah,* in NICOT (Grand Rapids: Eerdmans, 1980), 591, who both limit the comment on "signs & wonders" to Moses' time.

[15] For an in-depth analysis of Deere's theory that the miraculous continued beyond the apostles but at some substandard level, read Thomas R. Edgar, "An Analysis of Jack Deere on a Less Efficient Order of Miraculous Gifts" (unpublished paper presented at the 1991 ETS Eastern Regional Meeting).

[16] When someone reads Deere's discussion of miracles in post-biblical history (73–76) and compares it to the historical citations provided by Walter J. Chantry, *Signs of the Apostles,* 2d ed. (London: Banner of Truth, 1976), 140–46, he wonders what history books Deere has read.

[17] As do most theologians. Compare J. Oliver Buswell, *A Systematic Theology of the Christian Religion* (Grand Rapids: Zondervan, 1962), 1:177: "The great majority of miracles recorded in the Bible fall into three great epochs."

CHAPTER SIX

Freemasonry

Freemasonry and the Christian

Eddy D. Field II and Eddy D. Field III

Recently the largest Protestant denomination has ruled that member-ship in the Lodge is up to one's individual conscience. This position is contrary to a traditional Christian view of Freemasonry. Freemasonry is a fraternal order that advocates development of virtue and character among its members, as the authors can attest through their own past membership in it. The soteriology of Freemasonry is strongly antibiblical, as several of its teachings indicate—teachings associated with the Lamb-skin Apron, how to prepare for heaven, the Perfect Ashlar, the Common Gavel, and how to live a worthwhile life. Christian membership in the Lodge is, therefore, impossible to justify in light of Scriptural teachings.

* * * * *

RECENT DEVELOPMENTS

In 1992, Southern Baptist James Holly requested that the Southern Baptist Convention (SBC) conduct an investigation of Freemasonry. The SBC agreed and in June of 1993 approved a study of Freemasonry[1] which, though stating that some of Freemasonry is incompatible with Chris-tianity, concluded that membership in the Lodge is a matter of individual conscience.[2] This evaluation by the SBC has served as an endorsement of the Lodge.[3] In *The Scottish Rite Journal,* a Masonic periodical, one Mason has written,

> Because of your support, the vote of the Southern Baptist Convention is a historic and positive turning point for Free-masonry. Basically, it is a vitalization of our Fraternity by America's largest Protestant denomination after nearly a year of thorough, scholarly study. At the same time, it is a call to renewed effort on the part of all Freemasons today to re-

energize our Fraternity and move forward to fulfilling its mission as the world's foremost proponent of the Brotherhood of Man under the Fatherhood of God.[4]

The conclusion of the SBC surprised many who believe that the essential tenets of Freemasonry are contrary to those of Christianity. An overwhelming number of Christian denominations have condemned Freemasonry, including the Roman Catholic Church, the Methodist Church of England, the Wesleyan Methodist Church, the Russian Orthodox Church, the Synod Anglican Church of England, the Assemblies of God, the Church of the Nazarene, the Orthodox Presbyterian Church, the Reformed Presbyterian Church, the Christian Reformed Church in America, the Evangelical Mennonite Church, the Church of Scotland, the Free Church of Scotland, General Association of Regular Baptist Churches, Grace Brethren, Independent Fundamentalist Churches of America, The Evangelical Lutheran Synod, the Baptist Union of Scotland, The Lutheran Church—Missouri Synod, the Wisconsin Evangelical Lutheran Synod, and the Presbyterian Church in America.[5] Also, many prominent Christians have denounced the Lodge, including D. L. Moody, Jonathan Blanchard, Charles Blanchard, Alva McClain, Walter Martin, and Charles Finney.[6] So the Southern Baptist Convention is not in agreement with other Christians concerning the teachings of Masonry and Christian participation in it.[7] Christian membership in the Masonic Lodge is an issue that many churches must face and one that the SBC's *Report* has clouded.[8]

This chapter will explain the Lodge, tell of the authors' involvement in it, and their reasons for leaving it.

AN OVERVIEW OF FREEMASONRY

No formal definition of Freemasonry exists in its official literature,[9] but several descriptions are available elsewhere. For example, the *Monitor* says this of Freemasonry: "It is an institution having for its foundation the practice of the social and moral virtues."[10] It also makes the following statement:

> By speculative Masonry we learn to subdue the passions, act upon the Square, keep a tongue of good report, maintain secrecy, and practice charity. It is so far interwoven with religion as to lay us under obligations to pay that rational homage to the Deity which at once constitutes our duty and our happiness.[11]

Another statement reveals more about the nature of Freemasonry:

> Masonry is a progressive moral science, divided into different degrees; and, as its principles and mystic ceremonies are regularly developed and illustrated, it is intended and hoped that they will make a deep and lasting impression upon your mind.[12]

The *Monitor* also says,

> The Trowel is an instrument made use of by operative Masons to spread the cement which unites the building into one common mass; but we, as Free and Accepted Masons, are taught to make free use of it for the more noble and glorious purpose of spreading the cement of brotherly love and affection; that cement which unites us into one sacred band or society of friends and brothers, among whom no contention should exist, but that noble contention, or rather emulation, of who can work and best agree.[13]

The Lodge is a fraternal order—or brotherhood—that teaches its members to develop virtue and character. It distinguishes between the "operative" and the "speculative" mason. The operative mason is the literal mason who builds with stone and brick.[14] The speculative Mason is a member of the Masonic Lodge. The Lodge has adopted the symbols of stonemasonry related to temple-building because speculative Masons are also building a temple.[15] The teaching given to Masons is that they are building a spiritual temple in heaven. It instructs each Mason— regardless of his religion and by his own efforts—to fashion himself into a perfect living stone to fit into the spiritual temple being constructed in heaven. An explanation of this will come below.

Masons also refer to the Masonic Lodge as "the Blue Lodge." Individual Lodges are governed by a Grand Lodge. Nearly every state in the United States has a Grand Lodge, with many others existing throughout the world.

Requisite to being a Mason is belief in a deity. This may be any deity, meaning that a Mason may adhere to any religion. The details of a Mason's religious faith are irrelevant as pertains to membership in the Lodge. It is only necessary that he affirm a deity. So the Lodge includes Christians, Muslims, Hindus, and followers of other religions.

Upon approval of the application of a candidate for Masonic membership (i.e., an "initiate"), he must participate in three secret initiation ceremonies, called "degrees." After completion of the First Degree, the candidate becomes an "Entered Apprentice Mason." After completion of the Second Degree, he is a "Fellow Craft Mason." With completion of the third degree, he is a "Master Mason." This makes him a full member worldwide. The Master Mason can join other Masonic organizations such as Scottish Rite, York Rite, and the Shrine. Many Masons do not join these organizations and may know little about them.

THE AUTHORS' BACKGROUNDS IN FREEMASONRY

Eddy D. Field II (hereafter Mr. Field) was a member of the Blue Lodge and related organizations for twenty-five years. He was an officer of the Lodge for two of those years. He was a 32° Mason, a Royal Arch Mason, and an officer in his chapter. He held office in the Cryptic Council and was a Knight Templar and a Shriner. He also held membership in Eastern Star, Grotto, High 12, Amaranth, and White Shrine of Jerusalem.

Mr. Field's grandfather and father are both past Masters of the Lodge, with many of his family members being leaders of the various Masonic organizations. Mr. Field's son, coauthor of this article, was a member of the Order of DeMolay—a fraternity for males aged thirteen to twenty-one—founded and supervised by Masons.

For Mr. Field, the main appeal of the Lodge was a strong family tradition. This tradition helped bind his family together and instill in it a sense of pride. Another attraction to Masonry was a practical one. At the time, Freemasons exerted great social, political, and business influence.[16] Many politicians and businessmen were Masons. Since Masons tend to favor each other, it was sometimes easier for a man to advance his career if he was a Masonic "brother." A third feature that attracted Mr. Field to the Lodge was the mystique associated with it. The Lodge claims to be an ancient brotherhood that holds many secrets. This "gnostic" quality also drew him to Masonry.

After his conversion to Christ, Mr. Field carefully examined the origin and nature of the Lodge and discovered many grave problems with it. He compared the religious teachings of Freemasonry with those of Christianity and found them to be opposite. Therefore, he felt compelled to leave the Lodge. The following discussion will detail some results of his comparison.

THE SOTERIOLOGY OF FREEMASONRY

It is unnecessary and beyond the scope of this investigation to probe whether or not Masonry is a religion; most Masons deny that it is. Yet the Lodge explicitly teaches, "It is so far interwoven with religion as to lay us under obligations to pay that rational homage to the Deity which at once constitutes our duty and our happiness."[17] Religion or not, a comparison of the Lodge's religious teachings with Scripture is inevitable. The results of such a comparison make it clear that Freemasonry denies the teachings of Christianity. A theologian, who caused quite a stir with his critique of Freemasonry,[18] offered this evaluation:

> The actual secrets *are* for the most part trivial, and the esoteric moral symbolisms of geometry, astronomy, architecture, and the working tools of the operative stonemason, seem to the brethren to be in no way incompatible with, but rather supplementary to (though all too often they are substitutes for), a belief in the Christian Gospel. It is not difficult to show, however, that Freemasonry, in so far as it has a consistent teaching, is formally heretical.[19]

The Lodge teaches that every Mason should learn and obey its teachings, including its soteriology [i.e., doctrine of salvation], though the Lodge does not necessarily discipline anyone who does not. In the Third Degree, under "The Charge," the *Monitor* states,

> Duty and honor now alike bind you to be faithful to every trust; to support the dignity of your character on all occasions; and strenuously to enforce, by precept and example, a steady obedience to the tenets of Freemasonry.[20]

This applies to a Christian Mason as much as anyone.

Masonry teaches on many religious subjects, but of particular relevance to the present discussion is its soteriology. What follows is an analysis of five statements selected from the *Monitor* that expound the soteriology of the Lodge.

The Lambskin Apron

The First Degree includes a discussion of "The Lambskin Apron." As the Lambskin Apron is the most important emblem in the Freemasonry,[21] it is in order to discuss it first. Each candidate receives an apron in the First Degree. The *Monitor* says this about the apron:

> The Lamb, in all ages has been deemed an emblem of innocence. He, therefore, who wears the lambskin as the badge of a Mason, is continually reminded of that purity of life and

conduct so essentially necessary to his gaining admission into the Celestial Lodge above, where the Supreme Architect of the Universe presides.[22]

The "Celestial Lodge above" refers, of course, to heaven, and "the Supreme Architect of the Universe" is one of the names Masonry has for its god. The statement speaks of "gaining" admission into the Celestial Lodge. By the use of "gaining," the Lodge teaches that one earns or merits entrance into heaven on his own. That is, it is a matter of human effort. The statement also says that a person gains entrance into heaven by "purity of life and conduct." With this the Lodge teaches the achievement of salvation on the basis of human good works. This selection from the *Monitor* clearly states, then, that a person earns admission into heaven by living a pure life. As Masonry accepts any theist, the teaching on the Lambskin Apron holds true for anyone, regardless of that person's god or religion.

The statement about the Lambskin Apron creates several problems. It says that "purity of life and conduct" is necessary for admittance into heaven. If this means absolute purity, no one can in reality qualify. If it means relative purity, then what is the basis of measurement and how can one know if he has qualified? In fact, Christ is the Lamb of God who, by virtue of his purity, qualified as the sacrifice for the sins of the world (cf. John 1:29). In 1 Peter 1:18–19, the apostle writes to believers,

> You were not redeemed with perishable things like silver or gold from your futile way of life inherited from your forefathers, but with precious blood, as of a lamb unblemished and spotless, the blood of Christ.[23]

The Masonic teaching contradicts the gospel of Jesus Christ which says that salvation is through God's grace, being received through faith in Jesus Christ.[24] The *locus classicus* in this regard is Ephesians 2:8–9: "For by grace you have been saved through faith; and that not of yourselves, it is the gift of God; not as a result of works, so that no one may boast."[25]

Thus, the lesson taught with the most important symbol in the Lodge directly opposes the Christian gospel.

Preparation for Heaven
From the Third Degree of the *Monitor* comes another statement delineating the soteriology of the Lodge:

> Hence, my brother, how important it is that we should en-
> deavor to imitate *** in his truly exalted and exemplary char-
> acter, in his unfeigned piety to God, and in his inflexible
> fidelity to his trust, that we may be prepared to welcome death,
> not as a grim tyrant, but as a kind of messenger sent to trans-
> late us from this imperfect to that all perfect, glorious, and
> celestial Lodge above, where the Supreme Grand Master of
> the Universe forever presides.[26]

The three asterisks in the quotation stand in place of the words "the Grand Master Hiram Abiff." This is the chief character in Masonic lore. The exhortation to the candidate is to imitate three virtues of Hiram Abiff: his character, his devotion to god, and his trustworthiness. The reason that this imitation is so important is that it enables the Mason to be translated to heaven. As with the previous example of the Lambskin Apron, this excerpt demonstrates the Lodge's teaching that one attains entrance into heaven by living a virtuous life, regardless of religious orientation.

The Scriptures do not teach that a person goes to heaven by imitating even Christ Himself, much less anyone else. Salvation is a gift of God's grace. Paul writes in 2 Timothy 1:9–10 that God

> has saved us and called us with a holy calling, not according
> to our works, but according to His own purpose and grace
> which was granted us in Christ Jesus from all eternity, but
> now has been revealed by the appearing of our Savior Christ
> Jesus, who abolished death and brought life and immortality
> to light through the gospel.

Unlike a Mason, a Christian does not fear death because Christ has overcome it (1 Cor. 15:54–57).

The Perfect Ashlar

Part of the First Degree in the *Monitor* has a statement about "The Perfect Ashlar." Masonry calls a perfect stone a "Perfect Ashlar." The following describes the teaching symbolized by the Ashlar:

> The Rough Ashlar is a stone as taken from the quarry in its
> rude and natural state. The Perfect Ashlar is a stone made
> ready by the hands of the workman, to be adjusted by the
> working tools of the Fellow Craft. By the Rough Ashlar, we
> are reminded of our rude and imperfect state by nature; by
> the Perfect Ashlar, of that state of perfection at which we

hope to arrive by a virtuous education, our own endeavors, and the blessing of God.[27]

As explained below under a discussion of "The Common Gavel," a Mason intends to fashion himself from a rough stone to a perfect stone, for the purpose of fitting himself into the spiritual temple in heaven. The statement here means that the Mason can take himself from an imperfect state to a state of perfection by satisfying three requirements. First, he must obtain a virtuous education, which the Lodge claims to give. Second, he must apply in his life the knowledge gained. He accomplishes this by his own endeavors. Third, he must receive the blessing of his god, whatever that god may be. This statement plainly teaches that the Mason strives to achieve perfection by his own efforts.[28] By doing this he fits himself into the temple in heaven.

First Peter 2:5 teaches the opposite regarding Christians when it says that Christians "as living stones, are being built up as a spiritual house for a holy priesthood, to offer up spiritual sacrifices acceptable to God through Jesus Christ." God, not believers themselves, is the builder of believers, of course.[29]

The Common Gavel

A fourth statement in the First Degree portion of the *Monitor* reveals more of the Lodge's plan of salvation. As stated previously, Masons are building a spiritual temple in heaven. The instruction to each Mason is to fashion himself into a perfect living stone to fit into the spiritual temple in heaven. "The Common Gavel" symbolizes this concept:

> The common gavel is an instrument used by operative Masons to break off the rough and superfluous parts of stones, the better to fit them for the builder's use. But we, as Free and Accepted Masons, are taught to make use of it for the more noble and glorious purpose of divesting our hearts and consciences of all the vices and superfluities of life: thereby fitting our minds as living stones for that spiritual building, that house not made with hands, eternal in the heavens.[30]

For the operative mason, a gavel is a hammer used to shape stones. The speculative Mason is figuratively an imperfect stone with rough edges that he strives to break off with the gavel. This paragraph just quoted is quite clear in stating that the Mason makes himself fit for heaven by bettering himself through eliminating unwanted qualities.[31] This holds true for any Mason, regardless of his god or religious persuasion.

As the Common Gavel closely relates to the Perfect Ashlar, the criticism of the Perfect Ashlar applies to it. No one can make himself fit for heaven; only God can do this through Christ.[32]

The Well-Spent Life
A final example will aid in explaining the soteriology of the Lodge:

> In youth, as Entered Apprentices, we ought industriously to occupy our minds in the attainments of useful knowledge; in manhood, as Fellow Crafts, we should apply our knowledge to the discharge of our respective duties to God, our neighbor, and ourselves; that so, in age, as Master Masons, we may enjoy the happy reflection consequent on a well-spent life, and die in the hope of a glorious immortality.[33]

The "attainments of useful knowledge" here include the virtuous education to which the above discussion of "The Perfect Ashlar" referred. The "discharge of our respective duties" relates to applying that knowledge by one's own endeavors, as also indicated under "The Perfect Ashlar." This extraction indicates that the Mason's hope of eternal life hinges upon having lived a worthy life.

This contrasts directly with Christian teaching, according to which the hope of eternal life is Christ. In Colossians 1:27, Paul writes that God has made known to Christians "what is the riches of the glory of this mystery among the Gentiles, which is Christ in you, the hope of glory." The Lodge offers hope of eternal life apart from Christ. This hope for immortality is false, though, and a false hope for immortality is a false gospel.

CHRISTIAN MEMBERSHIP IN THE LODGE

The above five statements from the *Monitor* suffice to show the soteriology of the Lodge. A serious conflict exists between this soteriology and that of Christianity. The two are, in fact, contradictory. Freemasonry teaches that one may gain entrance into heaven through his good works, no matter who is his god and what is his religious affiliation. Christianity teaches that one gains entrance into heaven through Christ's work on the cross, appropriated by faith.

From this analysis of the five statements, the god of Masonry, often called "The Great Architect of the Universe," is identifiable. This god is one that will accept someone into heaven on the basis of works, regardless of religion. This is a false god, not the God of the Bible.[34]

A Biblical Appraisal of Masonic Soteriology

Paul was unequivocal in responding to anyone proclaiming a "gospel" contrary to[35] the true gospel:

> But even though we, or an angel from heaven, should preach to you a gospel contrary to that which we have preached to you, let him be accursed. As we have said before, so I say again now, if any man is preaching to you a gospel contrary to that which you received, let him be accursed. (Galatians 1:8–9)

Paul petitions that anyone distorting the gospel of Christ (v. 7) be cursed, that is, left outside of God's grace and subject to His disfavor.[36] This imprecation against anyone compromising the gospel is extremely strong.

As documented above, Freemasonry advocates a plan of salvation contrary to the gospel of Jesus Christ. Paul's curse would apply to proponents of the soteriology of Freemasonry.[37]

A Biblical Appraisal of Masonic Membership

In light of the foregoing, a Christian's participation in the Lodge is a significant issue. Masons consider themselves "one sacred band or society of friends and brothers."[38] In the First, Second, and Third Degrees, a Mason swears oaths to god, under penalty of death, to fulfill certain obligations.[39] He swears to this oath on a book considered by his Grand Lodge to be sacred. Thus, the book varies depending on the dominant religion of the area. So, it may be the Bible, the Koran, or the Bhagavad Gita, depending on where it occurs. Also, candidates take their oaths at the altar of the Masonic god, the same altar at which they all kneel, regardless of their religious persuasions.

At the end of each oath, the Worshipful Master (the local Lodge head) informs the Mason that he is bound to all Masons. After the First Degree, the Worshipful Master says, "Brother Senior Warden, release the candidate from the cable-tow, his being now bound to us by a stronger tie."[40] After the Second Degree, the Worshipful Master says, "Brother Senior Warden, release the candidate from the cable-tow, it being twice around his naked right arm, is to signify to him that he is now bound to the fraternity by a two fold tie."[41] After the Third Degree, the Worshipful Master says, "Brother Senior Warden, release the candidate from the cable-tow, it being thrice around his naked body, is to signify to him that he is now bound to the fraternity by a threefold tie."[42] These three statements illustrate the serious bond between Masons. As a further example of the extent of this bond, in the Third Degree each Mason swears to keep secret, if asked, the crimes committed by a fellow Mason. Murder and treason are the only exceptions. The oath reads, "Furthermore, that I will keep the secrets of a Master Mason as my own, when given to me in charge as such, murder and treason excepted."[43] Thus, by solemn oath the Mason binds himself as a brother to every other Mason, regardless of his god or religion.

Beyond this, though, in the Second Degree the candidate bows in reverence to the god of Freemasonry, called G.A.O.T.U.[44] He does this after the Worshipful Master utters the following call:

> I will again call your attention to the letter G for a more important purpose: *** *(Right hand, uncovers.)* It is the initial of the name of the Supreme Being, before whom all Masons, from the youngest Entered Apprentice in the north-east corner of the Lodge to the Worshipful Master in the east, should with reverence bow. (All bow.) *[45]

After this, all present bow toward the letter "G" suspended above the Worshipful Master in the east. Masons thereby pay homage to the false god of the Masonic Lodge. For a Christian to conceive that he is bowing to the true God does not mitigate this act of homage to a false god, because he is bowing to god as defined by the Lodge. One scholar has written the following to soften the offense of such worship:

> The uninstructed layman may in all good faith be unable to draw this distinction; to him God is God, whether addressed as the Great Architect or Grand Geometrician of the Universe, or as Father, Son, and Holy Ghost. But the position of the Masonic priest or bishop appears to be far less defensible.[46]

He means that a Christian Mason uninstructed in Freemasonry may not realize he is bowing to a false god. Yet an informed Christian Mason has no excuse. The only explanation is that a Mason bows before and pays homage to the Masonic idol.

In 2 Corinthians 6:14–18, Paul discussed the relationship of believers to unbelievers.[47] In 6:14–16a he wrote,

> Do not be bound together with unbelievers; for what partnership have righteousness and lawlessness, or what fellowship has light with darkness? Or what harmony has Christ with Belial, or what has a believer in common with an unbeliever? Or what agreement has the temple of God with idols?

Though it is not clear precisely what relationship to unbelievers Paul referred to in this context, it is apparently some intimate association with them and their false gods.[48] Webb summarizes,

> In conclusion, 2 Corinthians 6:14 prohibits believers from joining in any activity that forms a covenantlike *[sic]* bond with pagans and their idols (either through literal-physical or metonymical idolatry) and seriously violates the believer's covenant with God.[49]

Paul's counsel in such a situation was to abandon the relationship. In 6:14, the command "do not be bound together" calls for the readers to cease initiating relationships.[50] That such relationships already existed is confirmed by 2 Corinthians 6:17 where Paul counsels, "come out from their midst and be separate." The injunction of 2 Corinthians 7:1 also proves the preexistence of these relationships: "Therefore, having these promises, beloved, let us cleanse ourselves from all defilement of flesh and spirit, perfecting holiness in the fear of God."[51] Paul taught that a believer must not join himself to any unbeliever so as to associate himself with the unbeliever's idolatry. If he already had such a relationship, Paul insisted that he sever it. This has a direct application to Christian membership in the Lodge.[52]

INCOMPATIBILITY OF CHRISTIANITY AND FREEMASONRY

The Lodge teaches clearly that one may earn admittance into heaven on the basis of works, regardless of religion. This is a false gospel, which places those who advocate such a doctrine under Paul's imprecation. If this is not enough to convince a Christian not to involve himself in Masonry, it should be enough that a Christian Mason binds himself by oath to all other Masons in a way that associates him with their idolatry. In 2 Corinthians 6:14 Paul forbids such a relationship. The activity of a Christian Mason is even more unbiblical, though, when he kneels at the altar of the false god of the Lodge and pays homage to its deity. These facts demonstrate that Christian participation in the Lodge is more than a matter of individual Christian conscience. It is imperative that Christians not participate in this organization.[53]

One writer summarizes the church's appropriate response to Christian Masons:

> [The church can] make painstaking efforts when dealing with

lodge members to have them realize the incompatibility of membership in a society which ignores or even denies Jesus Christ and in a society which confesses and worships Him as the Savior of lost mankind and as the King of kings and Lord of lords.[54]

This entails telling Masons that they cannot be at once members of the Lodge—which denies Christ—and members of the church—which confesses Him as Lord.[55] The authors of this essay wish to communicate this message in the hope that Christian Masons will "come out from their midst and be separate."

ENDNOTES

[1] *A Study of Freemasonry* (Atlanta: Home Mission Board of the Southern Baptist Convention, 1993). See also *A Report on Freemasonry* (Atlanta: Home Mission Board of the Southern Baptist Convention, 1993).

[2] *Report,* 6.

[3] Joe Maxwell, "Baptist Battle over Freemasonry Erupts Anew," *Christian Research Journal* 16, no. 2 (fall 1993): 41; John Weldon, "The Masonic Lodge and the Christian Conscience," *Christian Research Journal* 16, no. 3 (winter 1994): 21.

[4] *The Scottish Rite Journal* (August 1993), cited by Weldon, "Masonic Lodge," 21.

[5] Maxwell, "Baptist Battle," 42; Dale A. Byers, *I Left the Lodge* (Schaumburg, Ill.: Regular Baptist Press, 1988), 114–18.

[6] Jack Harris, *Freemasonry: The Invisible Cult in Our Midst* (Chattanooga, Tenn.: Global Publishers, 1983), 111–12; Maxwell, "Masonic Lodge," 41; Alva J. McClain, *Freemasonry and Christianity* (Winona Lake, Ind.: BMH Books, 1951), 32.

[7] This disagreement is possibly traceable to the great number of Masons in the SBC (see Weldon, "Masonic Lodge," 39). Holly estimates the number to be between 500,000 and 1.3 million (Maxwell, "Baptist Battle," 42).

[8] Weldon, "Masonic Lodge," 22.

[9] *The Monitor and Officers' Manual* is the official textbook of the Lodge (*The Monitor and Officers' Manual,* rev. ed. [n.p.: Grand Lodge of California, 1985], 35). It contains *verbatim* extractions of teachings from the secret degree work (i.e., initiation ceremonies). The extractions printed in the *Monitor* become nonsecret in the process of being so reproduced. This is important because a Mason will not discuss secret teachings with non-Masons. For this reason this analysis in most cases refers to the *Monitor.* Some Masons refuse to discuss the teachings of even the *Monitor,* considering them to be secret. They are not, however. The teachings published in the *Monitor* are open for discussion by any Mason.

Each candidate learns these doctrines at the initiation ceremonies. He receives a copy of the *Monitor* and must memorize selections.

The present discussion refers to the California *Monitor,* and though it is typical of those in other jurisdictions, the content of the *Monitor* may vary slightly from jurisdiction to jurisdiction. The essential doctrine remains the same, however.

[10] Ibid., 15.

[11] Ibid., 20.

[12] Ibid., 27.

[13] Ibid., 30–31.

[14] Ibid., 19–20.

[15] Ibid., 20.

[16] Recently, though, membership in the Lodge has declined by two to three percent annually (Maxwell, "Baptist Battle," 41–44).

[17] *Monitor,* 20.

[18] The opinion of Paul M. Bretscher, "The Masonic Apostasy from Christ," *Concordia Theological Monthly* 26 (February 1955): 97.

[19] Walton Hannah, "Should a Christian be a Mason?" *Theology* 54 (January 1951): 4.

[20] *Monitor,* 36.

[21] Ibid., 4.

[22] Ibid., 5.

[23] All biblical quotations are from the New American Standard Bible.

[24] John Ankerberg and John Weldon, *The Secret Teachings of the Masonic Lodge* (Chicago: Moody, 1989, 1990), 78–79; Jim Shaw and Tom McKinney, *The Deadly Deception* (Lafayette, La.: Huntington House, 1988), 132; L. James Rongstad, *How to Respond to the Lodge* (St. Louis: Concordia, 1977), 11, 18; Ron Carlson and Ed Decker, *Fast Facts on False Teachings* (Eugene, Oreg.: Harvest House, 1994), 85; Harris, *Freemasonry*, 22–23.

[25] Cf. Romans 4:5; 6:23; 10:9–10; Titus 3:5–7.

[26] *Monitor*, 35–36.

[27] Ibid., 9–10.

[28] Harris, *Freemasonry*, 45–46.

[29] The context indicates that οἰκοδομεῖσθε (*oikodomeisthe*, "you are being built up") is passive indicative with God as the implied agent (cf. v. 9; see D. Edmond Hiebert, *1 Peter* [Chicago: Moody, 1984, 1992], 132; J. N. D. Kelly, *The Epistles of Peter and Jude* [Peabody, Mass.: Hendrickson, 1969], 89).

[30] *Monitor*, 5.

[31] Harris, *Freemasonry*, 17–18.

[32] McClain, *Freemasonry*, 31–32.

[33] *Monitor*, 38.

[34] Ankerberg, *Secret Teachings*, 176; McClain, *Freemasonry*, 18–19. See Ankerberg, *Secret Teachings*, chapter 8, for a further development of this point.

[35] Though it is preferable to render παρ᾽ ὅ (*par' ho*) as "besides that which" or "in addition to that which" (see J. B. Lightfoot, *The Epistle of St. Paul*

to the Galatians [Grand Rapids: Zondervan, 1957], 75), the adopted rendering—"contrary to"—is the more common translation. The point is the same in either case, because the Masonic teaching on salvation fits either rendering. It is both "contrary to" and "in addition to" the Christian gospel.

36 Ernest De Witt Burton, *A Critical and Exegetical Commentary on the Epistle to the Galatians,* ICC (Edinburgh: T & T Clark, n.d.), 28.

37 Byers, *I Left,* 81.

38 *Monitor,* 30–31.

39 *King Solomon and His Followers,* rev. Calif. ed. (Richmond, Va.: Allen, 1989), 22–23, 81–83, 135–38, respectively. This book contains the current secret ritual of the Lodge in code. The statements in this paper result from a decoding of the code-book. The earlier edition of the code-book is *King Solomon's Temple.* Those unable to use the code-book may consult Malcom C. Duncan, *Duncan's Masonic Ritual and Monitor,* 3rd ed. with add. and corr. (New York: David McKay, n.d.). This work contains the complete secret Masonic ritual (the three Degrees) in English. Because it is an older version it is somewhat different from the current edition, but the differences do not alter the present discussion.

The older code-books and older English-language ritual manuals containing all the secrets for the Lodge and related organizations are obtainable from Ezra A. Cook Publishers, 6604 West Irving Park Road, Chicago, Ill. 60634.

40 Ibid., 23.

41 Ibid., 83.

42 Ibid., 138.

43 Ibid., 136.

44 This is an acronym for "Great Architect of the Universe."

45 *King Solomon,* 100–101. The asterisks represent raps of the gavel by the Worshipful Master. The first three raps instruct all present to rise, the last tells all to be seated.

[46] Hannah, "Should a Christian," 5.

[47] The interpretation of ἄπιστοι *(apistoi)* as "unbelievers" is debatable, but has the best support (see William J. Webb, "Who Are the Unbelievers [ἄπιστοι] in 2 Corinthians 6:14?" *Bibliotheca Sacra* 149 [January–March 1992]: 27–44).

[48] Webb offers three reasons why 2 Corinthians 6:16 refers to literal, rather than metaphorical, idolatry: "That Paul intended literal idols in 2 Corinthians 6:16 is more likely in light of the living God-idols contrast, his pattern of clarifying metaphorical intent when referring to idolatry, and the major problem at Corinth with literal idols. Any references related to metaphorical idolatry, therefore, should probably be rejected" (William J. Webb, "What is the Unequal Yoke [ἑτεροζυγοῦντες] in 2 Corinthians 6:14?" *Bibliotheca Sacra* 149 [April–June 1992]: 170–71).

[49] Ibid., 179.

[50] A. T. Robertson, *Word Pictures in the New Testament* (Grand Rapids: Baker, 1931), 4:236.

[51] Webb, "Unequal Yoke," 170–71.

[52] Ankerberg, *Secret Teachings,* 91–92, 191; Byers, *I Left,* 81; Harris, *Freemasonry,* 36; McClain, *Freemasonry,* 36; R. A. Torrey, *Practical and Perplexing Questions Answered* (Chicago: Revell, 1908, 1909), 112.

[53] Weldon, "Masonic Lodge," 39.

[54] Bretscher, "Masonic Apostasy," 114.

[55] R. A. Torrey said, "The name of Jesus Christ is cut out of passages in which it occurs in the Bible so as not to offend Jews and other non-Christians. How a Christian can retain membership in a society that thus handles deceitfully the Word of God, and above all cuts out the name of his Lord and Master, I cannot understand" (*Perplexing Questions,* 112).

CHAPTER SEVEN

Feminism

The Hermeneutics
of Evangelical Feminism

Paul W. Felix Sr.

An evangelical feminist is one who has a high view of Scripture and be-lieves the Bible teaches the full equality of men and women without role distinctions between the two. Their principles for interpreting Scripture differ markedly from those of the advocates of role differences for men and women. A comparison of evangelical feminists' principles with the grammatico-historical method of interpretation clarifies what and how great they deviate from traditional views of a woman's role in church and at home. The disputed principles include the issues of ad hoc *documents, interpretive centers, the analogy of faith, slavery as a model for the role of women, culturally biased interpretation, cultural relativity, and patriar-chal and sexist texts. An examination of these issues shows evangelical feminist hermeneutics to fall short of the grammatico-historical method of interpretation.*

* * * * *

DEFINITIONS AND DIFFERENCES

The significant changes for women in society that began about thirty years ago have not bypassed the church. The changes have meant a chal-lenge to the Christian community to consider afresh the role of women in their relationship to men in the church and in the home. The instiga-tors of this challenge call themselves "feminists."

Feminist is a broad term that includes several groups. *Secular femi-nists* are those who do not accept the Bible as authoritative.[1] *Religious feminists* are "individuals who do not identify with Christianity, but whose beliefs nevertheless include a religious worldview."[2] *Christian feminists* work from the standpoint of a commitment to the Christian faith but ac-cept the authority of Scripture in only a limited way.[3] A final classification of feminists includes those identified as "evangelical feminists." An evangelical feminist has a high view of Scripture and is "one who believes that the Bible teaches the full equality of men and women without role distinctions based on gender."[4] The focus of this chapter is on this last group.

A group that best represents the position of evangelical feminism is Christians for Biblical Equality, organized in the latter part of 1987. A position paper—"Men, Women, and Biblical Equality"—published in 1989 stated the beliefs of this organization. The paper contained twelve "Biblical Truths" and five points of "Application."[5] Groothuis expresses the goal of this organization and of evangelical feminism well:

> The goal of evangelical feminism is that men and women be allowed to serve God as individuals, according to their own unique gifts rather than according to a culturally predetermined personality slot called "Christian manhood" or "Christian womanhood."[6]

The individuals primarily responsible for laying the foundation of evangelical feminism are Nancy Hardesty, Letha Scanzoni, Paul Jewett, Virginia Mollenkott, and Dorothy Pape. Prominent names currently associated with the movement are Gilbert Bilezikian, Mary Evans, W. Ward Gasque, Kevin Giles, Patricia Gundry, E. Margaret Howe, Gretchen Gaebelein Hull, Craig Keener, Catherine Clark Kroeger and Richard Kroeger, Walter Liefield, Alvera Mickelsen, David Scholer, Aida Besançon Spencer, and Ruth Tucker.

The purpose of this paper is to examine certain hermeneutical principles being implemented among those who are evangelical feminists.[7] As much as possible, the evaluation of these principles will use the standard of the grammatico-historical method of exegesis. The scope of this study necessitates focusing only on principles that differ from the hermeneutics of those called "hierarchialists,"[8] the ones frequently used in the Pauline "hard passages."[9]

There are two primary reasons why the role of women and their relationship to men in the church and the family is one of the "great divides" among Christians today. The first reason is a difference of opinion with regards to the exegesis of the relevant biblical texts.

The second reason is the role of hermeneutics in the debate. Johnston believes that this is what is behind the first reason. He comments,

> For behind the apparent differences in approach and opinion regarding the women's issue are opposing principles for

interpreting Scripture—i.e., different hermeneutics. Here is the real issue facing evangelical theology as it seeks to answer the women's question.[10]

It is the purpose of this essay to examine and evaluate seven relevant principles of hermeneutics of evangelical feminists and thereby provide a heightened mutual understanding of the basic difference between the two sides. This will hopefully lessen the "great divide" that exists in Christendom concerning a woman's role in the church and the home.

THE PRINCIPLE OF *AD HOC* DOCUMENTS

A prominent characteristic of evangelical feminism is its insistence that understanding the literary form of a passage plays a major role in adequate interpretation.[11] Sometimes the phrase describing this axiom is the "hermeneutics of *ad hoc* documents."[12] The principle is prominent in the interpretive scheme of 1 Timothy 2:8–15 by evangelical feminists.

The literary form of 1 Timothy closely relates to the purpose of the epistle. According to Scholer, Paul writes the letter to help Timothy handle the problem of false teachers in Ephesus: "The purpose of 1 Timothy is to combat the Ephesian heresy that Timothy faced."[13]

To some, a necessary corollary to this view of 1 Timothy's purpose is to perceive the epistle as an *ad hoc* letter.[14] The implication of this *ad hoc* perspective is to restrict the teaching of 2:9–15 to the original audience. Concerning the instructions in 2:9–10 and 15, Fee writes,

> All of these instructions, including 2:11–12, were *ad hoc* responses to the waywardness of the young widows in Ephesus who had already gone astray after Satan and were disrupting the church.
>
> It simply cannot be demonstrated that Paul intended 1 Timothy 3:11–12 [*sic*, 1 Tim. 2:11–12] as a rule in all churches at all times. In fact the occasion and purpose of 1 Timothy as a whole, and these verses in particular, suggest otherwise.[15]

It is impossible to deny the *ad hoc* nature of 1 Timothy. The inroads of false teachers into the church under Timothy's leadership are the evident occasion for the epistle. What is questionable, however, is the *ad hoc* interpretation that limits the teaching of 2:11–15 based on an *ad hoc* literary style. Paul's epistle to the churches of Galatia is *ad hoc* in nature.

Yet no one limits the teaching of Galatians 2:16 to the original recipients.[16] Also, Moo's observation is valid: "The isolation of local circumstances as the occasion for a particular teaching does not, by itself, indicate anything about the normative nature of that teaching."[17]

A further problem with the *ad hoc* interpretive principle is that it rests upon the assumption of 1 Timothy's sole purpose being to combat false doctrine. This purpose does find support in Paul's words in 1:3: "As I urged you upon my departure for Macedonia, remain on at Ephesus in order that you may instruct certain men not to teach strange doctrines." Yet it ignores the other purpose statement in 1 Timothy 3:14–15:

> I am writing these things to you, hoping to come to you before long; but in case I am delayed, I write so that you may know how one ought to conduct himself in the household of God, which is the church of the living God, the pillar and support of the truth.

These two verses support the view that Paul writes to his spiritual son to instruct him on how to order and direct the life of a Christian congregation. Hurley expresses this perspective:

> It is universally accepted that 1 Timothy was intended to provide a clear statement concerning certain issues which its author, whom I take to be Paul, felt needed attention. The letter forms a "spiritual will" from Paul to Timothy. In the letter, Paul indicates that he hopes to be able to come soon to Timothy, but fears that he will be delayed (3:14–15a). He writes, "I am writing you these instructions so that, if I am delayed, you will know how people ought to conduct themselves in God's household, which is the church of the living God . . ." [NIV].[18]

A "church manual" approach to 1 Timothy views the teaching of the epistle as normative.[19] Even if one agrees with this analysis of 1 Timothy, it does not follow that everything within the epistle is normative. Most agree that Paul's emphasis in 2:8—"I want the men in every place to pray, lifting up holy hands, without wrath and dissension"—is upon the manner of life of the one praying, not upon his posture.[20]

But neither of the above proposed purposes of 1 Timothy is preferable. It is best to understand 3:15 as the overarching purpose that embraces the purpose stated in 1:3.[21]

THE PRINCIPLE OF AN INTERPRETIVE CENTER

One of the hermeneutical questions related to the ecclesiastical and domestic roles of women is whether or not there is a single text that determines the interpretation of all the other passages. Stated another way, is there a clear text,[22] an interpretive center,[23] a theological and hermeneutical key,[24] a "*locus classicus,*"[25] a defining passage, a starting point that serves as a filter in analyzing the NT view regarding these female roles?[26]

Most evangelical feminists affirm the existence of such a starting point when seeking God's will on the role of women. Yet they do not agree on what that starting point is. They do agree that the interpreter should not start with the Pauline "hard passages." The comment of Gasque is informative:

> The Egalitarian View also takes these texts [1 Cor. 11:2–16; 14:33–35; 1 Tim. 2:11–15; Eph. 5:22–33; 1 Peter 3:1–7] seriously, but it does not begin with these. It points out that if you leave these texts to the side until the end of the discussion, you will come out with a different conclusion. If you look at these texts first, you have basically programmed yourself to come to the Traditional View; but if you put these texts aside for the time being and first study all else that the Bible has to teach theologically about the role of men and women—in society and in the created order, in the Old Testament people of God and the New Testament people of God, in the church and the home—then you come to a different position.[27]

One recommended starting place has been Galatians 3:28 where Paul declares to the Galatians that there is "neither male nor female." Some see this as the interpretive filter which determines the meaning of the other passages. Bruce represents this view when he writes,

> Paul states the basic principle here; if restrictions on it are found elsewhere in the Pauline corpus, as in 1 Corinthians 14:34f. or 1 Timothy 2:11f., they are to be understood in relation to Galatians 3:28, and not vice versa.[28]

Scanzoni and Hardesty concur with Bruce in stating,

> The biblical theologian does not build on isolated proof texts but first seeks the *locus classicus,* the major biblical statement,

on a given matter. (The doctrine of creation and fall, for example, is to be found most clearly spelled out in Gen. 1–3 and Rom. 5:12–21, not in 1 Cor. 11:2–16 or 1 Tim. 2:13–14.) Passages which deal with an issue systematically are used to help understand incidental references elsewhere. Passages which are theological and doctrinal in content are used to interpret those where the writer is dealing with practical local cultural problems. (Except for Gal. 3:28, all of the references to women in the New Testament are contained in passages dealing with practical concerns about personal relationships or behavior in worship services.)[29]

Another recommended interpretive center is Creation-Redemption. Weber comments, "Egalitarians, then, organize their understanding of the sweep of redemption history in terms of creation and redemption and believe that the women's issue should be seen in that context."[30]

To illustrate the lack of agreement among feminist writers further, a third suggested theological key identifies the highest norms or standards taught in the Bible as the starting point, and begins there. The source of these norms is usually the lofty standards emphasized by Jesus, as well as the statements about the purpose of Christ's ministry and the purpose of the gospel.[31]

Evangelical feminists have not listened to one of their own, David Scholer, on this subject. Scholer's says it is wrong to identify a controlling text regarding women's role and status in the church. His words are, "What I want to stress is that from a hermeneutical point of view the question of where one enters the discussion is really an open question to which no canonical text speaks with clarity."[32]

In essence, Scholer says that instead of attempting to identify an interpretive center, each text should have equal weight in developing a biblical theology of the role of women. Biblical theology should build upon all relevant texts. For several reasons, Scholer's proposal is the preferred solution to this hermeneutical issue. First, as already stated by Scholer, the NT does not specify a starting point for this or many other doctrines.[33] To choose a theological and hermeneutical key often reflects one's personal presuppositions.

Next, as Blomberg points out, the avoidance of an interpretive center is consistent with an evangelical doctrine of the plenary inspiration of Scripture. He comments,

> I think that if we as evangelicals take seriously our doctrine of the plenary inspiration of Scripture, then it is hermeneutically

impossible to set up one text as the interpretive grid through which everything else must be filtered.[34]

A third reason why this view is favored is that it allows for the hermeneutical principle universally agreed upon among those with a high view of biblical inspiration: it is necessary for all relevant texts to harmonize with each other.[35] This allows for input from each text that touches on the subject, without excluding the unique contribution of each to the doctrine.

Finally, to use Galatians 3:28 or any other starting point as the interpretive grid through which other passages are understood, automatically colors the meaning emerging from other passages. As Thomas argues, "It is impossible to deal with literature accurately if one's mind is already preconditioned to discover something that the literature does not relate to."[36]

THE PRINCIPLE OF THE ANALOGY OF FAITH

Closely related to the issue of a controlling text is the principle of "the analogy of faith." The principle of the analogy of faith says that Scripture cannot contradict Scripture.[37] In light of this internal agreement, no verse or passage can have a meaning isolated from the rest of Scripture.[38] Yet the role of the analogy of faith in the context of "clear" and "obscure" passages is debatable. The issue is how to handle "unclear" texts in light of the agreed upon truth that Scripture does not contradict Scripture. A resolving of this issue is key in the interpretation of women's place in the church and home.[39]

Feminists of the evangelical persuasion advocate that the analogy of faith principle means the clearer passages should determine the interpretation of the less clear ones.[40] They hold the "clear" text on women's roles to be Galatians 3:28[41] or one of other starting points referred to in the previous section, and perceive 1 Corinthians 11:2–16; 14:34–35, and 1 Timothy 2:11–12 to be the obscure passages.

Another way of applying the analogy of faith principle is to refrain from preferring one passage over another. The basic approach of this variation is to give equal attention to "obscure" or "disputed" texts.[42] This technique does not disregard the analogy of faith principle, but instead employs it after completion of the exegetical procedure, as more or less of a "double check" on the results of one's exegetical investigation.[43]

Two strong considerations make this second approach to the analogy of faith principle preferable. First, it keeps the influence of the interpreter's personal biases to a minimum. Piper and Grudem "hit the nail on the head" when they wrote, "We are all biased and would very likely use this principle of interpretation to justify neglecting the texts that do not suit our bias while insisting that the ones that suit our bias are crystal clear."[44]

Second, interpreting a passage in this way forces the interpreter to consider seriously all relevant passages. This prevents exegetical laziness by requiring an exegetical accounting for all passages germane to the issue. The following recommendation is fitting: "Our procedure should be rather to continue to read Scripture carefully and prayerfully, seeking a position that dismisses no texts but interprets all the relevant texts of Scripture in a coherent way."[45]

THE PRINCIPLE OF SLAVERY AS A MODEL FOR THE ROLE OF WOMEN

A predominant concept in the literature of evangelical feminism is that the relationship between slaves and masters parallels that between wives and husbands, thus impacting the issue of women and church leadership.[46] Proponents have offered two other justifications of the same principle. First, "Scriptural interpretation must allow for continuing actualization as necessary implications are drawn out."[47] A second justification is that "one is informed by the history of biblical interpretation, which may shed light on a passage at hand."[48]

Keener states the rationale of the principle clearly:

> Those who today will admit that slavery is wrong but still maintain that husbands must have authority over their wives are inconsistent. If they were consistent with their method of interpretation, which does not take enough account of cultural differences, it is likely that, had they lived one hundred fifty years ago, they would have had to have opposed the abolitionists as subverters of the moral order—as many Bible-quoting white slave owners and their allies did. Many of the traditions which today use Scripture to subordinate women once did the same for slavery before that idea was anathema in our culture. In contrast, the method of interpretation we favor in this book is closer to the methods favored by the abolitionists.[49]

The basis for treating the male/female relationship like the master/ slave relationship is the scriptural similarity between the two. Boomsma points this out when he says,

There are several comparable elements that suggest such a parallel. As we have seen, in Galatians 3:28 the distinctions between slave and free and male and female, although they continue to exist, are superseded by equality in Christ in the church. The instructions in Paul's letters prominently modify the relations between slaves and masters, and between husbands and wives, as in Ephesians 5:22–33. Similarly Paul places restrictions on both slaves and women by instructing slaves to obey their masters and women to be subservient to their husbands and to refrain exercising equality in the authoritative offices of the congregation.

What is of great significance is the parallelism between the grounds on which the apostle supports his instructions to both slaves and women. In 1 Timothy 6:1 he urges slaves to respect their masters "so that God's name and our teaching may not be slandered" [NIV]. In Titus 2:5 he requires women to be subject to their husbands "so that no one will malign the word of God" [NIV].[50]

Despite these impressive parallels, one major setback confronts this principle: "The existence of slavery is not rooted in any creation ordinance, but the existence of marriage is."[51] Additionally, Paul laid down principles in the book of Philemon that would ultimately destroy the institution of slavery. This is not true of the male/female relationship. Poythress is correct when he declares,

> In the NT, there are too many passages that never "drop the second shoe." The passages say that women must submit to their husbands. But they never say explicitly that husbands must submit to their wives. They explicitly instruct Timothy and Titus about appointing men as elders, but they never explicitly mention the possibility of women elders.[52]

Kassian states a final stumbling block for the slavery analogy in several ways when she writes,

> Biblical feminists view the Bible as open to alteration. One of the basic presuppositions of Biblical feminist theology is that the Bible is not absolute and that its meaning can "evolve" and "transform." Since the Bible presents no *absolute* standard of right and wrong, feminists maintain that they must decide this for themselves. This basic premise allows them to

interpret the Bible in *any manner* appropriate to their immediate circumstances.[53]

THE PRINCIPLE OF CULTURALLY BIASED INTERPRETATION

A recurring question in a quest to understand the biblical teaching on
the role of women is, "Can there be an objective understanding of Scripture?" Is it possible for a person to set aside biases and prejudices for the
purpose of ascertaining the meaning of the text?

"No" is the response of several in the evangelical feminist camp.
Scholer illustrates the negative answer: "Now, however, I feel that I have
come to understand for myself, along with many others, that in fact objective interpretation and objective hermeneutic is a myth."[54] One of the
"many others" is Johnston. His conviction is that the reason for the continuing spate of evangelical literature on women's role in the church and
family is the role of the reader/interpreter in determining the meaning of
the text:

> It is the reader who uses incomplete knowledge as the basis
> of judgment. It is the reader who chooses between equally
> valid possibilities based on personal preference. It is the reader
> who develops criteria for what is universal and what is cul-
> turally specific, what is translatable and what is transcultural.
> It is the reader who brings to a text a specific understanding
> of Scripture's overarching unity. It is the reader who finds it
> difficult to remain vulnerable to the text as it confronts Chris-
> tian and pagan alike.[55]

In light of this he concludes that evangelicals hide themselves behind
"the veneer of objectivity."[56]

The position that objectivity in interpretation is a false notion does
not demand the abandonment of all attempts to determine the meaning
of a text. What it does dictate is: (1) the exegete must recognize the
impact of his biases upon both his hermeneutic and interpretation[57] and
(2) a proper hermeneutical procedure.[58]

The view of the mythological nature of objective interpretation is contrary to the traditional grammatico-historical method of interpretation.
It is a standard corollary of the long-honored approach that one can in-
vestigate a passage in an unbiased manner. Kaiser's definition of interpretation clearly evidences this:

To interpret we must in every case reproduce the sense the Scriptural writer intended for his own words. The first step in the interpretive process is to link only those ideas with the author's language that he connected with them. The second step is to express these ideas understandably.[59]

Dockery concurs:

The goal of biblical interpretation is to approach the text in terms of the objective ideal. This goal does not mean approaching the Bible without any presuppositions at all, for the Bible itself provides the interpreter with certain presuppositions. Yet, the interpreter is expected to strive as diligently as possible for objective understanding.[60]

Is it possible for the interpreter to exclude bias in the hermeneutical process, or is this simply a delusion of grandeur or a hiding behind the veneer of objectivity? However one may answer these questions, all agree that the interpreter has prejudices in approaching the Word of God. Yet the grammatico-historical method of interpretation advocates the possibility and necessity of excluding these prejudices. The Reformers were well aware of this and consequently geared their approach to exegesis along lines of the *tabula rasa* idea. Commenting on this, Sproul says,

The interpreter was expected to strive as hard as possible for an objective reading of the text through the grammatico-historical approach. Though subjective influences always present a clear and present danger of distortion, the student of the Bible was expected to utilize every possible safeguard in the pursuit of the ideal, listening to the message of Scripture without mixing in his own prejudices.[61]

What response can a person offer to the claim that objective interpretation is a myth?[62] What procedures will exclude personal background and culture from hindering an understanding of the intent of the authors of Scripture? Piper and Grudem offer five suggestions to provide interpreters with confidence that they have excluded their biases and prejudices from the hermeneutical process. (1) Search your motives and seek to empty yourself of all that would tarnish a true perception of reality. (2) Pray that God would give you humility, teachability, wisdom, insight, fairness, and honesty. (3) Make every effort to submit your mind to the unbending and unchanging grammatical and historical reality of the biblical texts in Greek and Hebrew, using the best methods of study available to get as close as possible to the intentions of the biblical writers. (4) Test your conclusions by the history of exegesis to reveal any chronological snobbery or cultural myopia. (5) Test your conclusions in the real world of contemporary ministry and look for resonance from mature and godly people.[63]

To speak of objective interpretation is not to diminish the reality of the exegete's background and culture. As Thomas states,

> It must be granted that twentieth-century exegetes are outsiders to the cultures in which the Bible was written and for this reason can never achieve a complete understanding of the original meaning of the Bible in its historical setting. An undue emphasis upon this limitation, however, loses sight of the fact that all historical study is a weighing of probabilities. The more evidence we have, the higher degree of probability we can attain. The practice of exegesis, therefore, is a continued search for greater probability and a more refined understanding.[64]

THE PRINCIPLE OF CULTURAL RELATIVITY IN BIBLICAL REVELATION

The major hermeneutical issue in interpreting the Pauline "hard passages"—1 Timothy 2:11–15 in particular—is whether the teaching is cultural or normative. Quarrels about the meaning of the 1 Timothy passage are one issue, but even those who agree on its meaning disagree on how to apply it. Fee, who argues that the passage does not apply to the issue of women in ministry today, agrees with the interpretation of those who see it as restricting what women can do when the church meets for public worship. He writes,

> My point is a simple one. It is hard to deny that *this* text prohibits women teaching men in the Ephesian church; but it is the unique text in the NT, and as we have seen, its reason for being is *not* to correct the rest of the New Testament, but to correct a very *ad hoc* problem in Ephesus.[65]

The comment of Fee illustrates that the debate involving 1 Timothy 2:11–15 consists not only of how to interpret this passage but also of how to apply it. The primary hindrance to discerning the application is the ascertaining of whether the text is culture-limited or transcultural.

To state it another way, the concern is "discerning between the permanent, universal, normative teaching of Scripture on the one hand and, on the other hand, that which is transient, not applicable to every people in every culture, not intended to function as a mandate for normative behavior."[66] This is a major topic in contemporary studies of hermeneutics that is particularly relevant to determining women's roles in the home and the church.[67]

Evangelical feminist hermeneutics advocate widespread distinctions between universal principles and localized applications. In fact, Weber identifies this as one of the three distinguishing marks in the egalitarian reading of the Bible.[68] The problem is not with the principle but with how extensive its implementation should be. How to determine what is "cultural" or "normative" requires further discussion.

Resolving this matter requires answers to two important questions: (1) Does Scripture convey universal principles or culture-limited application? (2) What methodology should be followed to distinguish what is normative from what is cultural in Scripture?

Three suggestions of how to answer the former question are conceivable. The first recommendation is to view Scripture as conveying what is normative for all believers at all times unless Scripture itself explicitly expresses the limitation. McQuilkin represents this view when he writes, "My thesis is that a fully authoritative Bible means that every teaching in Scripture is universal unless Scripture itself treats it as limited."[69] Identifying criteria for nonnormativeness is the focus of this approach to distinguishing what is normative from what is cultural.[70]

The second recommendation is to see Scripture as conveying what is limited in application to its original context. Instead of Scripture relaying what is normative, it relays that which is culture-bound. The crucial question to be asked in discerning between the time-bound and the eternal is, "How can we locate and identify this permanent element or essence?"[71] This view assumes that Scripture is time-bound, not that which conveys what is basically normative.

The third recommendation mediates between the first two. Instead of assuming that Scripture conveys either what is normative or what is culture-bound, it assumes neither. This view allows the criteria to make this decision. Klein, Blomberg, and Hubbard write,

> We detect problems, however, with both of these views. The former [Scripture conveys what is cultural] makes it difficult to establish the timelessness even of fundamental moral principles such as prohibitions against theft or murder; the latter [Scripture conveys what is normative] would seem to require

us to greet one another with a holy kiss (1 Thess. 5:26) or drink wine for upset stomachs (1 Tim. 5:23).[72]

All three recommendations take seriously the need to distinguish between what is permanent and what is transient. Yet the suggestion that Scripture conveys what is culture-bound (recommendation two) does not harmonize with Paul's significant statement in 2 Timothy 3:16. Recommendations one and three both recognize the importance of this verse in their view. Knight, who agrees with McQuilkin that Scripture relays what is normative, has this to say about the thesis set forth by McQuilkin:

> In positing such a thesis, he is articulating the same absolute and universal language that the apostle Paul has used in asserting the Scripture's comprehensive didactic significance (2 Tim. 3:16). Since Christ's apostle indicates that this is true of *all* Scripture, then only it itself can teach us what it regards as limited and not universally normative.[73]

Likewise, the third recommendation (that criteria determines what is normative or cultural) regards 2 Timothy 3:16 as crucial to its formulation. Representatives of this position declare,

> With 2 Timothy 3:16 and related texts, we affirm that every passage (a meaningful unit of discourse that makes one or more points that can be restated, if necessary, in a proposition) has some normative value for believers in all times and places. But we presuppose nothing about whether the application for us today will come by preserving unchanged the specific elements of the passage or whether we will have to identify broader principles that suggest unique applications for new contexts. Instead we ask a series of questions of the text.[74]

The caveat offered in the last portion of the above quotation is what distinguishes this view from the position that Scripture presents what is normative. The distinction is that those who take Scripture as normative suggest "both the form and meaning of Scripture are permanent revelation and normative,"[75] but those who let the criteria determine what is normative accept the meaning as normative, but not the form. Elaborating on this difference, Larkin provides insight into why taking both the form and meaning of Scripture as normative is the best position:

The obvious reason for adopting the more comprehensive position affirming both form and meaning is that it best upholds the full authority of Scripture and to the same extent that Scripture itself does.[76]

The second question—"What methodology should be followed to distinguish what is normative from what is cultural in Scripture?"[77]— finds its answer in two primary methodologies that are foundational, but work from different perspectives, the ones proposed by McQuilkin[78] and Johnson.[79] Since the answer to the first question has ruled out Johnson's initial assumption that Scripture is culture-bound, it is unnecessary to review his proposal. Since Scripture conveys what is normative, McQuilkin's list is best in reflecting how to determine what is normative as opposed to cultural.[80] To discern this, the interpreter must ask the following questions: (1) Does the context limit the recipient or application? (2) Does subsequent revelation limit the recipient or the application? (3) Is this specific teaching in conflict with other biblical teaching?[81] (4) Is the reason for a norm given in Scripture, and is that reason treated as normative? (5) Is the specific teaching normative as well as the principle? (6) Does the Bible treat the historic context as normative? (7) Does the Bible treat the cultural context as limited?[82]

THE PRINCIPLE OF PATRIARCHAL
AND SEXIST TEXTS

Another hermeneutical mark of evangelical feminism is its detection of patriarchal and sexist texts in the Bible. The loudest advocate of this principle is Scholer, who writes, "Evangelical feminist hermeneutics must face patriarchal and sexist texts and assumptions within biblical passages and understand them precisely as limited texts and assumptions."[83]

The sample texts that Scholer sees as reflecting patriarchy, androcentrism, and possibly misogynism are: 1 Corinthians 11:2–16; Ephesians 5:24; 1 Timothy 5:3–16; Revelation 14:1–5. Concerning Revelation 14:1–5 he states:

> I submit that most of us have never really noticed how dramatically androcentric the text is: the redeemed are men, explicitly men. Nor do I think that most of us have noticed the sexual or sexuality assumptions behind the text: men who have not defiled themselves with women. This is a view of sexuality that most of us would like to explain away or ignore. It is a view rooted in the reality of the ancient world

that women were always understood to be the one primarily to blame for sexual sin. This view has haunted the question of rape even to this day.[84]

His comments on 1 Timothy 5:3–16 are along the same lines.

I submit again that the assumption behind this view is a view of sexuality that probably none of us really share or would admit to sharing. Again, it is rooted in the assumption that women are sexually irresponsible. If a fifty-nine-year-old or younger widow does not remarry, the odds are very great that she will follow Satan.[85]

The nature of these texts leads Scholer to the conclusion that they are limited texts and assumptions which reflect the historical-cultural realities from and in which biblical texts arose.[86] In essence, this hermeneutical principle helps him to affirm evangelical feminism by limiting the passages that speak against it.

Such a perspective toward the identified texts has several problems. First, it implies that the Bible cannot be interpreted in a regular fashion because of its male authorship.[87]

Second, it adds a further dimension to the historical aspect of the grammatico-historical method of interpretation, i.e., that the interpreter concern himself or herself with and know about the biases of the author. This is information that requires much guesswork on the part of the exegete.

A third reason to reject this principle as a valid hermeneutical rule is that it presents a writer of Scripture, such as Paul, in a contradictory light. On one hand, he advocates the full equality of men and women (cf. Gal. 3:28), but on the other, he capitulates to societal norms and writes from a sexist position (cf. 1 Tim. 5:3–16).

Furthermore, Scholer's stance assumes an evangelical feminist presuppositional perspective of the Old and New Testaments. He labels certain passages as sexist and patriarchal because an egalitarian position on the role of women in the church and home is a foregone conclusion.

Finally, a patriarchal culture does not necessarily mandate an improper view toward women. Poythress is helpful in this area when he states,

Note also that the patriarchy of OT and NT cultures did not necessarily exclude women from ever occupying a role of social and religious prominence. Proverbs 31 illustrates the breadth of scope possible even in ordinary circumstances. Moreover, Esther was a queen. Miriam, Deborah, Huldah, and Isaiah's wife were prophetesses (Exod. 15:20; Judg. 4:4; 2 Kings 22:14; Isa. 8:3). Deborah judged Israel (though this role functioned to rebuke the inadequate male leaders: Judg. 4:8–9; Isa. 3:12). Salome Alexandra, wife of Alexander Jannaeus, ruled over the Jews from 76 to 67 B.C. Women played an important role in Jesus' earthly ministry and as witnesses to his resurrection. Lydia, Priscilla, Phoebe, and others obviously had significant roles.[88]

RESULTS OF THE EVALUATION

This completes the evaluation of seven major principles that distinguish the hermeneutics of evangelical feminism from those of hierarchialists and, in many cases, from the grammatico-historical approach to interpreting Scripture.[89] This evaluation has shown the weaknesses of the hermeneutics of evangelical feminism. An *ad hoc* hermeneutic that limits the teaching of 1 Timothy 2:11–15 is inadequate, because it fails to consider both the purpose of 1 Timothy and the *ad hoc* nature of other Pauline epistles. Any attempt to establish one passage as the interpretive grid for all other passages is inconsistent with two standard tenets of the grammatico-historical method of interpretation: the plenary inspiration of Scripture and the necessary harmonization of texts. The principle of the analogy of faith is valid, but not when it is brought into the interpretation process too early, as evangelical feminists tend to do.

Furthermore, to parallel the role of women with the role of slaves is to assume that God ordained slavery, a teaching not found in Scripture. The role of women has its roots in the order of creation, however (Genesis 2). To argue that objective interpretation is a myth and that the Bible contains sexist and patriarchal texts is to differ again from the grammatico-historical method of exegesis. This preferred procedure for understanding Scripture has argued that objective interpretation is possible and that it is not necessary for the interpreter to be concerned with and knowledgeable of "the biases" of the author.

Finally, evangelical feminists are correct in observing that certain biblical texts are cultural. Yet their procedure for determining which ones is questionable. In light of 2 Timothy 3:16–17, it is best to consider all Scripture as normative, unless answers to the above questions presented by McQuilkin prove otherwise.

Evangelical feminists must take a hard look at their hermeneutics in view of evident weaknesses in the system. Many of these shortcomings contradict the grammatico-historical method of interpretation. Since these defects are present, then the position of evangelical feminism on the role of men and women in the church and home rests on less than a solid biblical foundation.

ENDNOTES

[1] Thomas J. Fricke, "What is the Feminist Hermeneutic? An Analysis of Feminist Interpretation of the Bible," *Wisconsin Lutheran Quarterly* 91 (winter 1994): 45.

[2] R. Letham, "The Hermeneutics of Feminism," *Themelios* 17 (April–May 1992): 4.

[3] Ibid., 4. Fricke refers to this category as "liberal feminists" ("Feminist Hermeneutic," 45).

[4] Daniel G. Lundy, "A Hermeneutical Framework for the Role of Women," *The Baptist Review of Theology* 2 (fall 1992): 57. Other labels that coincide with "evangelical feminists" are biblical feminists, conservative Christian feminists, and evangelical egalitarians.

[5] See "Men, Women, & Biblical Equality," *Journal for Biblical Equality* 3 (1991): 1–3; also cited in John Piper and Wayne Grudem, eds., *Recovering Biblical Manhood and Womanhood* (Westchester, Ill.: Crossway, 1991): 469–72, but without approval in this latter work.

[6] Rebecca Merril Groothuis, *Women Caught in the Conflict* (Grand Rapids: Baker, 1994), 110.

[7] Groothuis recently identified the following eight strategies as part of the biblical feminist hermeneutic: (1) Biblical interpretation is to endeavor to be faithful to the biblical author's intent in writing the specific passage in question. (2) It is important to know the accurate translation of the passages traditionally used to silence and subjugate women. (3) It is crucial to maintain interpretive consistency with the rest of a biblical author's writings as well as the whole of Scripture. (4) Texts couched in a context of culturally specific instructions are not to be taken *a priori* as normative for the present day. (5) Culturally specific instructions are to be interpreted not only in light of biblical doctrine and principle, but also in light of the culture to which they were written and the author's reason for writing them. (6) Events recorded in the Bible should be understood in light of the culture of that time. (7) In light of the progressive nature of God's revelation in the

Bible, NT texts concerning women should be considered more accurate indicators of God's intent for women than those provided in the OT. (8) The need to guard against interpreting the Bible in conformity with one's own cultural preunderstanding or personal expectations (*Caught in the Conflict,* 112–15).

[8] The hierarchialist position also has the labels "traditionalist" and "complementarian." Swartley sees the distinguishing marks of this view as: (1) Women are expected to be subordinate to men—in the home, church, and society. (2) Especially in the home, husbands are to exercise headship over wives, with roles prescribed in accord with this pattern. (3) Within the church, women are restricted from the preaching ministry and from teaching men. Other forms of leadership are to be exercised under the authority and leadership of men (Willard M. Swartley, *Slavery, Sabbath, War, and Women* [Scottdale, Pa.: Herald, 1983], 151). Eight points summarize the "Danvers Statement" with its more detailed description of the traditionalist position: (1) both Adam and Eve were created in God's image, equal before God as persons and distinct in their manhood and womanhood; (2) distinctions in masculine and feminine roles are ordained by God as part of the created order, and should find an echo in every human heart; (3) Adam's headship in marriage was established by God before the Fall, and was not a result of sin; (4) the Fall introduced distortions into the relationships between men and women; (5) the OT, as well as the NT, manifests the equally high value and dignity which God attached to the roles of both men and women, with both testaments also affirming the principle of male headship in the family and in the covenant community; (6) redemption in Christ aims at removing the distortions introduced by the curse; (7) in all of life Christ is the supreme authority and guide for men and women, so that no earthly submission—domestic, religious, or civil—ever implies a mandate to follow a human authority into sin; (8) in both men and women a heartfelt sense of call to ministry should never be used to set aside biblical criteria for particular ministries, but rather biblical teaching should remain the authority for testing our subjective discernment of God's will.

[9] Pauline "hard passages" are those that speak against the equality of roles between men and women in the church and home: 1 Corinthians 11:2–16; 14:33b–36; Ephesians 5:21–33; 1 Timothy 2:8–15; 1 Peter 3:1–7 (Robert K. Johnston, "The Role of Women in the Church and Family: The Issue of Biblical Hermeneutics," in *Evangelicals at an Impasse*, ed. Robert K. Johnston [Atlanta: John Knox, 1979], 52).

[10] Ibid., 50.

[11] Ibid., 70.

[12] Gordon D. Fee, "Reflections on Church Order in the Pastoral Epistles, with Further Reflection on the Hermeneutics of *Ad Hoc* Documents," *Journal of the Evangelical Theological Society* 28 (June 1985): 141–51.

[13] David M. Scholer, "1 Timothy 2:9–15 and the Place of Women in the Church's Ministry," in *Women, Authority, and the Bible,* ed. Alvera Mickelsen (Downers Grove, Ill.: InterVarsity, 1986), 199. Others taking this position are Bruce Barron, "Putting Women in Their Place: 1 Timothy 2 and Evangelical Views of Women in Church Leadership," *Journal of the Evangelical Theological Society* 33 (December 1990): 453; Gordon Fee, *1 and 2 Timothy, Titus* (San Francisco: Harper and Row, 1984), xx; Alan Padgett, "Wealthy Women at Ephesus," *Interpretation* 441 (January 1987): 20.

[14] Fee is reputedly the commentator who originated and popularized this view. He writes, "It must be noted again that 1 Timothy is not intended to establish church order but to respond in a very *ad hoc* way to the Ephesian situation with its straying elders" (Fee, "Reflections on Church Order," 146). Also prominent in the discussion about the *ad hoc* nature of 1 Timothy is Scholer, "1 Timothy 2:9–15," 200.

[15] Gordon D. Fee, "Issues in Evangelical Hermeneutics, Part III: The Great Watershed—Intentionality & Particularity/Eternality: 1 Timothy 2:8–15 as a Test Case," *Crux* 26 (December 1990): 35.

[16] Samuele Bacchiocchi, *Women in the Church: A Biblical Study on the Role of Women in the Church* (Berrien Springs, Mich.: Biblical Perspectives, 1987), 146–47.

[17] Douglas J. Moo, "The Interpretation of 1 Timothy 2:11–15: A Rejoinder," *Trinity Journal* 2 (fall 1981): 219.

[18] James B. Hurley, *Man and Woman in Biblical Perspective* (Grand Rapids: Zondervan, 1981), 196. Also agreeing with this viewpoint are Bacchiocchi, *Women,* 115; Douglas Moo, "What Does It Mean Not to Teach or Have Authority over Men? 1 Timothy 2:11–15," in *Recovering Biblical Manhood and Womanhood,* ed. John Piper and Wayne Grudem (Westchester, Ill.: Crossway, 1991), 180.

[19] Hurley holds this position and summarizes it by saying, "Despite the obviously general intention of the author, a large number of recent writers on the subject of the role of women have suggested that the matters discussed and the instructions given in this letter ought to be seen as relevant only in its particular time period. Even a superficial reading of the letter shows, however, that its author would not accept such a view of it" (*Man and Woman,* 196–97).

[20] E.g., ibid., 198.

[21] This is an improvement over the view of Gritz who sees a twofold purpose for writing given in 1:3 and 3:15 (Sharon Hodgin Gritz, *Paul, Women Teachers, and the Mother Goddess at Ephesus* [Lanham, Md.: University Press of America, 1991], 107–8).

[22] Scholer, "1 Timothy 2:9–15," 213.

[23] C. Powell, "A Stalemate of Genders? Some Hermeneutical Reflections," *Themelios* 17 (April–May 1992): 18.

[24] Grant R. Osborne, "Hermeneutics and Women in the Church," *Journal of the Evangelical Theological Society* 20 (December 1977): 348.

[25] Letha D. Scanzoni and Nancy A. Hardesty, *All We're Meant to Be* (Waco, Tex.: Word, 1974), 18–19.

[26] Scott E. McClelland, "The New Reality in Christ: Perspectives from Biblical Studies," in *Gender Matters,* ed. June Steffensen Hagen (Grand Rapids: Zondervan, 1990), 67.

[27] W. Ward Gasque, "The Role of Women in the Church, in Society, and in the Home," *Crux* 19 (September 1983): 4.

[28] F. F. Bruce, *The Epistle to the Galatians* (Grand Rapids: Eerdmans, 1982), 190. See also Richard N. Longenecker, *New Testament Social Ethics for Today* (Grand Rapids: Eerdmans, 1984), 74–75; McClelland, "New Reality," 65–67; Gasque, "Role of Women," 4.

[29] Scanzoni and Hardesty, *All,* 18–19. It is interesting that the authors removed this statement from their revised edition of this work (Letha Dawson Scanzoni and Nancy A. Hardesty, *All We're Meant to Be,* rev. ed. [Nashville, Tenn.: Abingdon, 1986], 25).

[30] Timothy P. Weber, "Evangelical Egalitarianism: Where We Are Now," *Journal for Biblical Equality* 1 (1987): 80.

[31] Alvera Mickelsen, "There Is Neither Male nor Female in Christ," in *Women in Ministry*, ed. Bonnidell and Robert G. Clouse (Downers Grove, Ill.: InterVarsity, 1989), 177–79.

[32] David M. Scholer, "Feminist Hermeneutics and Evangelical Biblical Interpretation," *JETS* 30 (December 1987): 417–18. Scholer appears to ignore his own advice, however, when he writes in his conclusion, "Such limited texts need not be ignored, excluded, or polemicised against. Rather, they should be interpreted from a particular vantage point—the dual commitments to the equal dignity and equality of men and women and to Scriptural authority" (419).

[33] Ibid., 418.

[34] Craig Blomberg, "Response to Catherine Kroeger on 1 Timothy 2," *Journal of Biblical Equality* 1 (December 1989): 44. Blomberg expresses agreement with Kroeger's proposal of evaluating and comparing all Scriptures to arrive at a proper position regarding women's role in the church (Catherine C. Kroeger, "Women in the Church: A Classicist's View of 1 Timothy 2:11–15," *Journal of Biblical Equality* 1 [December 1989]: 3).

[35] Powell, "Stalemate," 18.

[36] Robert L. Thomas, "Some Hermeneutical Ramifications of Contextualization and Feminist Literature" (paper read at Annual Meeting of the Evangelical Theological Society, Atlanta, November 1986), 18.

[37] "The analogy of faith" is defined by Ramm as "the system of faith or doctrine found in Holy Scripture." He goes on to say, "The basic assumption here is that there is one system of truth or theology contained in Scripture, and therefore all doctrines must cohere or agree with each other. That means that the interpretation of specific passages must not contradict the total teaching of Scripture on a point. This is similar to saying that Scripture interprets Scripture" (Bernard Ramm, *Protestant Biblical Interpretation* [Grand Rapids: Baker, 1970], 107).

[38] Susan T. Foh, *Women and the Word of God* (Phillipsburg, N.J.: Presbyterian and Reformed, 1979), 27.

[39] Johnston, "Role of Women," 73.

[40] Scholer, "Feminist Hermeneutics," 417; Powell, "Stalemate," 17; Gasque, "Role of Women," 6; Johnston, "Role of Women," 73.

[41] Pierce states, "The clearer, more general proclamation of Galatians 3:28 rightly serves as a foundation principle against which the more obscure text of 1 Timothy 2:8–15 can be interpreted" (Ronald W. Pierce, "Evangelicals and Gender Roles in the 1990s: 1 Timothy 2:8–15, a Test Case," *Journal of the Evangelical Theological Society* 36 [September 1993]: 353–54).

[42] John Piper and Wayne Grudem, "An Overview of Central Concerns: Questions and Answers," in *Recovering Biblical Manhood and Womanhood,* ed. John Piper and Wayne Grudem (Westchester, Ill.: Crossway, 1991), 90.

[43] Robert L. Thomas, "Introduction to Exegesis" (unpublished class notes, Greek Exegesis I, The Master's Seminary, Sun Valley, Calif., 1987), 17.

[44] Piper and Grudem, "Overview," 90.

[45] Ibid., 91.

[46] For a sampling, see Clarence Boomsma, *Male and Female: One in Christ* (Grand Rapids: Baker, 1993) 43–52; Kevin Giles, "The Biblical Argument for Slavery: Can the Bible Mislead? A Case Study in Hermeneutics," *Evangelical Quarterly* 66 (1994): 3–17; Craig Keener, *Paul, Women, and Wives* (Peabody, Mass.: Hendrickson, 1992), 184–224.

[47] Johnston, "Role of Women," 74. This is not a claim of progressive revelation, but of progressive understanding. This progressive understanding has manifested itself in the church's doctrine of the Trinity and the Christian abolitionist movement. It also is worthy of consideration in determining theological truth for women *in our day*.

[48] Gasque, "Role of Women," 9. The point is that the interpreter should be informed by the change in attitude among Christians toward slavery when considering the role of women.

[49] Keener, *Paul,* 207–8.

[50] Boomsma, *Male and Female,* 48. In addition to these scriptural parallels, Giles cites a number of general similarities between the biblical arguments for slavery and the permanent subordination of women (Giles, "Biblical Argument for Slavery," 17).

[51] Piper and Grudem, "Overview," 65. Contra Giles, who states, "The biblical case for slavery is the counterpart of the case for the subordination of women, the only difference being that the case for slavery has far more weighty biblical support" ("Biblical Case for Slavery," 16).

[52] Vern Sheridan Poythress, "Two Hermeneutical Tensions in Evangelical Feminism" (paper presented at the Eastern Regional Evangelical Theological Society Conference, Philadelphia, April 5, 1991), 2.

[53] Mary A. Kassian, *Women, Creation and the Fall* (Westchester, Ill.: Crossway, 1990), 147. Kassian has overstated her case regarding some biblical feminists. She probably has in mind primarily liberal feminists, but her point is valid regarding some evangelical feminists as Fricke comments: "Evangelical feminists follow the notion of a kind of progressive revelation, an evolutionary development of doctrine in the Christian church" ("Feminist Hermeneutic," 55).

[54] Scholer, "Feminist Hermeneutics," 412.

[55] Robert K. Johnston, "Biblical Authority and Interpretation: The Test Case of Women's Role in the Church and Home Updated," in *Women, Authority, and the Bible,* ed. Alvera Mickelsen (Downers Grove, Ill.: InterVarsity, 1986), 35.

[56] Ibid., 35.

[57] Powell, "Stalemate," 17.

[58] It is beyond the scope of this paper to identify and evaluate what is the currently recommended hermeneutical procedure to remedy the problem of bias in interpretation. For detailed presentations, see Anthony Thiselton, *The Two Horizons* (Grand Rapids: Eerdmans, 1980), and Grant R. Osborne, *The Hermeneutical Spiral* (Downers Grove, Ill.: InterVarsity, 1991).

[59] Walter C. Kaiser Jr., "Legitimate Hermeneutics," in *Inerrancy,* ed. Norman Geisler (Grand Rapids: Zondervan, 1979), 118.

[60] David S. Dockery, "The Role of Women in Worship and Ministry: Some Hermeneutical Questions," *Criswell Theological Review* 1 (1987): 376.

[61] R. C. Sproul, *Knowing Scripture* (Downers Grove, Ill.: InterVarsity, 1977), 105.

[62] As a proponent of the grammatico-historical hermeneutic, Thomas offers a ten-point response to those who insist on the impossibility of excluding the interpreter's biases in the hermeneutical process ("Hermeneutical Ramifications," 4–9).

[63] Piper and Grudem, "Overview," 84.

[64] Thomas, "Hermeneutical Ramifications," 10.

[65] Fee, "Issues in Evangelical Hermeneutics," 36.

[66] J. Robertson McQuilkin, "Problems of Normativeness in Scripture: Cultural Versus Permanent," in *Hermeneutics, Inerrancy, and the Bible,* ed. Earl D. Radmacher and Robert D. Preus (Grand Rapids: Zondervan, 1984), 222.

[67] William W. Klein, Craig L. Blomberg, Robert L. Hubbard Jr., *Introduction to Biblical Interpretation* (Dallas: Word, 1993), 409.

[68] Weber, "Evangelical Egalitarianism," 77.

[69] McQuilkin, "Normativeness," 230.

[70] William J. Larkin Jr., *Culture and Biblical Hermeneutics* (Grand Rapids: Baker, 1988), 316.

[71] Millard J. Erickson, *Christian Theology* (Grand Rapids: Baker, 1983), 1:120.

[72] Klein, Blomberg, and Hubbard, *Biblical Interpretation,* 410.

[73] George W. Knight III, "A Response to Problems of Normativeness in Scripture: Cultural Versus Permanent," in *Hermeneutics, Inerrancy, and the Bible,* ed. Earl D. Radmacher and Robert D. Preus (Grand Rapids: Zondervan, 1984), 243.

[74] Klein, Blomberg, and Hubbard, *Biblical Interpretation*, 410–11.

[75] McQuilkin, "Problems of Normativeness," 222.

[76] Larkin, *Culture*, 315.

[77] The importance, as well as the difficulty, of the question is seen in the many suggested methodologies. The cited references are just a sample of what is available: Bacchiocchi, *Women*, 147; Gordon D. Fee and Douglas Stuart, *How to Read the Bible for All Its Worth* (Grand Rapids: Zondervan, 1982), 66–68; Alan F. Johnson, "A Response to Problems of Normativeness in Scripture: Cultural Versus Permanent," in *Hermeneutics, Inerrancy, and the Bible*, ed. Earl D. Radmacher and Robert D. Preus (Grand Rapids: Zondervan, 1984), 279–80; Kaiser, "Legitimate," 142–44; Klein, Blomberg, and Hubbard, *Biblical Interpretation*, 411–21; Larkin, *Culture*, 354–356; McQuilkin, "Problems of Normativeness," 230–36; Osborne, *Hermeneutical*, 328–29; David M. Scholer, "Unseasonable Thoughts on the State of Biblical Hermeneutics: Reflections of a New Testament Exegete," *American Baptist Quarterly* 2 (June 1983): 139–40; Robert C. Sproul, "Controversy at Culture Gap," *Eternity* (May 1976): 14–15, 40; Michael F. Stitzinger, "Cultural Confusion and the Role of Women in the Church: A Study of 1 Timothy 2:8–14," *Calvary Baptist Theological Journal* 4 (fall 1988): 36–38; Terrance Tiessen, "Toward a Hermeneutic for Discerning Universal Moral Absolutes," *Journal of the Evangelical Theological Society* 36 (June 1993): 192–203; David P. Kuske, "What in Scripture Is Universally Applicable and What Is Historically Conditioned?" *Wisconsin Lutheran Quarterly* 91 (spring 1994): 83–105.

[78] McQuilkin, "Problems of Normativeness," 230–36. Knight is in substantial agreement with McQuilkin ("Response," 243–253; idem, "From Hermeneutics to Practice: Scriptural Normativity and Culture, Revisited," *Presbyterion: Covenant Seminary Review* 12 [fall 1986]: 93–104), as is Larkin (*Culture*, 354–56).

[79] Johnson, "Response," 279–80. The cited article is a response to the list offered by McQuilkin. Klein, Blomberg, and Hubbard state that their list shares important similarities with Johnson, but is by no means identical with it *(Biblical Interpretation*, 411). For an evaluation of the two foundational methodologies, see Larkin, *Culture*, 114–25.

[80] The preference of McQuilkin's list is not to reject wholesale the lists provided by others, especially Tiessen, "Toward a Hermeneutic," 193–207;

Larkin, *Culture,* 354–56; Kuske, "What in Scripture," 99–105; and Klein, Blomberg, and Hubbard, *Biblical Interpretation,* 411–21.

[81] A caveat to this question would be to add the words "my understanding of," so that the questions reads "Is my understanding of this specific teaching in conflict with other biblical teaching?" (Knight, "Response," 247).

[82] For a complete discussion of this list, see McQuilkin, "Problems of Normativeness," 230–36.

[83] David M. Scholer, "Contours of an Evangelical Feminist Hermeneutics," *Catalyst* 15 (April 1989): 4. See also: idem, "Feminist Hermeneutics," 413–17; idem, "Participation in the Issues of Women and Ministry in the New Testament," *Perspectives in Religious Studies* 15 (1988): 103–4.

[84] Scholer, "Feminist Hermeneutics," 414.

[85] Ibid., 415.

[86] Ibid., 419.

[87] Kassian, *Women,* 144.

[88] Poythress, "Two Hermeneutical Tensions," 7.

[89] The scope of this essay does not permit a consideration of other areas, such as the relationship between didactic and descriptive passages, Pauline use of the Old Testament, and the use of logic in understanding 1 Timothy 2:8–15.

CHAPTER EIGHT

Catholicism

Evangelicals and Catholics Together[1]

John F. MacArthur Jr.

A recent document entitled "Evangelicals and Catholics Together: The Christian Mission in the Third Millennium," signed by a number of prominent evangelicals, has neglected the wide doctrinal breach that separates evangelicalism and Roman Catholicism. It declares the unity of the two participating groups, emphasizes their common faith, allows for doctrinal differences, but states that the two nevertheless have a common mission. A fatal flaw in the document is its assumption that a common mission is possible in spite of the doctrinal differences. The alleged common mission is in effect a contradiction of the truths treasured among evangelicals. Reasons given by evangelical signers of the agreement are hollow and unconvincing. The statement in effect reverses what the Protestant Reformation advocated regarding sola Scriptura *and* sola fide. *The position of the Reformers regarding justification, which was quite biblical, was pronounced as anathema by the Roman Catholic Council of Trent in 1547. Other essential biblical doctrines have been denied by Roman Catholic pronouncements, even recent ones. Unity with Roman Catholicism is not a worthy goal if it means sacrificing the truth.*

* * * * *

March 29, 1994, saw a development that some have touted as the most significant development in Protestant-Catholic relations since the dawn of the Reformation. A document titled "Evangelicals and Catholics Together: The Christian Mission in the Third Millennium" was published with a list of more than thirty signatories—including well-known evangelicals Pat Robertson, J. I. Packer, Os Guinness, and Bill Bright. They were joined by leading Catholics such as John Cardinal O'Connor, Bishop Carlos A. Sevilla, and Catholic scholar Peter Kreeft.

A team of fifteen participants led by Richard John Neuhaus and Charles

Colson drafted the twenty-five-page document. Neuhaus is a former Lutheran minister who converted to Catholicism in 1990 and has since been ordained to the priesthood. Like Colson, he is an influential author and speaker.

Colson explained that "Evangelicals and Catholics Together" resulted from a series of meetings sponsored by Neuhaus a few years ago in New York. The original purpose of the meetings was to discuss tensions in Latin America between Protestant missionaries and Catholic officials. "In some countries the Catholic Church was using political power to suppress Protestant evangelistic efforts; Protestant missionaries were being persecuted for their faith," Colson said. "On the other side, some evangelicals were promoting the gospel by calling the Catholic Church the 'whore of Babylon'; the Pope, the 'antichrist'; and the like."[2]

Colson says he and others at the meetings "were moved by the words of our Lord, calling us to be one with one another as He is one with us and with the Father, in order that the world might know, as Jesus prayed, that 'Thou didst send me.'" Colson added, "We were agreed that the Scripture makes the unity of true Christians an essential—a prerequisite for Christian evangelism."[3]

The lengthy statement of accord that resulted has been praised in both the secular and Christian press as a landmark ecumenical agreement. Especially notable is the fact that the Catholics who signed are not from the liberal wing of Catholicism. Signatories on both sides are conservatives, many of whom are active in the pro-life movement and other right-wing political causes. Historically, evangelicals and conservative Catholics have opposed ecumenical efforts.

An article in *Christianity Today* praised the accord for bringing conservatives into the ecumenical movement: "For too long, ecumenism has been left to Left-leaning Catholics and mainline Protestants. For that reason alone, evangelicals should applaud this effort and rejoice in the progress it represents."[4]

But does this new accord really represent progress, or are the essentials of the gospel being relegated to secondary status? Is the spirit of the Reformation quite dead? Should we now rejoice to see conservative evangelicals pursuing ecumenical union with Roman Catholicism?

The list of Protestant signatories to the document is certainly impressive. Some of these are men who have given their lives to proclaiming and defending Reformation theology. J. I. Packer's work is well known through his many valuable books. His book *Evangelism and the Sovereignty of God,* in print for several decades, has introduced multiplied thousands to the Reformed emphasis on divine sovereignty. He has capably defended the key Reformation doctrine of justification by faith in several of his books. His book *Fundamentalism and the Word of God* is an able defense of the authority of Scripture. Few in our generation have been more effective advocates of Reformation theology than Packer.

Charles Colson is one of evangelicalism's most capable writers. Many of the recurring motifs in his writings over the years sound very much like echoes of Reformation themes—the sovereignty of God, the lordship of Christ, and the authority of Scripture. In fact, several of the teachers whom Colson himself names as his mentors are men whose ministries are closely aligned with the ideals and objectives of the Protestant Reformation.

Both of these men surely understand the gulf that divides Roman Catholicism from the evangelical faith. It is not a philosophical or political difference, but a theological one. And it is not a matter of trivia. The key difference between evangelicalism and Roman Catholicism is a difference over the *gospel*. The issues that separated the Reformers from the Roman Catholic Church go to the heart of what evangelicals believe about salvation.

Many people assume that with signatures from men of this stature on it, "Evangelicals and Catholics Together" must be a trustworthy document, not a compromise of Reformation distinctives. But is that a safe assumption to make?

"Evangelicals and Catholics Together" is an object lesson on the importance of biblical discernment. But it is much, much more than that. As the pressure mounts for evangelicals to succeed in the political realm and fight for cultural morality, they capitulate to the new ecumenism. This may become one of the most hotly contested issues of the decade. The future of evangelicalism may hang in the balance.

WHAT DOES THE DOCUMENT SAY?

"Evangelicals and Catholics Together" is a lengthy document. Unfortunately, it is impossible to reproduce the entire text here. But here are some of the highlights:

A Declaration of Unity

The document begins with this: "We are Evangelical Protestants and Roman Catholics who have been led through prayer, study, and discussion to common convictions about Christian faith and mission. This statement cannot speak officially for our communities. It does intend to speak responsibly from our communities and to our communities."[5]

Later in the Introduction, the document states, "As Christ is one, so the

Christian mission is one. That one mission can and should be advanced in diverse ways. Legitimate diversity, however, should not be confused with existing divisions between Christians that obscure the one Christ and hinder the one mission" (2).

"Visible unity" is the stated goal (2). The document quotes John 17:21, where the Lord Jesus prayed "that they may all be one; even as Thou, Father, art in Me, and I in Thee, that they also may be in Us; that the world may believe that Thou didst send Me." Then this follows: "We together, Evangelicals and Catholics, confess our sins against the unity that Christ intends for all His disciples" (2).

At this point the document's drafters are very explicit about who they believe is included in Christ's prayer for unity: "The one Christ and one mission includes many other Christians, notably the Eastern Orthodox and those Protestants not commonly identified as Evangelical. All Christians are encompassed in the prayer, 'May they all be one'" (2).

The section that follows has the heading "We Affirm Together." It includes this:

> All who accept Christ as Lord and Savior are brothers and sisters in Christ. Evangelicals and Catholics are brothers and sisters in Christ. We have not chosen one another, just as we have not chosen Christ. He has chosen us, and he has chosen us to be his together (John 15). However imperfect our communion with one another, we recognize that there is but one church of Christ. There is one church because there is one Christ and the Church is his body. However difficult the way, we recognize that we are called by God to a fuller realization of our unity in the body of Christ (5).

Similar declarations of unity—and appeals for more visible manifestations of unity—are included in every section of the document.

A Statement of Common Faith

The document highlights areas of common faith between Catholics and evangelicals. It affirms the lordship of Christ as "the first and final affirmation that Christians make about all of reality" (5). It identifies Christ as "the One sent by God to be Lord and Savior of all" (5). It declares that the Scriptures are divinely inspired and infallible (6). And it affirms the Apostles' Creed "as an accurate statement of Scriptural truth" (6). The Apostles' Creed is reproduced in its entirety as a part of the document.

The pact also includes this statement about salvation:

> We affirm together that we are justified by grace through faith
> because of Christ. Living faith is active in love that is noth-
> ing less than the love of Christ, for we together say with Paul:
> "I have been crucified with Christ; and it is no longer I who
> live, but Christ lives in me; and the life which I now live in
> the flesh I live by faith in the Son of God, who loved me, and
> delivered Himself up for me" (Gal. 2:20). (5)

Although that statement has been celebrated as a remarkable concession
on the Catholic participants' part, it actually says nothing that has not
been affirmed by the Catholic Church since the time of the Reformation,
as will be shown below. The real issue under debate between Roman
Catholicism and historic evangelicalism—justification by faith *alone*—
is carefully avoided throughout "Evangelicals and Catholics Together."

A Statement of Doctrinal Differences

Those who drafted the accord did acknowledge other important areas
of doctrinal difference between Roman Catholicism and evangelicalism.
Further, they correctly observed that real unity cannot be achieved merely
by glossing over Catholic-evangelical differences. In fact, near the end
of the Introduction, they state, "We reject any appearance of harmony
that is purchased at the price of truth" (4).

In a section titled "We Search Together," they said, "We do not presume to suggest that we can resolve the deep and long-standing differences between Evangelicals and Catholics. Indeed these differences may
never be resolved short of the Kingdom Come" (9).

How are differences to be addressed? They "must be tested in disci-
plined and sustained conversation. In this connection we warmly commend and encourage the formal theological dialogues of recent years
between Roman Catholics and Evangelicals" (9).

The document continues,

> We note some of the differences and disagreements that must
> be addressed more fully and candidly in order to strengthen
> between us a relationship of trust in obedience to truth. Among
> points of difference in doctrine, worship, practice, and piety
> that are frequently thought to divide us are these:
>
> • The church as an integral part of the Gospel, or the church
>   as a communal consequence of the Gospel.
> • The church as visible communion or invisible fellowship
>   of true believers.

- The sole authority of Scripture *(sola Scriptura)* or Scripture as authoritatively interpreted in the church.
- The "soul freedom" of the individual Christian or the Magisterium (teaching authority) of the community.
- The church as local congregation or universal communion.
- Ministry ordered in apostolic succession or the priesthood of all believers.
- The Lord's Supper as eucharistic sacrifice or memorial meal.
- Remembrance of Mary and the saints or devotion to Mary and the saints.
- Baptism as sacrament of regeneration or testimony to regeneration.

This account of differences is by no means complete. (9–10)

The document even acknowledges the solemn importance of many Catholic-evangelical differences. The signers expressly confess that some of the differences are so profound that they impinge on the gospel itself:

> On these questions, and other questions implied by them, Evangelicals hold that the Catholic Church has gone beyond Scripture, adding teachings and practices that detract from or compromise the Gospel of God's saving grace in Christ. Catholics, in turn, hold that such teachings and practices are grounded in Scripture and belong to the fullness of God's revelation. Their rejection, Catholics say, results in a truncated and reduced understanding of the Christian reality. (10–11)

A Mandate for Common Mission

But the theme that runs like a thread through "Evangelicals and Catholics Together" is identified by the document's subtitle: "The Christian Mission in the Third Millennium." The primary motivation behind the accord is the desire to eradicate differences that supposedly "obscure the one Christ and hinder the one mission" (2). How this can be done without *resolving* doctrinal matters that affect the gospel is not explained.

But the gospel is clearly *not* the driving concern of "Evangelicals and Catholics Together." The "one mission" envisioned by the accord places temporal goals alongside—and in effect ahead of—eternal ones. Much of the document focuses on "the right ordering of society" (12). The longest section, "We Contend Together," states that "politics, law, and culture must be secured by moral truth" (12). The mandate they assume is cultural and temporal, not spiritual and eternal.

Therefore the catalog of issues which the document's signers "contend together" for is made up of religious freedom, right-to-life issues, moral education, parental choice in education, antiobscenity laws, human equality, a free-market economy, esteem for Western culture, pro-family legislation, and a responsible foreign policy.

Another section, "We Witness Together," deals with evangelism. No attempt is made to outline the *content* of the gospel message. Indeed, since the document already lists key elements of the gospel as points of disagreement, consensus on this would seem utterly impossible. Nevertheless, as if oblivious to the insurmountable difficulty this poses, the document unequivocally calls for evangelicals and Catholics to demonstrate "the evidence of love" toward one another that "is an integral part of [our] Christian witness" (20).

Beyond that, it gives no positive guidelines for *how* Catholics and evangelicals can "witness together." Instead, the primary concern of this entire section on evangelism is to "condemn the practice of recruiting people from another community for the purposes of denominational or institutional aggrandizement" (22).

The document states unequivocally that our witness is *not* toward people already in the "Christian community." That is, evangelicals are not supposed to proselytize active Roman Catholics (22–23). This is labeled "sheep stealing" (22). Signers of the document believe that such "attempt[s] to win 'converts' from one another's folds . . . undermine the Christian Mission" (20). Besides, proselytizing one another is deemed utterly unnecessary, because "we as Evangelicals and Catholics affirm that opportunity and means for growth in Christian discipleship are available in our several communities" (22).

Much of the controversy regarding "Evangelicals and Catholics Together" stems from this statement:

> "In view of the large number of non-Christians in the world and the enormous challenge of our common evangelistic task, it is neither theologically legitimate nor a prudent use of resources for one Christian community to proselytize among active adherents of another Christian community." (22–23)

THE FATAL FLAW

But it is another statement in the section "We Witness Together" that betrays the document's fundamental weakness:

There are, then, differences between us that cannot be resolved here. But on this we are resolved: All authentic witness must be aimed at conversion to God in Christ by the
power of the Spirit. Those converted—whether understood
as having received the new birth for the first time or as *having experienced the reawakening of the new birth originally
bestowed in the sacrament of baptism*—must be given full
freedom and respect as they discern and decide the community in which they will live their new life in Christ. (24, emphasis added)

The document acknowledges "a major difference in our understanding of the relationship between baptism and the new birth in Christ. For
Catholics, all who are validly baptized are born again and are truly, however imperfectly, in communion with Christ" (23). But how "major" is
this difference? Signers of the accord evidently did not feel it was anything fundamental. *"There are,"* after all, *"different ways of being Christian"* (22, emphasis added). The temporal, cultural, political issues are
so compelling that the gospel must be ameliorated to whatever degree
necessary to achieve a superficial "Christian" morality.

So people who believe they are "born again" because they were baptized Catholic "must be given full freedom and respect" to remain Catholic. That is, they should not be approached by evangelicals and told that no
amount of sacraments or good works can make them acceptable to God.

Having declined to address the profound difference between the evangelical message of justification by faith *alone* and the Roman Catholic
gospel of faith plus works, the document here simply treats that difference as an optional matter of preference.

It is not. Catholicism places undue stress on human works. Catholic
doctrine denies that God "justifies the ungodly" (Rom. 4:5) without first
making them godly. Good works therefore become the ground of justification. And Scripture says that relegates people to an eternal reward that
is reckoned not of grace, but of debt (v. 4). As thousands of former Catholics will testify, Roman Catholic doctrine and liturgy obscure the essential truth that we are saved by grace through faith and not by our own
works (Eph. 2:8–9). It has trapped millions of Catholics in a system of
superstition and religious ritual that insulates them from the glorious
liberty of the true gospel of Christ

Adding works to faith as the ground of justification is precisely the
teaching Paul condemned as "a different gospel" (cf. 2 Cor. 11:4;
Gal. 1:6). It nullifies the grace of God. If meritorious righteousness
can be earned through the sacraments, "then Christ died needlessly"

(Gal. 2:21). "For we maintain that a man is justified by faith apart from works of the Law" (Rom. 3:28).[6]

Furthermore, justification by faith *plus* works was exactly the error that condemned Israel: "Pursuing a law of righteousness, [they] did not arrive at that law. Why? Because they did not pursue it by faith, but as though it were by works" (Rom. 9:31–32). "For not knowing about God's righteousness, and seeking to establish their own, they did not subject themselves to the righteousness of God" (Rom. 10:3). Throughout Scripture teaches that "a man is not justified by the works of the Law but through faith in Christ Jesus . . . since by the works of the Law shall no flesh be justified" (Gal. 2:16).

Yet ignoring the gravity of this defect in the Roman Catholic system, evangelical signers of the document in effect pledge that none of their evangelistic work will ever be aimed at guiding Catholic converts out of Roman Catholicism—with its daily sacrifices, meritorious sacraments, confessional booths, rosary beads, fear of purgatory, and prayers to Mary and the saints. The document insists that "opportunity and means for growth in Christian discipleship are available" in the Catholic Church (22). Therefore winning a Catholic to the evangelical faith is nothing but "sheep stealing"—a sin against the body of Christ.

Having declared all active Catholics "brothers and sisters in Christ," and having given *de facto* approval to baptismal regeneration and justification by faith plus works, the accord has no choice but to pronounce Catholic Church members off limits for evangelism.

A STEP IN THE RIGHT DIRECTION?

Signers of the document nonetheless hailed what they had done "as historic." Some applauded it as a major step toward healing the breach caused by the Reformation. Catholic signatories said the document had even circulated inside the Vatican, where it was received with great enthusiasm. *Christianity Today* ran an editorial welcoming the new ecumenism as a reflection of the changing pattern of American church life. Two major agency heads from the Southern Baptist Convention were signatories to the document. One of them wrote me to say this accord fulfills the whole intent of the Reformation!

But not all evangelicals responded so warmly. Many see the document as confusing, misleading. Some have said it sells out the gospel. Evangelicals who are former Catholics have called the accord a betrayal. Missionaries taking the gospel to predominantly Roman Catholic nations read it as an attack on their ministries. Evangelicals in Latin America fear that the pact will be used as a weapon against them.

Even some Catholics have taken exception. Christians United for Reformation (CURE) featured on their weekly radio broadcast a dialogue with a leading Catholic apologist who agreed with CURE's assessment: the document muddles and simply sweeps aside the important doctrinal differences that prompted the Reformation. CURE scrambled to produce an alternative document that would affirm Catholic-evangelical cobelligerence on moral and political issues without validating Roman Catholicism as authentic Christianity.

I am convinced that "Evangelicals and Catholics Together" is a step in exactly the *wrong* direction. It contradicts the very truths it professes to stand for. It expresses a wish for unity but threatens to split the evangelical community. It claims to reject the appearance of harmony purchased at the price of truth, but it treats precious truths thousands have died for as if they were of negligible importance. It calls for the removal of tensions that supposedly hinder the testimony of the gospel, then renders the gospel moot by suggesting that perhaps "the sacrament of baptism" is efficacious for spiritual regeneration. It condemns moral relativism and nihilism, yet it attacks the very foundation of absolute truth by implying that all forms of "Christianity" are equally valid. It calls for a clearer witness, but it denigrates evangelism among active Catholics as "sheep stealing"—while unduly elevating the importance of social and political issues. It is, frankly, an assault *against* evangelism. It suggests that "the right ordering of society" takes precedence over discerning between true Christianity and "a different gospel." It sets aside personal salvation in favor of national morality. It is nothing but the old ecumenism with moral conservatism rather than radical politics as its real agenda.

In an age already prone to reckless faith and lacking in biblical discernment, this accord seems fraught with potential mischief. It blurs doctrinal distinctives and therefore inflames the very worst tendencies of modern religion. It falls lock-step into line with our culture's minimalist approach to truth issues. Far from signaling "progress," it may mark the low point of post-Reformation evangelicalism.

That may seem like a harsh judgment of a document endorsed by so many stellar evangelicals. But quite honestly, one of the most distressing aspects of "Evangelicals and Catholics Together" is that men of such caliber would lend their support to an effort that camouflages the lethal errors of the Roman Catholic system. Having studied both the document and the different rationales for signing given by various signatories, I am convinced that no matter how noble the motives, "Evangelicals and Catholics Together" is a grave mistake, and it poses profound dangers for the future of evangelicalism.

WHY WOULD KNOWLEDGEABLE EVANGELICALS SIGN THIS ACCORD?

I wrote to the men I know personally who signed the accord and asked them to explain their position. Most responded with very gracious letters. Virtually all who replied explained that their signatures on the document do not necessarily indicate *unqualified* support, and they admitted they have concerns about the document. Most said they signed in spite of concerns because they wanted to express support for evangelical-Catholic alliances against social and moral ills. Some said they hoped the document would open the door for more dialogue on the pivotal doctrinal issues.

I must confess that I find all such explanations unsatisfying, because both the public perception of the accord and the language of the document itself send the signal that evangelicals now accept Roman Catholicism as authentic Christianity. That grants an undeserved legitimacy to Roman Catholic doctrine.

Moreover, the document confuses Christendom with the true church. It makes the unwarranted and unbiblical assumption that every breach of unity between professing Christians wounds the body of Christ and violates the unity Christ prayed for. The reality is that the true body of Christ is far less inclusive than the document implies. The document wants to include "many other Christians, notably the Eastern Orthodox and those Protestants not commonly identified as Evangelical." Who could this latter group include besides theological liberals? Yet Eastern Orthodoxy and most Protestant liberals would side with Rome in rejecting justification by faith alone. Having abandoned the true faith for "another gospel," these groups are not entitled to be embraced as members of Christ's body (Gal. 1:9).[7]

The evangelical signers of the document—particularly those who have studied Reformation theology—surely are aware that official Roman Catholic doctrine is antithetical to the simple gospel of grace. So why would theologically informed evangelical leaders sign a document like this? Here is what some of them say.

One writes,

> This document is not about theology or doctrine. From the outset we admit that there are doctrinal differences that are irreconcilable and we specifically identify many of these. This document is about religious liberty (i.e., the right of all Christians to share their faith without interference from church or state), evangelism and missions (e.g., not only the right but

the responsibility under the Great Commission of all Christians to share Christ with all nations and all people), and the need all Christians have to cooperate, without compromise, in addressing critical moral and social issues, such as abortion, pornography, violence, racism, and other such issues. In our battle for that which is good and godly, we must stand with those who will stand at all.[8]

Another signer wrote,

Why did I sign the recent statement 'Evangelicals and Catholics Together: The Christian Mission in the Third Millennium'? I did so because the document—though by no means perfect—presents an unusually strong combination of basic Christian truth and timely Christian response to the modern world.

Another suggested,

To non-Christians and the non-believing world who know nothing about Christianity and who may think Protestants and Catholics worship a different God, this affirmation should be a great testimony to the Lordship of Christ and the truth of His Word.

And one well-respected, evangelical leader wrote,

It was and is in harmony with the two-pronged approach to Rome that I have pursued for three decades: maximizing fellowship, cooperation, and cobelligerence with Roman Catholics on the ground, at grass roots level, while maintaining the familiar polemic against the Roman church and system as such. The document is not official, it is *ad hoc* and informal, and is designed to lead honest cobelligerence against sin and evil in evangelism and community concerns.

Here are some other reasons evangelical signers give to justify their support for the document. All of these are taken verbatim from letters these men wrote or papers they have circulated:

- I think the document is correct in saying that the scandal of conflict between Christians often has overwhelmed the scandal of the cross.

- I also thought the document's stand for life (especially in protest against abortion) and against the "relativism, anti-intellectualism, and nihilism" that are rampant today are exactly the stands that all Christians should be taking.
- The document is clear about what it is *not* trying to do. It is not put forth as an anticipation of church union, it does not hide the fact that real differences continue to divide Catholics and evangelicals, and does not hide the fact that conditions outside North America are often different from those here.
- We have differences, but on the ancient creeds and the core beliefs of Christianity we stand together. Christianity is besieged on all sides—by a militant nation of Islam, by pantheists who have invaded many areas of life through the New Age Movement, and by aggressive secularism of Western life.
- If we are to reverse the surging tides of apostasy in Western culture and resist the advancing forces of secularism, then it is absolutely vital that those of us who share conservative, biblically-based views stand together, that we make common cause. Regardless of one's Christian tradition or even past prejudices, should we not affirm John Paul II and Mother Teresa for their uncompromising and stirring defense of the sanctity of human life?
- [The document states] "All who accept Christ as Lord and Savior are brothers and sisters in Christ." Isn't "accepting Christ as Lord and Savior" what it means to be saved?
- The issue addressed is not theology. The primary issues addressed are missions, evangelism, societal concerns, and religious liberty.
- I believe the document represents the ultimate victory of the Reformation!

There, in the words of the evangelical signers themselves, is as complete a list of their arguments as I can assemble. To those must be added, of course, the arguments contained in the document itself.

But all those reasons ring hollow in view of everything the agreement surrenders.

WHAT IS COMPROMISED BY THE AGREEMENT?

Notice that a common theme that runs through the signers' arguments is the protest that "this document is not about doctrine." After all,

"Evangelicals and Catholics Together" explicitly disavows any intent to seek resolution of any doctrinal differences (24). All those who signed point to the document's long list of doctrinal differences as proof that no crucial doctrine was compromised.

But the incredible naivete of that perspective is unworthy of any of the men who attached their signatures to this document. Far from safeguarding evangelical distinctives, the document relegated them all to the status of nonessentials. By expressly stating, "Evangelicals and Catholics are brothers and sisters in Christ," the document suggests that none of the differences between Catholics and evangelicals involve any doctrines of eternal significance.

Yet that was the whole point of the Reformation. Rome viewed the Reformers as apostates and excommunicated them. The Reformers became convinced that Rome's deviation from biblical doctrine was so serious that the Papal system represented false Christianity. Both sides understood that the doctrines at stake were fundamental. "Evangelicals and Catholics Together," while acknowledging that *all* those doctrinal differences still exist, simply assumes without discussion that none of them makes the difference between authentic Christianity and "a different gospel." That assumption itself is a monumental doctrinal shift— abandoning more than four hundred years of evangelical consensus. So it is disingenuous to suggest that the document "is not about doctrine."

In fact, one might argue that the document is *against* doctrine. By downplaying or denying the importance of crucial doctrinal distinctions, "Evangelicals and Catholics Together" amounts to a virtual assault against discernment. The sort of Christianity it proposes—broad fellowship based on the barest possible confession of faith—will provide a hothouse environment for reckless faith.

The *Christianity Today* editorial I mentioned earlier includes this welcome caveat: "Lest anyone be carried away by the ecumenical euphoria of the moment, it needs to be stated clearly that the Reformation was not a mistake." But quite unaccountably, the editorial also assures readers that the accord as it stands sufficiently safeguards the essential doctrines of the Reformation: "Both the formal and material principles of the Reformation—that is, the infallibility of Holy Scripture and justification by faith—are duly affirmed in this statement."[9]

That language may be unfamiliar to some readers, but "the formal principle" and "the material principle" are terms most students of Reformation doctrine will immediately recognize. One excellent textbook on Reformation doctrine says this: "Historians have frequently referred to the doctrine of *sola Scriptura* as the *formal* principle of the Reformation, as compared to the *material* principle of *sola fide*."[10] The *formal* principle has to do with the form, or the essence, of the theological debate between Rome and the Reformers: the sufficiency of the Scriptures alone *(sola Scriptura)*. The *material* principle defined the matter in question: whether sinners are justified by faith alone *(sola fide)* or by faith plus works.

The truth is, *Christianity Today*'s endorsement notwithstanding, "Evangelicals and Catholics Together" utterly compromises both the formal and the material principles of the Reformation.

Sola Scriptura—*The Formal Principle*

Notice that the *Christianity Today* editorial identifies the formal principle of the Reformation as "the infallibility of Holy Scripture." But the actual issue under debate in the Reformation was the *sufficiency,* not the *infallibility,* of Scripture. From the beginning of the Reformation, Catholics and Protestants have agreed on the questions of biblical inspiration and infallibility. Even in Luther's day, church officials "were in perfect agreement with him" on biblical infallibility.[11] What the papists objected to was Luther's doctrine of *sola Scriptura*. In Luther's own words, *sola Scriptura* means that "what is asserted without the Scriptures or proven revelation may be held as an opinion, but need not be believed."[12]

Catholicism flatly rejects that principle, adding a host of traditions and Church teachings and declaring them binding on all true believers—with the threat of eternal damnation to those who hold contradictory opinions. In Roman Catholicism, "the Word of God" encompasses not only the Bible, but also the Apocrypha, the Magisterium (the Church's authority to teach and interpret divine truth), the Pope's *ex cathedra* pronouncements, and an indefinite body of church tradition, some formalized in canon law and some not yet committed to writing. Whereas evangelical Protestants believe the Bible is the ultimate test of all truth, Roman Catholics believe *the Church* determines what is true and what is not. In effect, this makes the Church a higher authority than Scripture.

The documents of the Second Vatican Council affirm that "it is not from sacred Scripture alone that the [Catholic] Church draws her certainty about everything which has been revealed," but "sacred tradition [transmits] in its full purity God's word which was entrusted to the apostles."[13] *"Therefore both sacred tradition and sacred Scripture are to be accepted and venerated with the same sense of devotion and reverence."*[14]

How does "Evangelicals and Catholics Together" address the issue of biblical authority? As *Christianity Today* pointed out, the document expressly affirms "that Christians are to teach and live in obedience to the divinely inspired Scriptures, which are the infallible Word of God" (6). But the document lists the question of the Bible's *sufficiency* as one of the disputed issues: "The sole authority of Scripture *(sola Scriptura)* or Scripture as authoritatively interpreted in the church" (10).

The manner of framing that statement implies that the difference between evangelicals and Catholics has to do with the question of who is authorized to interpret Scripture. It implies that evangelicals allow for individuals to interpret the Bible according to their personal preferences while Catholics insist on following the hierarchy of Church authority. But that is a gross misstatement of the issue.

Evangelicals certainly believe in interpreting Scripture correctly. That is why they have creeds and doctrinal statements. But evangelicals believe that creeds, decisions of church councils, all doctrine, and even the church itself *must be judged by Scripture*—not vice versa. Scripture is to be interpreted accurately in its context by comparing it to Scripture (1 Cor. 2:13; Isa. 28:9–13)—certainly not according to anyone's personal whims. Scripture itself is thus the *sole binding rule of faith and practice* for all Christians. Protestant creeds and doctrinal statements simply express the churches' collective understanding of the proper interpretation of Scripture. In no sense do the creeds or pronouncements of the churches constitute an authority equal to or higher than Scripture. Scripture always takes priority over the church in the rank of authority.

Catholics, on the other hand, believe the infallible touchstone of truth is the Church itself. The Church not only infallibly determines the proper interpretation of Scripture, but also *supplements* Scripture with additional traditions and teachings. That combination of Church tradition plus the Church's interpretation of Scripture is what constitutes the binding rule of faith and practice for Catholics. *De facto,* the Church sets herself *above* Holy Scripture in rank of authority.

Therefore the real point of disagreement between evangelicals and Catholics regarding *sola Scriptura* is not the question of *who* should interpret Scripture but whether Scripture alone is a sufficient rule of faith and practice.

"Evangelicals and Catholics Together" not only misrepresents *sola Scriptura,* but it also consigns the whole issue to the status of secondary, nonessential point of disagreement. In that regard, it represents a major victory for Rome and a sorry defeat for the Reformation.

Sola Fide—*The Material Principle*
The other great plank in the Reformers' platform—the material principle—was justification by faith alone. *Christianity Today's* contention that *sola fide* was "duly affirmed in this statement" is mystifying. In the entire twenty-five-page document, not one reference to *sola fide*

appears anywhere! Yet this is what Martin Luther called "the article of the standing or falling church." In other words, Luther believed—and the rest of the Reformers were of one accord on this—that the test of authentic Christianity is the doctrine of justification by faith alone. Rome disagreed, declared the doctrine a damnable heresy, and pronounced a series of anathemas against anyone who dared to side with the Reformers.

It is surely significant that in "Evangelicals and Catholics Together" the issue of justification—the doctrine that launched the Reformation—is not even mentioned in the list of points of disagreement! Are the drafters of the document satisfied that evangelicals and Catholics now agree on this issue? Indeed, where justification is mentioned, it is given as a point of *agreement*: "We affirm together that we are justified by grace through faith because of Christ" (5).

What is wrong with that? many evangelicals will ask. So what if it leaves out the disputed word *alone?* After all, the phrase "justification by grace through faith" is certainly biblical as far as it goes. It may not be a full discourse on the doctrine of justification, but is it not really adequate? Does it not seem like theological nitpicking to insist on technical precision in an informal statement like this?

But it is *not* nitpicking to fault this statement. For five hundred years the question of whether people are justified by faith *alone* has been the main point of theological dispute between Catholics and evangelicals. Both sides have taken rather clearly defined positions on the issue. Any document that purports to bring Catholicism and evangelicalism into harmony *must* address this fundamental disagreement. The difference is so crucial that it cannot and should not merely be glossed over with ambiguous language.

In fact, it does not overstate the case to say that on the matter of justification the difference between the Roman Catholic view and that of Protestant evangelicalism is so profound as to constitute *two wholly different religions*. Error at this point is damning heresy. If one view represents authentic Christianity, the other certainly cannot. They are antithetical. There is no common ground here.

The doctrine of justification by faith has been something of a focus in my personal study for the past few years. It rose to prominence as a major point in the so-called "lordship controversy"—a debate between evangelicals about the role of good works in the Christian life. That debate was sparked by several prominent evangelicals who insisted that people can be saved by accepting Jesus as Savior—even if they choose to defer obedience to His lordship indefinitely. Justification by faith was the issue on which they staked their claim. If we are truly justified by faith *alone,* they reasoned, all good works must remain optional for Christians. That position, known as *antinomianism,* I rejected on biblical grounds.

But the lordship controversy launched me on a very profitable study of justification by faith from both the biblical and the historical perspectives. As I read what the Reformers had to say about justification, I gained a new appreciation for their biblical thoroughness. I also began to see in a clearer light than ever before how vitally important it is to be absolutely sound on the doctrine of justification by faith. Luther did not overstate the case when he called justification the article by which the church stands or falls. A right understanding of justification is the only safe course between the Scylla of works-righteousness and the Charybdis of radical antinomianism.

The Reformers' Firm Stance on Justification

The Roman Catholic Church defined its views on justification at the Council of Trent. That Council began its work in 1545 and continued for nearly twenty years. The doctrine of justification was high on the Council's list of priorities. The canons and decrees on justification were written in 1547 at the Council's sixth session.

Trent was the Catholic Church's answer to the Reformation. In 1517, when Martin Luther nailed his Ninety-Five Theses to the door of the castle church at Wittenberg, attacking the sale of indulgences, he "cut a vein of mediæval Catholicism."[15] The bleeding continued for at least three decades. The Council of Trent was a desperate attempt to staunch the flow.

Philip Schaff described the work of Trent:

> The decisions of the Council relate partly to doctrine, partly to discipline. The former are divided again into Decrees *(decreta),* which contain the positive statement of Roman dogma, and into short Canons *(canones),* which condemn the dissenting views with the concluding *"anathema sit"* ["let him be damned"]. The Protestant doctrines, however, are almost always stated in exaggerated form, in which they could hardly be recognized by a discriminating Protestant divine, or they are mixed up with real heresies, which Protestants condemn as emphatically as the Church of Rome.[16]

So rather than replying to the Reformers' teaching, Trent often attacked straw men of its own making. Bear that in mind during the discussion below regarding some of the Council's pronouncements about justification. Sometimes the view they condemn is merely a caricature of Reformation teaching.

On the other hand, many of Trent's decrees sound quite evangelical. For example, the Council of Trent explicitly denied that anyone can be justified by good works apart from grace: "If anyone says that man may be justified before God by his own works . . . without the grace of God through Jesus Christ—let him be anathema" (*Trent,* sess. 6, canon 1).[17]

The council also affirmed that "God justifies sinners by his grace, through the redemption that is in Christ Jesus" (*Trent,* sess. 6, chap. 6) and that "we are said to be justified by faith because faith is the beginning of human salvation" (*Trent,* sess. 6, chap. 8). It also stated that the *meritorious* cause of justification is "our Lord Jesus Christ, who . . . merited justification for us by His most holy passion on the wood of the cross, and made satisfaction for us unto God the Father" (*Trent,* sess. 6, chap. 7).

So when the recent "Evangelicals and Catholics Together" document stated that "we are justified by grace through faith because of Christ," *it was saying nothing that the Roman Catholic Church has not consistently affirmed for the past 450 years.*

If that is true, why did the Reformers object so strenuously to the Roman Catholic Church's doctrine of justification? The dispute had to do with the very nature of justification. The Reformers said justification is an act of God whereby the believing sinner is *declared* righteous. The Council of Trent argued that justification is a process that actually *makes* the sinner righteous. Here is Trent's definition: "[Justification is] not remission of sins merely, but *also the sanctification and renewal of the inward man,* through the voluntary reception of the grace and gifts by which an unrighteous man *becomes righteous*" (*Trent,* sess. 6, chap. 7, emphasis added).

Certainly all true evangelicals believe that the believer's "inward man" is renewed and sanctified in the salvation process. But, as we shall see momentarily, evangelicals are careful to distinguish between *justification* and *sanctification.* The distinction must be drawn in order to make clear that it is Christ's righteousness imputed to us—not something in the "inward man"—not even an infusion of divine grace—that makes us acceptable to God. *This is the essential theological difference that underlies every other point of disagreement between Catholicism and evangelicalism.* Only if this issue is settled can there ever be any real spiritual unity between Rome and evangelicals.

According to Trent, justification is a lifelong process (*Trent,* sess. 6, chap. 10). Perseverance is not guaranteed (*Trent,* sess. 6, chap. 13); but "those who, by sin, have fallen from the received grace of justification may be again justified . . . through the sacrament of penance" (*Trent,* sess. 6, chap. 14). The council also stated that justification must be preserved through good works, which are energized by the grace of God infused into the believer (*Trent,* sess. 6, chap. 16).

What consistently comes through in Trent's pronouncements is a clear and definite repudiation of the doctrine of justification by faith *alone.* According to the Council, "unless hope and love are *added to faith,* it neither unites a man perfectly with Christ nor makes him a living member of His body" (*Trent,* sess. 6, chap. 7, emphasis added). In the Catholic scheme, justification means that God's grace pours forth into the sinner's heart, making the person progressively more righteous. It then becomes the sinner's responsibility to preserve and increase that grace by various good works. The system mixes works with grace, so that justification is not *sola fide,* by faith alone. And it makes justification an ongoing process, never an accomplished fact.

Here are the Council of Trent's own words:

- If anyone says that *by faith alone* the sinner is justified, so as to mean that nothing else is required to cooperate in order to obtain the grace of justification . . . let him be anathema. (*Trent,* sess. 6, canon 9)
- If anyone says that men are justified either by the imputation of the righteousness of Christ alone, or by the remission of sins alone, to the exclusion of the grace and love that is poured forth in their hearts by the Holy Spirit and is inherent in them; or even that the grace by which we are justified is only the favor of God—let him be anathema. (*Trent,* sess. 6, canon 11)
- If anyone says that the righteousness received is not preserved and also not increased before God *by good works,* but that those works are merely the fruits and signs of justification obtained, but not a *cause* of its increase, let him be anathema. (*Trent,* sess. 6, canon 24)
- If anyone says that the guilt is remitted to every penitent sinner after the grace of justification has been received, and that the debt of eternal punishment is so blotted out that there remains no debt of temporal punishment to be discharged either in this world or in the next in Purgatory, before the entrance to the kingdom of heaven can be opened let him be anathema. (*Trent,* sess. 6, canon 30)
- If anyone says that the Catholic doctrine of justification set forth in this decree by this holy Synod derogates in any way the glory of God or the merits of our Lord Jesus Christ,

and not rather that the truth of our faith and the glory of
God and of Jesus Christ are rendered more illustrious—let
him be anathema. (*Trent,* sess. 6, canon 33)

Trent also declared that the *instrumental* cause of justification (the
means by which it is obtained) is not faith, but "the sacrament of baptism" (*Trent,* sess. 6, chap. 7). The Council also said justification is for-
feited whenever the believer commits a mortal sin (*Trent,* sess. 6, chap.
15)—clearly making justification contingent on human works. So according to Trent, justification is neither procured nor maintained through
faith; works are necessary both to begin and to continue the process.

The Reformers objected to Trent's pronouncements solely on biblical
grounds. They filled many thick volumes with Scriptural proofs against
Rome's position. But since the Council of Trent's rulings were deemed
infallible and those who questioned them threatened by the Church with
eternal damnation, the breach between Rome and the Reformers was in
effect made irreparable.

The Biblical Doctrine of Justification

The Reformers' objections to the Catholic Church's stance on justification may be summed up in four biblical arguments.

First, Scripture presents justification as *instantaneous, not gradual.*
Contrasting the proud Pharisee with the broken, repentant tax-gatherer
who smote his breast and prayed humbly for divine mercy, Jesus Himself said that the tax-gatherer "went down to his house justified" (Luke
18:14). His justification was instantaneous, complete before he performed
any work, based solely on his repentant faith. Jesus also said, "Truly,
truly, I say to you, he who hears My word, and believes Him who sent
Me, has eternal life, and does not come into judgment, but has passed
out of death into life" (John 5:24). Eternal life is the present possession
of all who *believe*—and by definition eternal life cannot be lost. The one
who believes immediately passes from spiritual death to eternal life,
because that person is instantaneously justified. "Therefore having been
justified by faith, we have peace with God through our Lord Jesus Christ"
(Rom. 5:1). A few verses later we read, "Having now been justified by
His blood, we shall be saved from the wrath of God through Him" (v. 9).
Those verses put justification for the believer in the past tense, not the
present or the future. Justification occurs in an instant. At the first moment of faith it is already an accomplished fact: "There is therefore now
no condemnation for those who are in Christ Jesus" (Rom. 8:1).

Second, justification means the sinner is *declared righteousness,
not actually made righteous.* This goes hand in hand with the fact that

justification is instantaneous. There is no process to be performed. Justification is a purely forensic reality, a declaration God makes about the sinner. Justification takes place in the court of God, not in the sinner's soul. It is an objective fact, not a subjective phenomenon. It changes the sinner's status, not his nature. Certainly at the moment of conversion the sinner's nature *is* changed miraculously; old things pass away and all things are made new (2 Cor. 5:17). But the actual changes that occur in the believer have to do with *regeneration* and *sanctification,* not justification. Again, it is absolutely vital to keep these ideas separate. Regeneration is a spiritual quickening in which the sinner is born again with a new heart (Ezek. 36:26; John 3:3); sanctification is a lifelong process whereby the believer is conformed to the image of Christ (2 Cor. 3:18). But *justification* is an immediate decree, a divine "not guilty" verdict on behalf of the sinner. This is inherent in the meaning of the word *justify*. The word itself (*dikaioō* in the Greek) means "to declare righteous"; the sense it conveys is the exact opposite of the word *condemn*.

Third, the Bible teaches that justification means righteousness is *imputed, not infused*. Righteousness is "reckoned," or credited to the account of those who believe (Rom. 4:3–25). They stand justified before God not because of their own righteousness, but because of a perfect righteousness outside themselves that is reckoned to them by faith (Phil. 3:9). Where does that perfect righteousness come from? It is God's own righteousness (Rom. 10:3), and it is ours in the person of Jesus Christ (1 Cor. 1:30; cf. Jer. 23:6; 33:16). We are united to Christ by faith—we are "in Christ"—and therefore accepted by God in His beloved Son (Eph. 1:6–7). Christ's own perfect righteousness is credited to our personal account (Rom. 5:17–19), just as the full guilt of our sin was imputed to Him. "He made Him who knew no sin to be sin on our behalf, that we might become the righteousness of God in Him" (2 Cor. 5:21). So once again we see that the ground on which we stand before God is the perfect righteousness of Christ imputed to us by faith, and not (as the Catholic Church teaches) the imperfect righteousness that is wrought by God's grace infused into us. The point is that the only merit God accepts for salvation is that of Jesus Christ; nothing we can ever do could earn God's favor or add anything to the merit of Christ.

Finally, Scripture clearly teaches that we are justified *by faith alone, not by faith plus works*. "If it is by grace, it is no longer on the basis of works, otherwise grace is no longer grace" (Rom. 11:6). Contrast that with Trent's ruling:

> If anyone says that by the said sacraments of the New Law[18]
> grace is not conferred through the act performed [*ex opere*

> *operato,* lit., "the work worked"] but [says] that faith alone in
> the divine promises is sufficient for the obtaining of grace, let
> him be anathema." (*Trent,* sess. 7, canon 8)

In other words, grace is received not by faith but through works—
specifically, through the Roman Catholic sacraments.

But again, the Bible says, "By grace you have been saved *through faith;*
and that not of yourselves, it is the gift of God; *not as a result of works,*
that no one should boast" (Eph. 2:8–9, emphasis added). The only correct
answer to the question "What must I do to be saved?" is the one the Bible
gives: "*Believe* in the Lord Jesus, and you shall be saved" (Acts 16:31).

> For what does the Scripture say? "And Abraham believed
> God, and it was reckoned to him as righteousness." Now to
> the one who works, his wage is not reckoned as a favor, but
> as what is due. But *to the one who does not work, but believes*
> *in Him who justifies the ungodly, his faith is reckoned as righ-*
> *teousness,* just as David also speaks of the blessing upon the
> man to whom *God reckons righteousness apart from works.*
> (Romans 4:3–6, emphasis added)

None of this renders good works, obedience, or sanctification optional in Christian living, as I have argued at length in two other books.[19]
But it does mean emphatically that works play no role in justification.
Works of righteousness and religious ritual can never make anyone acceptable to God. For that, we must depend wholly by faith on the merit
of the Lord Jesus. Any system that mingles works with grace is "a different gospel" (Gal. 1:6), a distorted message that is anathematized (v. 9)—
not by a council of medieval bishops, but by the very Word of God that
cannot be broken.

Other Essentials of the Faith

"Evangelicals and Catholics Together" compromises and obfuscates
several other essential evangelical truths. Notice, for example, that fourth
from the end in the document's list of "differences and disagreements"
is this: "The Lord's Supper as eucharistic sacrifice or memorial meal"
(10). Here it treats another fundamental doctrine as though it were a
peripheral matter.

Roman Catholicism teaches that the communion wafer is transformed
through a miracle into the literal body of Christ and the wine is transformed into the literal blood of Christ. Trent stated, "The whole Christ is
contained under each form of the communion elements" (*Trent,* sess. 13,

canon 3). Therefore, whoever participates in the Mass actually eats the flesh of Jesus Christ, and the priests who partake of the wine actually drink His blood. This is the doctrine known as *transubstantiation.*

Its corollary is the teaching that every time Mass is said, the sacrifice of Christ is offered over again. "A true and real sacrifice" is offered to God in the Mass and "Christ is given to us to eat" (*Trent,* sess. 22, canon 1). Rome believes that the "Savior instituted the Eucharistic Sacrifice of His Body and Blood. He did this in order to perpetuate the sacrifice of the Cross throughout the centuries until He should come again."[20]

That nullifies the crucial biblical truth that

> we have been sanctified through the offering of the body of Jesus Christ *once for all.* And every priest stands daily ministering and offering time after time the same sacrifices, which can never take away sins; but He, having offered *one sacrifice for sins for all time,* sat down at the right hand of God. (Hebrews 10:10–12, emphasis added)

There is no more need for daily sacrifices or an intercessory priesthood.

In fact, those things have encumbered the Roman Catholic system with pure idolatry. Each Mass features the holding up of the consecrated wafer ("the host") and the bowing and worshiping the communion elements by all present. The Council of Trent ruled,

> If anyone says that in the holy sacrament of the Eucharist, Christ the only begotten Son of God [in the form of the wafer], is not to be adored with the worship of *latria* [worship due God alone], also outwardly manifested; and is consequently neither to be venerated with a special festive solemnity, nor to be solemnly borne about in procession according to the laudable and universal rite and custom of Holy Church; or is not to be proposed publicly to the people to be adored and that the adorers of it are idolaters—let him be anathema. (*Trent,* sess. 13, canon 6)

In other words, the host—the transubstantiated wafer—is deemed worthy of the kind of worship reserved only for God.

On the other hand, Mary, the saints, and relics are objects for *veneration,* which is supposed to be something less than *worship*—but practically it is difficult to see any meaningful difference. Indeed, the word *venerate* originally meant "worship"—from a Latin, rather than Anglo-Saxon root.

Mary is practically vested with attributes of deity. The Church teaches—with no biblical warrant whatsoever—that she is sinless, that she "was taken up body and soul into heavenly glory," and that "she was exalted by the Lord as Queen of all."[21] The current Pope is well known for his devotion to Mary. He and millions of other Catholics pray to Mary daily—as if she were omniscient. She is said to have a "saving role" because of her heavenly intercession and is deemed "Advocate, Auxiliatrix, Adjutrix [words meaning "Helper," "Benefactor"], and Mediatrix"[22]—all roles mirroring those ascribed in Scripture to both Christ and the Holy Spirit. Vatican II specifically ordered "that the cult, especially the liturgical cult, of the Blessed Virgin, be generously fostered" and that "exercises of devotion toward her . . . [as well as] decrees issued in earlier times regarding the veneration of images of Christ, the Blessed Virgin, and the saints, be religiously observed."[23]

The Second Vatican Council stated at least one thing accurately:

> When Christians separated from us [Protestants] affirm the divine authority of the sacred Books, *they think differently from us.* . . . According to Catholic belief, an authentic teaching office plays a special role in the explanation and proclamation of the written Word of God.[24]

In other words, in Catholicism, the plain sense of Scripture apart from the authoritative interpretation of the Church has no relevance whatever. So Catholics can quote and affirm 1 Timothy 2:5: "There is one God, and one mediator also between God and men, the man Christ Jesus." But "they think differently from us" about whether God speaks directly to people through the plain sense of His Word. According to Roman Catholicism 1 Timothy 2:5—and every other verse of Scripture—is subject to the Church's infallible interpretation. The Scriptures do not speak for themselves as the Word of God. *The Church* determines what the Bible means, and *that authoritative interpretation* becomes the infallible Word of God.

Thus—ironically—the section of the Vatican II document that asserts Mary's "saving role" as intercessory Mediatrix *begins* by quoting 1 Timothy 2:5![25] In a popular edition of the Vatican II documents, a footnote after the word *Mediatrix* explains,

> The Council applies to the Blessed Virgin the title of Mediatrix, but carefully explains this so as to remove any impression that it could detract from the uniqueness and sufficiency of Christ's position as Mediator (cf. 1 Tim. 2:5).[26]

Of course, simply *denying* their violation of 1 Timothy 2:5 does not resolve the obvious contradiction between ascribing to Mary an ongoing "saving role" as intercessory "Mediatrix" and Scripture's plain meaning. But that does not matter in Catholicism, since authoritative truth is not determined by the plain sense of Scripture, but by the church's teaching authority. If the Church says Mary's "saving, mediatorial role" does not encroach on Christ's uniqueness as sole Mediator between God and men, Catholics are supposed to believe it with unquestioning faith.

That is reckless faith. Evangelicals must continue to oppose it.

IS UNION WITH ROME A WORTHY GOAL?

Should evangelicals wish to see the Protestant Reformation undone? Certainly not. The Reformation was not a tragedy but a glorious victory. The result of the Reformation was not a breach in the true body of Christ but the recovery of the gospel of grace from the near obscurity it had fallen into under Catholic abuses. Protestants who doubt that ought to study church history.

Some claim the Second Vatican Council in the 1960s brought Rome and evangelicals closer together doctrinally. They say Rome further reformed herself and opened the door for ecumenical rapprochement. But Vatican II only solidified the stance Rome took against the Reformation. Rome declared herself "irreformable."[27]

It would certainly be wonderful for the Roman Catholic Church to repudiate her opposition to justification by faith and abandon her extrabiblical doctrines. Yet nothing suggests that it might happen. All the dialogue between evangelicals and Roman Catholics has not brought Rome one hair's breadth closer to a biblical position on any pivotal doctrinal issue. Nor is there any sensible reason to think that *more* dialogue could accomplish this. On the contrary, changes in Rome's doctrinal position have never been a matter for discussion.

The fact is that the Colson-Neuhaus accord became possible not because Roman Catholicism moved closer to the evangelical position, but because the evangelical drafters of the document either downplayed, compromised, or relinquished all the key evangelical distinctives. "Evangelicals and Catholics Together" capitulated precisely where the Reformers stood firm. Far from being an incentive for Rome to reconsider her position, this document grants an unwarranted stamp of legitimacy on the Roman Catholic system. It makes it harder than ever for doctrinally-minded evangelicals to mount an effective polemic against Rome's "different gospel."

Now is the time when evangelicals must carefully reexamine how dearly they hold their doctrinal convictions. We ought to pause and ask ourselves if we really are willing to consider all who recite the Apostles' Creed as true members of the body of Christ. Either the Protestant Reformation was all a big mistake, or we must be willing to stand with the Reformers. Are we ready to concede that the thousands of martyrs who gave their lives to oppose the tyranny and false doctrine of Rome all died for an unworthy cause?

These are not minor issues. Nor will they go away if evangelical leaders merely keep silent. Other treaties and more doctrinal compromise will follow "Evangelicals and Catholics Together." Those who hold biblical convictions will find themselves forced either to make peace with enemies of the gospel or to take a clear and vigorous stand against Rome's "different gospel" and against ecumenical homogeneity.

Someone who had heard of my stand against "Evangelicals and Catholics Together" asked, "Don't you want to see Christian unity?" I certainly do want to see *true* Christian unity. Remember, however, that the unity our Lord prayed for goes hand in hand with His request that we be sanctified in the *truth* (John 17:17–21). The familiar principle in 2 Corinthians 6:14–17— though it certainly applies to marriage—is actually far broader, encompassing all forms of spiritual union:

> Do not be bound together with unbelievers; for what partnership have righteousness and lawlessness, or what fellowship has light with darkness? Or what harmony has Christ with Belial, or what has a believer in common with an unbeliever? Or what agreement has the temple of God with idols? For we are the temple of the living God; just as God said, "I will dwell in them and walk among them; and I will be their God, and they shall be My people. Therefore, come out from their midst and be separate," says the Lord. "And do not touch what is unclean; and I will welcome you."

Unity at the expense of truth is never a worthy goal. "Evangelicals and Catholics Together" gave lip service to that principle but failed to follow through.

To those who ask "Don't you want to see unity?" I ask in return, "Are you willing to allow souls to be led into darkness by false religion and error?"

"Evangelicals and Catholics Together" practically demands that evangelicals regard all active Catholics as true Christians and refrain from "proselytizing" them. To accede to that request is to capitulate to reckless faith.

I have heard testimonies from literally hundreds of former Roman Catholics who affirm unequivocally that while they were in the Catholic Church they did not know Christ at all. They were blindly following the religious system, attempting to earn grace and work their way into divine favor. They actively partook in the sacraments and ceremonies and rituals, but they had unregenerate hearts. Hardly a Sunday evening passes without at least one or two former Roman Catholics giving a testimony to that effect from our church baptistery. None of these people passed from death to life until they abandoned their blind faith in the Roman Catholic system and embraced the message of God's free grace.

For evangelicals to sign a pact labeling such conversions "sheep stealing" is in my mind unconscionable. And for the document to declare that "it is neither theologically legitimate nor a prudent use of resources for one Christian community to proselytize among active adherents of another Christian community" (23) is incredible. By the document's own definitions, that puts all churchgoers who are Catholic, Eastern Orthodox, or liberal Protestant off-limits for evangelism.

But *most* "active adherents" of those communities simply do not know Christ as Lord and Savior. The christ they worship is not the One who offers full salvation freely to those who trust Him. Most of them are feverishly trying to earn divine favor for themselves through good works and religious ritual—as if Christ had never said, "It is finished!" (John 19:30). Those people desperately need to hear the liberating message of the gospel of grace. For evangelicals to sign a document agreeing to place them off-limits for evangelism is a gross act of betrayal.

Ecumenical unity with Roman Catholicism is not essential to the furtherance of the kingdom of God. Evangelism of Roman Catholics is. To waive the latter goal in pursuit of the former is a serious mistake. One wonders what the evangelical leaders who signed "Evangelicals and Catholics Together" were thinking when they approved such strictures against evangelizing Catholics.

Do the evangelical signers of the document really intend to follow the path it lays out? Let us fervently pray that they will not. Those who pursue that course will find that they have traded away their evangelical birthright for a mess of ecumenical pottage. Rather than honoring our Lord, they will dishonor Him. Rather than clarifying the gospel for a watching world, they will be substituting a muddled message. And rather than steering people to the small gate and the narrow way, they will be pointing multitudes to the wide gate and broad way that lead to destruction.

ENDNOTES

[1] The source of this essay is the volume entitled *Reckless Faith: When the Church Loses Its Will to Discern* (Wheaton, Ill.: Crossway, 1994). It is adapted and used here by permission.

[2] "Evangelicals and Catholics Together: Comments from Chuck Colson and Prison Fellowship Ministries," news release from Prison Fellowship dated June 15, 1994.

[3] Ibid.

[4] Timothy George, "Catholics and Evangelicals in the Trenches," *Christianity Today* 38, no. 6 (May 16, 1994): 16.

[5] "Evangelicals and Catholics Together: The Christian Mission in the Third Millennium" (29 March 1994), 1. All page numbers refer to the twenty-five-page version of the document as originally distributed by Prison Fellowship. Hereafter quotations from this document are cited in parentheses with a page number only.

[6] All Scripture quotations in this chapter are from the New American Standard Bible unless otherwise indicated.

[7] This is by no means meant to imply that none who identify with these groups are truly saved. There are undoubtedly people within Roman Catholicism and Eastern Orthodoxy who really do trust Jesus Christ alone for salvation without realizing that their evangelical faith is a wholesale departure from official Catholic and Orthodox Church doctrines. Yet the Catholic Church's anathemas against anyone who affirms justification *sola fide* (see section below on "The Reformers' firm stance on justification") amounts to an automatic excommunication of all who sincerely trust in Christ alone for salvation. Such people—though they may call themselves Catholic—are officially sentenced by Rome to eternal damnation. Hence the expression "evangelical Catholic" is something of a contradiction in terms.

[8] Most quotations from the document's signatories are from personal letters. Their comments are cited anonymously unless quoted from published sources.

[9] George, "Catholics and Evangelicals," 16.

[10] Timothy George, *Theology of the Reformers* (Nashville: Broadman, 1988), 82. Ironically, George is also the author of the *Christianity Today* editorial.

[11] Ibid., 82–83.

[12] Ibid., 80–81.

[13] *Dei verbum,* 9 (emphasis added). All citations from the Vatican II documents are quoted from Walter M. Abbot, S. J., ed., *The Documents of Vatican II* (New York: America Press, 1966).

[14] Ibid.

[15] Philip Schaff, *History of the Christian Church,* 8 vols. (New York: Scribner's, 1910), 7:160.

[16] Philip Schaff, *The Creeds of Christendom,* 3 vols. (reprint, Grand Rapids: Baker, 1983), 1:94.

[17] Quotations from the Canons and Decrees of the Council of Trent are cited in parentheses as *Trent.*

[18] "New Law" refers to the Council of Trent's canons and decrees on the sacraments. The seventh session established seven sacraments: baptism, confirmation, the eucharist, penance, extreme unction, order, and matrimony—then pronounced the usual anathema on anyone who says that there are more or less than these seven sacraments (*Trent,* sess. 7, canon 1).

[19] *The Gospel According to Jesus,* rev. ed. (Grand Rapids: Zondervan, 1994); *Faith Works: The Gospel According to the Apostles* (Dallas: Word, 1992), esp. 90–121, 242–43.

[20] *Sacrosanctum Concilium* (Vatican II), 47.

[21] *Lumen Gentium* (Vatican II), 59.

[22] Ibid., 62.

[23] Ibid., 67.

[24] *Unitatis Reditegratio,* 21.

[25] *Lumen Gentium,* 60.

[26] Abbot, ed., *The Documents of Vatican II,* 91. Catholic apologist Karl Keating says any contradiction between 1 Timothy 2:5 and Mary's "saving role" as "Mediatrix of all graces" is "illusory" (Karl Keating, *Catholicism and Fundamentalism: The Attack on "Romanism" by "Bible Christians"* [San Francisco: Ignatius, 1988], 278). The inescapable fact Catholic apologists must deal with, however, is that multitudes of Catholics "venerate" Mary with a devotion that far outdoes their "worship" of Christ.

[27] *Lumen Gentium,* 25.

CHAPTER NINE

Progressive Dispensationalism

The Hermeneutics of Progressive Dispensationalism[1]

Robert L. Thomas

Progressive Dispensationalism differs from dispensationalism in a number of ways, one of them being in not viewing the time of the rapture to be as crucial. Progressive dispensationalists view themselves as a continuation of the dispensational tradition, but realize they are moving toward nondispensational systems. The movement's desire for rapprochement with other theological systems has involved a hermeneutical shift in its understanding of Scripture. It has replaced grammatical-historical interpretation with a system of hermeneutics called historical-grammatical-literary-theological. Several comparisons that illustrate the differences between the two hermeneutical systems relate to the function of the interpreter, the historical dimension, the "single-meaning" principle, the issue of sensus plenior, and the importance of thoroughness. The bottom line is that a choice between dispensationalism and Progressive Dispensationalism amounts to a choice of which system of hermeneutics an interpreter chooses to follow.

* * * * *

A recent development related to the pretribulational rapture has come from a relatively new movement calling itself Progressive Dispensationalism (hereafter usually designated by "PD"). For the most part, progressive dispensationalists believe in a rapture prior to the future seven-year tribulation, but they do so in a rather tentative fashion.[2] Their system could dispense with this doctrine without altering their position significantly.

A closer look at PD will clarify why its adherents do not hold the pretrib view to be crucial. The name "Progressive Dispensationalism" derives from the proclivity of its adherents to see the movement in the lineage of dispensational theology and from the understanding of dispensations as not being different arrangements between God and the human race but as successive arrangements in the progressive revelation and accomplishment of redemption.[3] An attempt at defining PD must remain vague because progressive dispensationalists themselves are still in the process of trying to define it. The title of a recent book, *Dispensationalism, Israel, and the Church: The Search for Definition* (1993), reflects the uncertainty of those within the movement about definition.

LINEAGE AND MEDIATING STANCE OF PROGRESSIVE DISPENSATIONALISM

The leaders in the movement[4] view themselves and their supporters as taking a further step in the continuing development of dispensational theology.[5] For example, Bock sees himself as combining two elements, one from what he calls Scofieldian dispensationalism and the other from so-called essentialist dispensationalism, into his system.[6] Advocates of PD, in other words, see themselves in the lineage of dispensational theology.

Yet they do so with a realization that they are moving toward theological systems that are nondispensational. Saucy's quest is for a mediating position between traditional dispensationalism and nondispensationalism.[7] In this quest, however, some of his PD associates have gone far enough to suggest to outside observers a nondispensational orientation in their systems.[8] Bock admits the closeness of his views regarding a present kingdom to those of George Ladd's historic premillennialism—a system adverse to dispensationalism—though claiming a distinction regarding the future kingdom.[9] In fact, the desire for rapprochement with theologians of other systems appears to be a primary motivation behind the emergence of PD.

HERMENEUTICAL SELF-ASSESSMENT OF PD

With PD's desire for rapprochement, however, has come a hermeneutical shift away from literal interpretation—also call the grammatical-historical method—that has been one of the ongoing hallmarks of dispensationalism.[10] In late twentieth-century writings, advocates of this developing theological perspective have shifted in the direction of nondispensational systems by adopting some of the same hermeneutical practices as found in these other systems. For whatever reason, proponents of PD sometimes call their hermeneutics by the name "grammatical-historical," but they mean something quite different by the phrase. Blaising and Bock confirm this difference:

> . . . Evangelical grammatical-historical interpretation was . . . broadening in the mid-twentieth century to include the field of biblical theology. Grammatical analysis expanded to include developments in literary study, particularly in the study of genre, or literary form, and rhetorical structure. Historical interpretation came to include a reference to the historical and cultural context of individual literary pieces for their overall interpretation. And by the late 1980s, evangelicals became more aware of the problem of the interpreter's historical context and traditional preunderstanding of the text being interpreted. These developments . . . have opened up new vistas for discussion which were not considered by earlier interpreters, including classical and many revised dispensationalists. These are developments which have led to what is now called "progressive dispensationalism."[11]

So the hermeneutics of PD represent a significant discontinuity in their alleged lineage of dispensationalism. The recent and more sophisticated "grammatical-historical" interpretation does not lead to dispensationalism in its traditional sense, but to PD.[12]

Blaising and Bock see the continued use of "grammatical-historical" in its traditional sense as running the risk of anachronism,[13] presumably because their analysis of consensus is that *all* agree on the new principles of interpretation.[14] This appraisal of current views on hermeneutics is open to serious question. No such unanimity in favor of new interpretive approaches exists. Even if it did, who is guilty of anachronism? Is it not those who have taken traditional terminology and read into it new connotations?

Recent additions that differentiate the hermeneutics of PD from traditional dispensational hermeneutics include rhetorical and literary matters, the history of interpretation, the matter of tradition, and the historical context of the interpreter.[15] The method advocates consideration of the problem of historical distance between the text and the interpreter, the role of the interpreter's preunderstanding, and methodological applications of the hermeneutical spiral.[16] In fact, Blaising and Bock in at least one place call the approach by the name "historical-grammatical-literary-theological,"[17] which, of course, is more sophisticated and therefore quite different from simple grammatical-historical hermeneutics. It emphasizes the subjective element in its reasoning and hence is more provisional in its conclusions.[18]

This is not the appropriate forum for evaluating recent developments in hermeneutics as a whole—the trends to which these authors refer[19]—

but it is appropriate to compare perspectives regarding several of the new hermeneutical principles with traditional grammatical-historical hermeneutics. For purposes of comparison, Milton S. Terry and Bernard Ramm will furnish principles pertaining to traditional grammatical-historical interpretation in the following discussion.[20]

COMPARISON OF OLD AND NEW HERMENEUTICAL MAXIMS

The following rules of interpretation will illustrate the acknowledged difference in approach to Scripture between PD and dispensationalism. They compare historical-grammatical-literary-theological interpretation with grammatical-historical interpretation.

The Function of the Interpreter
One principle that conspicuously distinguishes the two systems of interpretation relates to the role of the interpreter. Traditionally, the interpreter has sought to suppress any of his own viewpoints regarding what he thinks the passage should mean so as to allow the exegetical evidence from the passage under investigation to speak for itself. Terry writes,

> In the systematic presentation, therefore, of any scriptural doctrine, we are always to make a discriminating use of sound hermeneutical principles. We must not study them in the light of modern systems of divinity, but should aim rather to place ourselves in the position of the sacred writers, and study to obtain the impression their words would naturally have made upon the minds of the first readers. . . . Still less should we allow ourselves to be influenced by any presumptions of what the Scriptures *ought* to teach. . . . All such presumptions are uncalled for and prejudicial.[21]

He adds,

> He [the interpreter] must have an intuition of nature and of human life by which to put himself in the place of the biblical writers and see and feel as they did. . . . He must not allow himself to be influenced by hidden meanings, and spiritual-izing processes, and plausible conjectures. . . . Such a dis-criminating judgment may be trained and strengthened, and no pains should be spared to render it a safe and reliable habit of the mind.[22]

Ramm puts the principle this way:

> It is very difficult for any person to approach the Holy Scrip-
> tures free from prejudices and assumptions which distort the
> text. The danger of having a set theological system is that in
> the interpretation of Scripture the system tends to govern the
> interpretation rather than the interpretation correcting the sys-
> tem. . . . Calvin said that the Holy Scripture is not a tennis
> ball that we may bounce around at will. Rather it is the Word
> of God whose teachings must be learned by the most impar-
> tial and objective study of the text.[23]

The hermeneutics of PD are a bold contrast to this principle of seeking objectivity through repression of one's biases. Its relevant principle
advocates the inclusion of one's preunderstanding in the interpretive process as a starting point. Leaders in the movement pointedly advocate
allowing one's biblical theology and other elements of preunderstanding
to influence interpretive conclusions. Blaising and Bock note this in a
number of places and affirm it as a proper evangelical procedure of interpretation.[24] For example, Bock's preunderstanding in coming to Scripture includes the assumption that a NT appearance of several elements
of an OT promise constitutes an initial or partial fulfillment of that promise
as a whole.[25] This foregone conclusion with which he initiates his research is what ultimately leads him to conclude that Christ is presently
ruling from the Davidic throne in heaven.

In the words of Blaising and Bock, "Each of us has our own way of
seeing, a grid for understanding, that impacts what we expect to see in
the text, the questions we ask of it, and thus the answers we get."[26] They
apparently agree with McCartney and Clayton that preunderstanding,
not interpretive methodology, determines the end result of interpretation.[27] This, of course, differs radically from the quest of traditional hermeneutics for objectivity in hermeneutical investigations.

Though not as specific as Blaising and Bock, Saucy apparently shares
this view of the hermeneutical role of preunderstanding. He writes, "The
fact that earthly human ministry still has significance after the finality of
Christ's coming leads to a second truth with hermeneutical implications.
The application of Christ's fulfillment of the eschatological promises is
progressive."[28] In coming to the NT, he assumes that it contains a progressive unfolding of the dispensations rather than seeing the church as
a parenthesis. This, of course, colors his interpretation of many aspects
of revelation regarding the church.

Quite clearly, the issue of preunderstanding distinguishes the hermeneutics of PD from principles of traditional grammatical-historical interpretation.

The Historical Dimension

Another contrast between the two approaches to hermeneutics lies in an understanding of the meaning of "historical" in the expression "grammatical-historical." Traditionally, the historical dimension in interpretation has referred to the historical setting of the text's origin, as Terry describes:

> The interpreter should, therefore, endeavour to take himself from the present, and to transport himself into the historical position of his author, look through his eyes, note his surroundings, feel with his heart, and catch his emotion. Herein we note the import of the term grammatico-*historical* interpretation.[29]

He states further, "Subject and predicate and subordinate clauses must be closely analyzed, and the whole document, book, or epistle, should be viewed, as far as possible from the author's historical standpoint."[30] In support of history's importance, Ramm writes, "Some interaction with the culture and history of a book of Holy Scripture is mandatory,"[31] and "The interpreter must know *Biblical history*. . . . Every event has its historical referent in that all Biblical events occur in a stream of history."[32]

Bock, on the other hand, advocates a multilayered reading of the text which results in a "complementary" reading (or meaning) that adds to the original meaning determined by the text's original setting. The "complementary" perspective views the text from the standpoint of later events, not the events connected with the text's origin.[33] He proposes a third layer of reading also, that of the entire biblical canon.[34] In essence, he sees three possible interpretations of a single text, only one of which pertains to the text's original historical setting. He refers to his method as a historical-grammatical-literary reading of the text.[35] He notes that "such a hermeneutic produces layers of sense and specificity for a text, as the interpreter moves from considering the near context to more distant ones."[36]

By thus ignoring the way the original historical setting "freezes" the meaning of a text, Bock concludes that the meaning of any given passage is not static, but dynamic. It is ever changing through the addition of new meanings.[37] In principle, Saucy indicates the same perspective. Though acknowledging that Jesus' Sermon on the Mount in its original utterance had pre-Christian Judaism as its target,[38] he views the sermon as directly applicable to the church.[39] This can be true only if that portion of Scripture at some point received additional connotations that were not part of its original historical utterance. Adapting Saucy's words from another setting, this amounts to "a bending [of the text] that would have been quite foreign to the original readers [i.e., listeners]."[40]

For PD hermeneutics, "historical" has apparently come to incorporate not just the situation of the original text, but also the ongoing conditions throughout the history of the interpretation of that text.[41] According to traditional hermeneutical principles, such a "bending" is impossible because the historical dimension fixes the meaning of a given passage and does not allow it to keep gaining new senses as it comes into new settings.

The "Single-Meaning" Principle

Closely related to the dimension that, according to the traditional method, fixes the meaning of a text in relation to its original historical surroundings is the guiding principle that a given text has one meaning and one meaning only. Terry states the principle thus: "A fundamental principle in grammatico-historical exposition is that the words and sentences can have but one significance in one and the same connection. The moment we neglect this principle we drift out upon a sea of uncertainty and conjecture."[42]

Ramm states the same another way: "But here we must remember the old adage: 'Interpretation is one, application is many.' This means that there is only one meaning to a passage of Scripture which is determined by careful study."[43]

The position of PD, however, is to refrain from limiting a passage to a single meaning, and to allow for later complementary additions in meaning, which of necessity alter the original sense conveyed by the passage.[44] These later alterations are in view when Blaising and Bock write, ". . . There also is such a thing as complementary aspects of meaning, where an additional angle on the text reveals an additional element of its message or a fresh way of relating the parts of a text's message."[45]

In part, Bock admits this characteristic of his hermeneutics:

> Does the expansion of meaning entail a change of meaning?
> . . . This is an important question for those concerned about consistency within interpretation. The answer is both yes and no. On the one hand, to add to the revelation of a promise is to introduce "change" to it through addition.[46]

He tries to justify this change by calling it revelatory progress, but whatever the attempted justification, the fact remains that change is present.[47]

This contrasts with traditional grammatical-historical hermeneutics' denial of the possibility of a passage's having multiple meanings.

Saucy practices the hermeneutics of multiple meanings also. Acknowledging the reference of "seed" in Genesis 12:7 to the physical posterity of Abraham, he assigns the term an additional meaning by including Jews and Gentiles who follow Abraham's pattern of faith.[48] He finds that an original meaning of Psalm 110 received added meaning through Peter's sermon at Pentecost.[49] This leads him to assign two meanings to the OT throne of David: one a throne in heaven and the other a throne on earth.[50]

In other instances, however, he strongly opposes a reinterpretation of the OT, when it comes to equating the church with the new Israel.[51] Yet this is precisely what he has done in instances when necessary to fit his system of PD. One can but wonder why he does not treat these passages as he does Hosea 1:9–10; 2:23 and make them an *application* of OT passages rather than an added interpretation of them.[52]

To theorize that the apostles assigned additional meanings to OT texts, as Saucy does,[53] cannot qualify as grammatical-historical interpretation, because in numbers of cases the meanings they added to the OT were beyond the reach of human recipients of those OT Scriptures. Yes, God knew all along that the passages would ultimately attain these added nuances, but the additions were unavailable to human interpreters until the time of the NT spokesmen and writers.[54] It is an example of anachronistic hermeneutics to read NT revelation back into the context of the OT under the banner of grammatical-historical methodology, a method that limits a passage to one meaning and one meaning only.

The Issue of Sensus Plenior (i.e., "Fuller Meaning")

The issue of whether to assign a fuller sense to a passage than grammatical-historical examination warrants is not too remote from the issue of the principle of single meaning. The practice of doing so has characterized Roman Catholicism for centuries,[55] and amounts to an allegorical rather than a literal method of interpretation. Terry strongly repudiates this practice: "He [the systematic expounder of Scripture] must not import into the text of Scripture the ideas of later times, or build upon any words or passages a dogma which they do not legitimately teach."[56] Recently Protestant evangelicals have begun advocating the incorporation of this "fuller meaning" too.[57] Remarks in the earlier discussion of "historical dimension" and "single-meaning" reflect the disharmony of *sensus plenior* with traditional grammatical-historical interpretation.

Facing the issue of "fuller meaning," PD comes down clearly on the side of incorporating it into hermeneutical methodology. Its delineation of "complementary hermeneutics," as described above, is clearly of this nature. Blaising and Bock explicitly refuse to limit textual meaning to a reproduction of what the author meant.[58] Regarding this issue they state, "These texts have a message that extends beyond the original settings in which they were given. Something about what they say lives on."[59] They deny the well-known maxim of "one interpretation, many applications" by referring to later applications as added meanings that accrue to various biblical texts.[60] This opinion is in essence none other than an advocacy of *sensus plenior,* when they endorse a meaning beyond that determined by the historical circumstances of the text's origin.[61] When in referring to the possibility of later revelation's expanding of previous revelation, one means an addition to the original text,[62] it is tantamount to the principle of assigning a meaning beyond that yielded through grammatical-historical study.

In his expansion of the meaning of "seed" in Genesis 12:7,[63] Saucy follows the same pattern of assigning a fuller meaning than called for by traditional hermeneutics. He also points out that Peter's preaching in Acts 2 added something to the meaning of Psalm 110 that was unrecognized in earlier interpretations.[64] All such interpretations by PD—of which there are many—fall into the category of historical-grammatical-literary-theological hermeneutics and are a distinguishing mark of this new system.

Saucy, on the other hand, sometimes takes NT uses of the OT not as fulfillments, but as new applications of the OT. He summarizes an extended discussion of how Hebrews uses the OT in these words: "In this connection it is important to recognize that the purpose of the writer to the Hebrews is not to give us an interpretation of Old Testament prophecy. The book is rather a 'word of exhortation' (13:22). . . ."[65] He also notes,

> . . . The Scriptures frequently reveal different applications of similar language without implying a change in identity. The fact that the same phrase about God's son being called out of Egypt applies to both Israel and Christ does not make these objects identical (cf. Hos. 11:1 and Matt. 2:15).[66]

This principle of seeing the NT use of the OT as applications rather than as interpretations is more in accord with grammatical-historical practices. The fact that the added meanings supplied in the NT did not become discernible until provided by inspired NT writings means that the authority for such interpretations derives from the NT citation, not from the OT passages themselves. This being the case, the support for

PD vanishes when evaluated by grammatical and historical criteria. Of course, God knew from eternity past that fuller meanings would eventually emerge, but so far as human beings were concerned, such meanings were nonexistent until the time that NT apostles and prophets disclosed them.

The Importance of Thoroughness

The expression "hermeneutical hopscotch" describes a final characteristic of PD hermeneutics. Hopscotch is a game in which players choose which squares they want to hop into and avoid stepping in the squares that would lose the game for them. Hermeneutical procedures of PD resemble this game through a selective use of passages seemingly in support of their system—while avoiding others that do not—and through selective comments regarding the passages they cite. The following instances illustrate this fact.

Traditional grammatical-historical exegesis refrains from such passage selectivity. Ramm warns against the danger of *apparent* cross references—i.e., places where a word or words may be the same in two passages, but when equating the two misrepresents the meaning of one or both passages.[67] The practice to which this warning applies is remarkably close to Bock's treatment of the words "light" and "sit" in some of Luke's writings.[68] He builds major doctrinal conclusions on the repetitions of these words in contexts that differ considerably from one another. Another instance of selectivity—this time of a thematic type—is Bock's survey of Luke's gospel and Acts to prove that Christ's promised kingdom rule presently exists. He selects scattered passages in the two books that allegedly prove his point, but omits those that are destructive to his theory, such as Luke 8:10 where Christ through His use of "mysteries" indicates He is talking about a kingdom unforeseen in the OT.[69]

Traditional grammatical-historical exegesis also refrains from making only selective comments regarding texts that are crucial to the point to be proven. Careful study of a passage is the way to obtain the one and only meaning of that passage.[70] Progressive dispensationalists do not exhibit "careful study" in their handling of critical texts. Regarding Romans 16:25–27, the three principal spokesmen fail to acknowledge another interpretation of the passage that refutes their use of it.[71] They consistently interpret "the Scriptures of the prophets" (lit., "the prophetic Scriptures") (16:26) as referring to the OT. They conclude on the basis of this assumption that "the mystery which has been kept secret for long ages past" (16:25) was made known in the OT. They nowhere in their major writings on the subject show an awareness that another very viable interpretation of "the Scriptures of the prophets" exists, i.e., that it refers to the utterances and/or writings of NT prophets.[72] This latter meaning would negate the conclusion they draw from the passage. Thoroughgoing grammatical-historical interpretation does not condone this kind of superficial treatment of texts, particularly when they are critical to support a doctrine being propounded.

In the matter of hermeneutical hopscotch, then, lies another distinction between grammatical-historical interpretation and the methodology of PD. The five principles, of which this is the last, are not all that distinguish the two approaches, but they are sufficient to illustrate that significant differences exist.

THE BOTTOM LINE

The difference in hermeneutical methodology summarized above explains why PD is less clear-cut in its support of a pretribulational rapture of the church as well as of a number of other long-standing distinctives of dispensationalism. It is not the purpose of this essay to raise the question of how proper it is to apply the name "dispensational" to the new theological system. The discussion above has only sought to clarify wherein lies the basic difference between dispensationalism and PD.

By now it has become quite evident both from the self-assessment of progressive dispensationalists and from the comparison of illustrative hermeneutical principles that a choice between the two systems amounts to a choice between two systems of interpretation. If one endorses recent trends in evangelical hermeneutics, that person may very easily fit into the camp of PD or perhaps even into a theological system that is decidedly nondispensational. On the other hand, a choice of grammatical-historical interpretation must lead to dispensational conclusions.

In the latter case, a consideration of the hermeneutics of PD is beneficial in sharpening an appreciation for some of the finer points of the traditional method. Positive lessons from above comparisons include the importance of interpretive objectivity, of a passage's historical and cultural background, of limiting each passage to a single meaning, of avoiding the temptation to assign a "fuller meaning," and of thoroughness in letting each passage have its complete contribution to the totality of biblical revelation. Practicing these lessons will have a stabilizing and building effect in the growth of Christ's body.

ENDNOTES

[1] This chapter appeared in the volume *When the Trumpet Sounds,* ed. Thomas Ice and Timothy Demy (Eugene, Oreg.: Harvest House, 1995)

under the title "A Critique of Progressive Dispensational Hermeneutics." It is adapted here and used by permission.

[2] E.g., Robert L. Saucy, *The Case for Progressive Dispensationalism: The Interface Between Dispensational & Non-Dispensational Theology* (Grand Rapids: Zondervan, 1993), 8–9; Craig A. Blaising and Darrell L. Bock, *Progressive Dispensationalism* (Wheaton: Victor, 1993), 317 n. 15; cf. Walter A. Elwell, "Dispensationalists of the Third Kind," *Christianity Today* 38, no. 10 (September 12, 1994): 28.

[3] Blaising and Bock, *Progressive Dispensationalism,* 48.

[4] For purposes of this article, Craig A. Blaising, Darrell L. Bock, and Robert L. Saucy—sometimes called "the father of Progressive Dispensationalism"—will receive major attention because of their key leadership roles among progressive dispensationalists.

[5] E.g., Craig A. Blaising, "Dispensationalism: The Search for Definition," *Dispensationalism, Israel, and the Church: The Search for Definition,* ed. Craig A. Blaising and Darrell L. Bock (Grand Rapids: Zondervan, 1992), 16–34; Saucy, *Case for Progressive Dispensationalism*, 9.

[6] Darrell L. Bock, "The Son of David and the Saints' Task: The Hermeneutics of Initial Fulfillment," *Bibliotheca Sacra* 150, no. 600 (October–December 1993): 442.

[7] Robert L. Saucy, "The Church as the Mystery of God," *Dispensationalism, Israel, and the Church: The Search for Definition,* ed. Craig A. Blaising and Darrell L. Bock (Grand Rapids: Zondervan, 1992), 150; idem, *Case for Progressive Dispensationalism,* 9, 29.

[8] E.g., Elwell, "Dispensationalists of the Third Kind," 28.

[9] Darrell L. Bock, "Current Messianic Activity and OT Davidic Promise: Dispensationalism, Hermeneutics, and NT Fulfillment," *Trinity Journal* 15NS (1994): 70 n. 29; cf. Elwell, "Dispensationalists of the Third Kind," 28.

[10] See Charles Caldwell Ryrie, *Dispensationalism Today* (Chicago: Moody, 1965), 20, 45–46, 86–90; J. Dwight Pentecost, *Things to Come* (Findlay, Ohio: Dunham, 1958), 11–12, 33, 60–61; Thomas D. Ice, "Dispensational Hermeneutics," in *Issues in Dispensationalism,* ed. Wesley R. Willis and

John R. Master (Chicago: Moody, 1994), 32. Ice points out the error of Poythress and Blaising in attributing a spiritualized hermeneutics to early dispensationalists such as Darby and Scofield. Dispensationalism has always practiced a literal method of interpretation (Ice, "Dispensational Hermeneutics," 37–38).

[11] Blaising and Bock, *Progressive Dispensationalism,* 35–36.

[12] Ibid., 36.

[13] Ibid., 37.

[14] Ibid., 58, 77.

[15] Ibid., 52.

[16] Blaising, "Dispensationalism: The Search," 30.

[17] Blaising and Bock, *Progressive Dispensationalism,* 77.

[18] Ibid., 83.

[19] Cf. Robert L. Thomas, "Current Hermeneutical Trends: Toward Explanation or Obfuscation?" *Journal of the Evangelical Theological Society* 39, no. 2 (June 1996): 241–56.

[20] Milton S. Terry, *Biblical Hermeneutics,* 2d ed. (Grand Rapids: Zondervan, n.d.); Bernard Ramm, *Protestant Biblical Interpretation: A Textbook of Hermeneutics,* 3rd rev. ed. (Grand Rapids: Baker, 1970).

[21] Terry, *Biblical Hermeneutics,* 595 [emphasis in the original].

[22] Ibid., 152–53.

[23] Ramm, *Protestant Biblical Interpretation,* 115–16. Ramm also quotes Luther to emphasize this point: "The best teacher is the one who does not bring his meaning into the Scripture but gets his meaning from Scripture" (Ibid., 115, citing Farrar, *History of Interpretation,* 475).

[24] E.g., Craig A. Blaising and Darrell L. Bock, "Dispensationalism, Israel, and the Church: Assessment and Dialogue," *Dispensationalism, Israel, and the Church: The Search for Definition,* ed. Craig A. Blaising and

Darrell L. Bock (Grand Rapids: Zondervan, 1992), 380; Blaising and Bock, *Progressive Dispensationalism,* 58–61.

[25] Bock, "Current Messianic Activity," 72.

[26] Blaising and Bock, *Progressive Dispensationalism,* 59.

[27] Dan McCartney and Charles Clayton, *Let the Reader Understand: A Guide to Interpreting and Applying the Bible* (Wheaton, Ill.: Victor, 1994), 65; cf. Millard J. Erickson, *Evangelical Interpretation: Perspectives on Hermeneutical Issues* (Grand Rapids: Baker, 1993), 88.

[28] Saucy, *Case for Progressive Dispensationalism,* 32.

[29] Terry, *Biblical Hermeneutics,* 231 [emphasis in the original].

[30] Ibid., 205.

[31] Ramm, *Protestant Biblical Interpretation,* 150.

[32] Ibid., 154 [emphasis in the original].

[33] Bock, "The Son of David," 445.

[34] Ibid., 445 n. 9. Blaising and Bock elsewhere call the three levels of reading the historical-exegetical, the biblical-theological, and the canonical-systematic (Blaising and Bock, *Progressive Dispensationalism,* 100–101).

[35] Bock, "The Son of David," 447.

[36] Ibid., 447.

[37] Bock, "Current Messianic Activity," 71; cf. Blaising and Bock, *Progressive Dispensationalism,* 64.

[38] Saucy, *Case for Progressive Dispensationalism,* 87 (see also n. 24).

[39] Ibid., 18.

[40] Ibid., 235.

[41] Blaising and Bock, *Progressive Dispensationalism,* 29–30.

[42] Terry, *Biblical Hermeneutics,* 205.

[43] Ramm, *Protestant Biblical Interpretation,* 113.

[44] Blaising and Bock, "Dispensationalism, Israel, and the Church," 392–93.

[45] Blaising and Bock, *Progressive Dispensationalism,* 68.

[46] Bock, "Current Messianic Activity," 71.

[47] Ibid. Progress in divine revelation is quite apparent in tracing through the books of the Old and New Testaments chronologically, but "progress" in the sense only of adding to what has already been revealed, not in any sense of a change of previous revelation. To change the substance of something already written is not "progress"; it is an "alteration" or "change" that raises questions about the credibility of the text's original meaning.

[48] Saucy, *Case for Progressive Dispensationalism,* 42–43.

[49] Ibid., 71.

[50] Ibid., 72.

[51] E.g., ibid., 134, 211.

[52] Cf. ibid., 205–6.

[53] Ibid., 33.

[54] Saucy himself illustrates the difference between divine and human perspectives in his defense of the validity of an offer of the kingdom to Israel prior to the prophesied cross of Christ: "We suggest that the solution lies in the same realm as other problems related to the sovereign decree of God for history and the responsible actions of mankind. The idea that God could offer humankind a real choice and opportunity, knowing all the while that humankind would fail (and, in fact, having decreed a plan on the basis of that failure), is expressed in other passages of Scripture. In Eden, humankind was given a genuine opportunity to choose holiness, yet Scripture indicates that God's plan already included the sacrifice of Christ 'from the creation of the world' (Rev. 13:8; cf. Acts 2:23; 4:28). Thus in this instance, a similar unanswerable question as

that related to the offer of the kingdom might be posed: What would have happened to the death of Christ if Adam and Eve had not sinned?" (ibid., 92). The analogy holds here too: The humanly discernible meaning of these OT passages was limited to the single connotation determined by grammatical and historical factors, the additional divine nuance being reserved for later NT revelation to humans. The answer to the question, "What would have happened to the added meanings if the NT writers had never penned new meanings to OT passages?" is also unanswerable. Would the meanings have remained unknown to men?

[55] Ramm, *Protestant Biblical Interpretation,* 40–42.

[56] Terry, *Biblical Hermeneutics,* 583.

[57] E.g., McCartney and Clayton, *Let the Reader,* 162, 164; cf. William W. Klein, Craig L. Blomberg, and Robert L. Hubbard Jr., *Introduction to Biblical Interpretation* (Dallas: Word, 1993), 139, 145–50; Moisés Silva, *An Introduction to Biblical Hermeneutics: The Search for Meaning,* co-authored with Walter C. Kaiser (Grand Rapids: Zondervan, 1994), 267.

[58] Blaising and Bock, *Progressive Dispensationalism,* 64.

[59] Ibid., 64.

[60] Ibid.; cf. also ibid., 65–68.

[61] Bock elsewhere denies that this hermeneutical principle amounts to *sensus plenior* or spiritualizing interpretation, choosing to refer to it as "pattern" fulfillment or typological-prophetic fulfillment ("Current Messianic Activity," 69; cf. Blaising and Bock, *Progressive Dispensationalism,* 102–4). Whatever name one applies to the practice, it still violates the strict standards of a consistent grammatical-historical interpretation.

[62] Bock, "The Son of David," 446.

[63] Saucy, *Case for Progressive Dispensationalism,* 49.

[64] Ibid., 71.

[65] Ibid., 56.

[66] Ibid., 206.

[67] Ramm, *Protestant Biblical Interpretation,* 140–41. Terry also warns, ". . . We must avoid the danger of overstepping in this matter [i.e., the matter of using cross-references too carelessly]" (Terry, *Biblical Hermeneutics,* 222), and "There may be a likeness of sentiment without any real parallelism [i.e., in regard to verbal parallels between separate passages]" (ibid., 223).

[68] Bock, "The Son of David," 447–48, 451–52.

[69] Cf. ibid., 449–54.

[70] Ramm, *Protestant Biblical Interpretation,* 113.

[71] Cf. Blaising and Bock, "Dispensationalism, Israel, and the Church," 393 n. 8; Bock, "The Son of David," 456 n. 26; idem, "Current Messianic Activity," 84; Saucy, "The Church as the Mystery," 144.

[72] Cf. Frederic Louis Godet, *Commentary on Romans* (1977 reprint, Grand Rapids: Kregel, 1883), 504–5; James M. Stifler, *The Epistle to the Romans* (Chicago: Moody, 1960), 254–55.

CHAPTER TEN

The Jesus Seminar

Evangelical Responses
to the Jesus Seminar[1]

Robert L. Thomas

Evangelicals have reacted strongly against the conclusions of the Jesus Seminar. Yet their methodologies in studying the Gospels fit the pattern of methods employed by that Seminar, particularly the assumption that the composition of the Gospels involved some form of literary dependence. Ten Scriptures illustrate how this assumption leads inevitably to assigning historical inaccuracies to various portions of the Synoptic Gospels. Only one alternative avoids a dehistoricizing of the Gospels, that of concluding that the synoptic problem does not exist—and is therefore unsolved—because the writers did not depend on one another's works. They wrote independently of each other but in dependence on the Holy Spirit who inspired them to compose books that were historically accurate in every detail.

* * * * *

The Jesus Seminar, composed of liberal scholars under the leadership of Robert Funk, began its twice-a-year meetings in 1985. Its highly publicized findings have denied the authenticity of 82 percent of what the four Gospels indicate that Jesus said. Their conclusions about Jesus' sayings appeared in *The Five Gospels: The Search for the Authentic Words of Jesus* in 1993.[2] The Seminar continues its meetings currently to vote on the deeds of Jesus in anticipation of publishing a similar work treating that subject. The already published work prints Jesus' sayings in four colors—red, pink, gray, and black—to match the colors of the symbolic beads members used to cast votes in their meetings—red, Jesus definitely said it; pink, Jesus probably said it; gray, Jesus probably did not say it; black, Jesus definitely did not say it. Only one red statement appears in the Gospel of Mark and none in the Gospel of John. In comparison, the appearance in red of three sayings in the Gospel of Thomas illustrates the skepticism of this group toward the canonical Gospels.

The evangelical[3] community has reacted strongly against the pronouncements of the Jesus Seminar because of that group's rejection of many historical aspects of the Gospels.[4] The number of specific evangelical responses to this Seminar is growing.[5] Yet most of these responses come from those who utilize the same methodology in gospel study as do the Jesus Seminar personnel. Further, a closer look at studies done by some of these evangelical critics yields results that show their goal of refuting Seminar findings to be quite challenging if not impossible to achieve. To a degree, they must attack the same presuppositional framework that they themselves utilize. In their acceptance of the same historical-critical assumptions, they have rejected the wisdom of B. B. Warfield who many years ago wrote, "And in general, no form of criticism is more uncertain than that, now so diligently prosecuted, which seeks to explain the several forms of narratives in the Synoptics as modifications of one another."[6] The following discussion will reflect this.

EVANGELICAL SIMILARITIES TO THE JESUS SEMINAR

Outspoken evangelical critics have engaged in the same type of dehistoricizing activity as the Jesus-Seminar people with whom they differ. If they were to organize among themselves their own evangelical "Jesus Seminar,"[7] the following is a sampling of the issues they would vote on, most of which they would probably pass:[8]

1. The author of Matthew, not Jesus, created the Sermon on the Mount.
2. The commissioning of the twelve in Matthew 10 is a group of instructions compiled and organized by the author of the first gospel, not spoken by Jesus on a single occasion.
3. The parable accounts of Matthew 13 and Mark 4 are anthologies of parables that Jesus uttered on separate occasions.
4. Jesus did not preach the Olivet Discourse in its entirety as we have it in three of the gospel accounts.
5. Jesus gave His teaching on divorce and remarriage without the exception clauses found in Matthew 5:32 and 19:9.
6. In Matthew 19:16–17, the writer changed the words of Jesus and the rich man to avoid a theological problem

involved in the wording of Mark's and Luke's accounts
of the same event.

7. The scribes and Pharisees were in reality decent people
whom Matthew painted in an entirely negative light because of his personal bias against them.

8. The genealogies of Jesus in Matthew 1 and Luke 3 are
figures of speech and not accurate records of Jesus' physical and/or legal lineage.

9. The magi who according to Matthew 2 visited the child
Jesus after His birth are fictional, not real, characters.

10. Jesus uttered only three or four of the eight or nine beatitudes in Matthew 5:3–12.

Recognizably, the listed conclusions impinge upon the historical accuracy of the gospel records. Various evangelicals have opted for the stated
unhistorical choice in each of the suggested instances. Granted, their re-
duction of historical precision in the Gospels is not the wholesale repudiation of historical data as is that of the original Jesus Seminar, but that it is
a repudiation is undeniable. An acceptance of imprecision is even more
noticeable in light of the fact that the above questions are only the tip of
the iceberg. An exhaustive list would reach staggering proportions.[9]

In the spring of 1991, the *Los Angeles Times* religion staff planned to
run two articles, one a pro-Jesus Seminar piece and the other an anti-
Jesus Seminar one. The cochairman of the Jesus Seminar—Robert
Funk—wrote the former and a professor at a prominent evangelical seminary—Robert Guelich—wrote the other.[10] The plan to represent the two
sides failed, however. Some staff person for this newspaper recognized
that the anti-Seminar article was not "anti" at all, but took the same
essential viewpoint as the Jesus Seminar. This came to light when a *Times*
editor called me and asked if I would do an "anti" article the following
week because the evangelical contributor approached the Gospels in the
same way as those he was supposed to oppose.[11] This observation by
someone on the editorial staff—to this day I do not know who—was
shrewd because it recognized that the evangelical in what was to have
been the "con" article supported the same general methodological and
presuppositional mold as those whom he purposed to refute.

A STANDARD METHODOLOGY

Methodological Framework

What do evangelical scholars who surrender this or that historical
aspect of the first three Gospels have in common? They all build on the

same presuppositional construct, which also happens to be the one followed by the more radical Jesus Seminar.[12] They thereby render themselves all but powerless to respond to the radical conclusions of that Seminar.

A title appropriate to the methodology common to Jesus-Seminar personnel and many evangelicals is Historical Criticism. Various subdisciplines that have come into vogue under this broad heading include Source Criticism, Tradition Criticism, Form Criticism, and Redaction Criticism. Source Criticism was the earliest of these to arise, having its origin in the nineteenth century. The others sprang up at various points in the twentieth century. The stated purpose of all the subdisciplines is to *test* the historical accuracy of NT historical narrative,[13] but in one way or another, they *reduce* the historical accuracy of the Synoptic Gospels.

The claim of these evangelical scholars is that the widely practiced Historical Criticism is not necessarily antithetic to finding the Gospels historically reliable. Yet the results of their research belie their claim. They profess that their methodology is neutral and does not necessitate negative presuppositions regarding the integrity of the gospel accounts,[14] but the same people question Matthew's and Mark's representation that Jesus taught the parables of Matthew 13 and Mark 4 on a single occasion[15] and Matthew's and Luke's indications that Jesus preached the whole Sermon on the Mount and Sermon on the Plain to one audience.[16] The evangelical stance of those who thus question historicity dictates that in all probability the theories do not arise from conscious antisupernaturalistic predispositions. Their questionings must issue from a flawed methodology, one that inevitably leads to diminishing historical accuracy in the Gospels.

A basic tenet of Historical Criticism is the assumption that the authors of the three Synoptic Gospels depended on one another's writings. Various schemes regarding who depended on whose writings have surfaced, the most widely held current theory being that Mark wrote first and Matthew and Luke depended on Mark.[17] The other element of the theory maintains the existence of another document called "Q" on which Matthew and Luke depended also. No one in recent centuries has ever seen Q, if indeed it ever existed.[18]

Attempted Proof of Literary Dependence

Rarely does one find a defense of the general theory of literary dependence. It is most often just an assumption with no serious attempt at proof.[19] One exception to the unsupported assumption is the argumentation by Stein favoring a common literary source for the Synoptic Gospels. He cites agreements (1) in wording, (2) in order, and (3) in parenthetical material and (4) the Lukan prologue (Luke 1:1–4) as proof of literary dependence.[20]

1. He lists a number of places to illustrate agreements in wording, but makes no allowance in his argument for places of disagreement. He fails to note that these disagreements include three categories: Matthew and Mark against Luke, Matthew and Luke against Mark, and Mark and Luke against Matthew.[21] This factor argues strongly against any type of literary dependence and favors a random type of composition through which no writer ever saw another's work before writing his own gospel.[22]

2. Stein also notices agreements in sequence in the Gospels,[23] but fails to give more than passing notice to disagreements in order which are adverse to the case he builds for literary dependence. He does not endorse or even mention the possibility that agreements in order could result from the sequence of historical occurrences they describe. Yet such a possibility offers a natural explanation for the agreements in essentially all cases.

3. His first illustration of agreements in parenthetical material lies in the words "let the reader understand," found in Matthew 24:15 and Mark 13:14. Yet he cites this without acknowledging the widely held opinion that these words were not parentheses added by Matthew and Mark, but were the words of Jesus Himself, referring to the reader of Daniel, not the reader of Matthew and Mark.[24] His other three instances of agreement in parenthetical material are not verbatim agreements with each other and could easily be coincidental words of explanation from writers working independently, without seeing each other's work.

4. His final reason in proof of literary dependence is the prologue of Luke's gospel. In defending his use of the prologue for this purpose, he reflects no awareness of the possibility that Luke's sources mentioned therein do not include another canonical book.[25] This is the traditional understanding of the prologue, an understanding quite defensible exegetically, modern Source Criticism notwithstanding. The best understanding of Luke's prologue excludes Mark from, not includes Mark among, the sources used by the author of the third gospel.

So a tabulation of tangible evidence shows the case for literary dependence is essentially nonexistent. It is merely an assumption, incidentally an assumption known to be shared by only one early church figure. Besides Augustine, the church for her first eighteen hundred years held the first three gospels to be independent of each other in regards to literary matters.[26] Substantial opinion in support of independence has emerged recently,[27] but most in the historical-critical school apparently do not take the possibility seriously.

CONSEQUENCES OF LITERARY DEPENDENCE

Where has the theory of literary dependence among the Synoptists led? Does it impact one's view of the inerrancy of Scripture? To many, this foundational plank of Historical Criticism appears inconsequential. Yet when pursued to its logical end, the theory has quite significant repercussions.

The type of dependence advocated by most is the one described above, i.e., Mark and Q are the earliest documents and Matthew and Luke are copies of and elaborations on these two. The usual name assigned to this theory is the Two-Source (or Two-Document) Theory.[28] To many, this assumption does no harm. After all, literary collaboration between the writers of Kings and Chronicles in the OT is obvious,[29] and did not Jude depend on 2 Peter in writing his epistle (or vice versa, as some would have it)?

Yet the consequences are more serious when dealing with Matthew, Mark, and Luke and their similar records of the life of Christ. McKnight elaborates on the nature of the consequences in his observations about comparing the Gospels and identifying authorial reasons for editorial changes:

> For example, a redaction critic, usually assuming Markan priority, inquires into the nature of and rationale for Matthew's addition of Peter's unsuccessful attempt to walk on the water (cf. Mark 6:45–52 with Matt. 14:22–33). The critic seeks to discover whether the confession at the end of the story (Matt. 14:33) is materially different from Mark's rather negative comment (Mark 6:52). . . .
>
> Alteration . . . involves direct alterations of the tradition to avoid misunderstandings, as when Matthew alters Mark's comment which could suggest inability on the part of Jesus (Mark 6:5; Matt. 13:53) or when he changes Mark's form of address by the rich young ruler (Mark 10:17–18; Matt. 19:16–17).[30]

To illustrate how authorial changes impact historical accuracy, a closer look at the ten sample issues listed above in this essay is in order. For clarity's sake, presentation of the illustrations will be in three categories that redaction critics find useful to describe the types of editorial changes allegedly made by the Synoptic Gospel writers: arrangement, modification, and creativity.[31] The first category is that of arrangement of material, by which they mean the writer rearranged material from a chronological to a nonchronological sequence. Four samples are of this type.[32]

Arrangement of Material

1. The Sermon on the Mount. According to many evangelical practitioners of Historical Criticism, the traditional credit given to Jesus for preaching the Sermon on the Mount is a mistake. Guelich has written,

> When one hears the phrase "the Sermon on the Mount," one generally identifies it with Matthew's Gospel and correctly so, not only because of the presence of the Sermon in the first Gospel but because the Sermon on the Mount, as we know it, is ultimately the literary product of the first evangelist.[33]

Mounce's opinion clarifies Guelich's position somewhat: "We are not to think of the Sermon on the Mount as a single discourse given by Jesus at one particular time. Undoubtedly there was a primitive and historic sermon, but it has been enlarged significantly by Matthew. . . ."[34] Stein goes even further regarding the creativity of the gospel writers:

> The Sermon on the Mount (Matt. 5:1–7:29) and the Sermon on the Plain (Luke 6:20–49) are literary creations of Matthew and Luke in the sense that they are collections of Jesus' sayings that were uttered at various times and places and have been brought together primarily due to topical considerations, i.e., in order to have an orderly account (Luke 1:3). There is no need, however, to deny that a historical event lies behind the scene. Jesus' teaching on a mountain/plain has been used as an opportunity by the Evangelists (or the tradition) to bring other related teachings of Jesus in at this point.[35]

Hagner concurs: "The 'sermon' is clearly a compilation of the sayings of Jesus by the evangelist, rather than something spoken by Jesus on a single occasion."[36] Others share the view that teachings in the Sermon on the Mount did not all come at the same time in Jesus' ministry, but were the result of the "clustering" of similar themes by the gospel writers.[37]

Going the route of these evangelical scholars entails explaining away Matthew's introduction to the Sermon (5:1–2)—which indicates Jesus began at a certain point to give the Sermon's contents—and his conclusion to the Sermon (7:28)—which indicates Jesus' conclusion of that same portion. Dispensing with the factuality of the introduction is what Wilkins does in his remarks:

> Instead Matthew's editorial activity in the introduction to the Sermon serves to make an explicit distinction between them

[i.e., the μαθηταί (*mathētai,* "disciples") and the ὄχλοι (*ochloi,* "crowds"]. . . . Since the underlying Sermon tradition clearly had the disciples as the audience (cf. Luke 6:20), this writer suggests that Matthew has maintained that tradition and has added that the crowds were also there, but as a secondary object of teaching because of their interest in his mission (4:23–25).[38]

In other words, the introductory and concluding formulas are no more than literary devices adopted by Matthew to give the impression (for whatever reason) that Jesus preached just such a Sermon to the crowds and the disciples on one given occasion. The historical reality of the situation was that Jesus did not preach it all at that time. Rather, Matthew grouped various teachings of Jesus given at different times to create the Sermon.

It is difficult to locate an explanation for why Matthew bracketed the Sermon with "And seeing the crowds, He ascended into the mountain; and having sat down, His disciples came to Him; and having opened His mouth, He began teaching them, saying" (5:1–2) and "it came about that when Jesus finished these words, the crowds were amazed at His teaching" (7:28). If Jesus did not preach such a sermon on a single occasion, why would the gospel writer mislead his readers to think that He did? This question has no plain answer.[39]

Yet the proponent of Historical Criticism, because of his proclivity to compare parts of the Sermon with words of Christ uttered at other times and to assume Matthew's dependence on other writings (such as Mark and Q), finds himself compelled to visualize the Sermon as made up of many small pieces that the writer of Matthew assembled in a masterful manner. This theory devastates the historical accuracy of the Gospels.

2. Commissioning of the Twelve. A number of evangelical leaders have proposed that Jesus did not on a single occasion commission the twelve disciples as described in Matthew 10:5–42, but that Matthew has drawn together sayings of Jesus from a number of different occasions and combined them into a single flowing discourse. Carson, for example, is of the opinion that if the sermon came from Q, conceived as a variety of sources, oral and written and not necessarily recorded in the historical setting in which the teaching was first uttered, the effect on historical conclusions would be "not much."[40] He finds it plausible that Matthew, without violating the introductory and concluding formulas in 10:5a and 11:1, collapsed the discourse to the seventy in Luke 10:1–16 with the commissioning of the twelve in Matthew 10 to form a single discourse.[41] Carson thus concludes that the Matthew 10 instructions are a mingling of what Jesus gave the seventy with what He told the twelve when He sent them out.[42]

Carson's explanation of how such liberties are possible without violating the sermon's introduction and conclusion is unconvincing, however. Certainly Matthew left no clues for his first readers to alert them to the fact that this sermon was a compilation of Jesus' teachings from more than one occasion.[43]

Wilkins agrees that Matthew 10:5–42 is a composite of Jesus' utterances on several occasions. He evidences his agreement in allowing that Matthew used a statement from a separate occasion when he borrowed from Mark 9:41–42 in recording Jesus' words in the last verse of Matthew 10.[44] The episode in Mark came later in Jesus' life when Jesus warned His disciples against causing believers to stumble and is parallel to Matthew 18:6. Wilkins shows his view further in stating that the interpretation and context of Matthew 10:24–25 differs from that of the similar statement in Q (Luke 6:40).[45] The context of the latter is that of Luke's Sermon on the Plain, which came chronologically earlier than the commissioning of the twelve in Matthew 10. His conclusion is that Matthew used the statement from Q in two different places, once in its correct historical context and once in the context of Matthew 10. Thus Wilkins groups himself with those who view Matthew 10:5–42 as a combination of Jesus' words from different periods of His ministry, in disregard for the historical markers found in the discourse's introduction and conclusion.

Blomberg also notes how the latter part of the discourse in Matthew 10 (Matt. 10:17–42) parallels Jesus' eschatological discourse (esp. Mark 13:9–13; Luke 21:12–17) and scattered excerpts in Luke elsewhere (e.g., 12:2–9, 51–53; 14:26–27). On this basis and because of what he calls the vague wording of Matthew 11:1, he concludes that a theory of composite origins is more plausible here than it is in Matthew's other four discourses.[46]

Gundry joins in the opinion that in Matthew 10:16–42 "Matthew brings together various materials scattered in Mark and Luke and relates them to the persecution of the twelve disciples, who stand for all disciples of Jesus."[47]

The theory of literary dependence has done it again. It has caused its advocates to sacrifice historical particularity in the gospel accounts. It has caused a disregard for the discourse's introduction (Matt. 10:5a)—"Jesus sent these twelve, charging them, saying"—and conclusion (Matt. 11:1a)—"and it came about when Jesus finished giving orders to His twelve disciples"—which to Matthew's earliest readers and to readers for almost twenty centuries have meant that Matthew 10:5–42 constituted a commissioning of Jesus delivered on one occasion, not several.

3. The Parables of Mark 4 and Matthew 13. Bock proposes that the parable accounts of Mark 4 and Matthew 13 are probably anthologies.[48] He notes the difficulty in placing the parable of the soils chronologically in light of the possibility that either Matthew or Mark, or both, may have done some rearranging of material. He sees the parables as having been uttered by Jesus on separate occasions and grouped in these chapters for topical reasons. He gives little or no historical weight to Matthew 13:1–3 and 13:53, another introduction and conclusion that bracket the parabolic teachings in 13:4–52.[49]

In dealing with the Mark sequence of parables, Brooks isolates 4:10–12 and 4:21–25 as words not spoken by Jesus on this particular occasion.[50] Regarding the former, he favors those as words applying to Jesus' whole ministry and not just to Jesus' teachings in parables as Mark indicates. Regarding the latter, he sees those as five or six sayings of Jesus spoken at various times, with Mark bringing them together and attributing them to Jesus at this point in His ministry. It is clear that Mark's introduction and conclusion to the parabolic discourse (Mark 4:1–2, 33) are of no historical consequence to Brooks.

Stein suggests the possibility that the three synoptic writers, Luke in particular (Luke 8:11–15), interpreted the parable of the soils in light of their own theological interests.[51] Without concluding that the interpretation was a pure creation of the early church, he still sees that interpretation as being strongly influenced by early church circumstances in which existed a real danger of falling away from allegiance to Christ. Again, this questions the historical integrity of such indicators as Luke's clear statement that Jesus Himself gave the interpretation of Luke 8:9–10.

Stein's statement about the parabolic series in Mark 4:3–32 confirms his reluctance to attribute historical worth to introductory and concluding formulas: "It is clear that Mark sees the parables of Mark 4:3–32 as a summary collection and not a chronology of consecutive parables that Jesus taught in a single day."[52] With this perspective he can allow Matthew to add parables to Mark's collection and Luke to put some of the parables in other locations.[53] This is all without regard to how it erodes historicity.

4. The Olivet Discourse. Brooks expresses the following opinion regarding Jesus' Olivet Discourse:

> This claim that the substance of the discourse goes back to Jesus himself should not be extended to claim that it is a verbatim report or free from any adaptation and application on Mark's part or spoken on one occasion. That portions of it are found in

other contexts in Matthew and Luke suggests Mark included some comments Jesus spoke on other occasions.[54]

Blomberg concurs with this position:

> Sayings of Jesus may appear in different contexts. The Sermon on the Mount (Matthew 5–7) and the Olivet Discourse (Matthew 24–25) gather together teachings which are scattered all around the Gospel of Luke. Some of these may simply reflect Jesus' repeated utterances; others no doubt reflect the common practice of creating composite speeches. Again, no one questioned the integrity of ancient historians when they utilized a device that modern readers often find artificial.[55]

Yet one must ask Brooks and Blomberg what to make of the introductory and concluding formulas of this discourse, which in Matthew read, "Jesus answered and said to them" (Matt. 24:4) and "it came about when Jesus finished all these words" (Matt. 26:1). Despite what the practice of ancient historians may have been, Matthew's intention to cite a continuous discourse from a single occasion is conspicuous. Was he mistaken? Hopefully, an evangelical would not propose that he was.

Regarding the discourse, Stein writes,

> Although Luke added additional material to the discourse (cf. 21:12, 15, 18, 20–22, 23b–26a, 28), his main source appears to have been Mark. Whether his additional material came from another source or sources (L, proto-Luke, some apocalyptic source) is debated.[56]

Like others of the historical-critical school, he sees in this discourse as recorded in all three Synoptic Gospels sayings that Jesus uttered on other occasions.[57] He even attributes to Luke a widening of the audience of the discourse from that to whom it was addressed in Mark, his source.[58] Later in his comments, he suggests, "Luke changed Mark 13:19; Matthew 24:21 . . . in order to avoid confusing Jerusalem's destruction, which he was describing, with the final tribulation that precedes the return of the Son of Man, which Mark and Matthew were describing."[59] All this raises the question as to what were the circumstances and words of Jesus on the occasion of the sermon. Were they as Mark and Matthew described them, as Luke described them, or neither?

Modifying of material

The second type of alteration is that of modifying material. This editorial activity accounts for places where a writer changed material when incorporating it into his gospel. Illustrations 5, 6, and 7 are of this type.

5. The Exception Clause. Hagner is one of those who cannot endorse the exception clauses in Matthew 5:32 and 19:9 as having come from Jesus. One of the reasons he gives for this is the absolute prohibition of divorce in Mark 10:11 which Matthew used as his source.[60] With this to work from, either Matthew or someone else in the traditional handling of Jesus' teaching must have added it.[61]

Gundry's reasoning is similar as he draws the conclusion, "It [the exception clause in Matt. 5:32] comes from Matthew, not from Jesus, as an editorial insertion to conform Jesus' words to God's Word in the OT."[62] Stein likewise reasons that "the 'exception clause' is an interpretative comment added by Matthew" because of its nonappearance in Mark, Q, and Paul.[63] Bruner says the exception clause came from the creative thought of Jesus' spokesman, not from Jesus Himself.[64] In other words, Jesus never uttered the clause.

Here is another instance where the assumption of literary dependence forces scholars to diminish the historical precision of a gospel account. This is no different in kind from decisions of the Jesus Seminar. Granted, these evangelicals do not carry their dehistoricizing to the same degree as those who radically reduce the biographical data in the Gospels, but it is nevertheless the same type of dehistoricizing.

6. Dialogue with the Rich Man. The writer of Matthew supposedly found the words of Jesus and the rich man in Mark 10:17–18 theologically unacceptable and changed them in his account to solve a Christological problem:

Mark 10:17–18	**Matthew 19:16–17**
. . . Having run up and knelt before Him, one was asking Him, "Good Teacher, what should I do to inherit eternal life?" And Jesus said to Him "Why do you call me good? No one is good but God alone."	. . . Having come up to Him, one said, "Teacher, what good thing should I do to have eternal life?" And He said to him "Why do you ask me about what is good? One there is who is good."

The impression given by Stein and others is that Mark's wording implies that Jesus was less than Deity, so Matthew felt compelled to change the young man's question and Jesus' answer to convey a high view of Christology.[65] Even Stonehouse sacrificed the historical accuracy of Matthew's account in theorizing Matthew's change of Mark's wording.[66]

All these recent writers part company with Warfield on this issue. It was in connection with this passage that Warfield reached the sensible conclusion already noted: "And in general, no form of criticism is more uncertain than that, now so diligently prosecuted, which seeks to explain the several forms of narratives in the Synoptics as modifications of one another."[67] It is not difficult to harmonize Matthew's account of the rich man with the one in Mark and Luke if one drops the assumption that Matthew embellished Mark's account and assumes that all three writers worked independently of each other.[68]

7. The Pharisees. It is a recent tendency among evangelicals to dwell on the positive qualities of the Pharisees of Jesus' time, even though Jesus emphatically denounced the group on many occasions, such as when He pronounced woes against them and the scribes in Matthew 23:13–36. Hagner laments,

> It is a tragedy that from this chapter in Matthew [chap. 23] that the word "Pharisee" has come to mean popularly a self-righteous, hypocritical prig. Unfortunately not even Christian scholarship was able over the centuries to rid itself of an unfair bias against the Pharisees.[69]

Wyatt proposes that an accurate description of the Pharisees is possible only by a comparison of three major sources: Josephus, the NT, and the rabbinic literature.[70] The resultant picture differs from how the NT pictures them, i.e., almost always in a negative light.

Hagner notes, "Pharisaism was at heart, though tragically miscarried, a movement for righteousness. . . . This basic drive for righteousness accounts for what may be regarded as attractive and Biblical both about Pharisaic and rabbinic Judaism."[71] One can only marvel at how radically this appraisal differs from that of Jesus: "For I say to you, unless your righteousness exceeds that of the scribes and Pharisees, you shall in no way enter the kingdom of heaven" (Matt. 5:20).

How has Historical Criticism managed to formulate a picture of this group so different from the one painted by Jesus? Largely through assuming that the gospel writers, particularly Matthew, took great editorial liberties in describing the life of Christ. Matthew was writing about the church of his day late in the first century more than about the actual experiences and words of Jesus. By comparing Matthew with his source,

Mark, one can see how his embellishments were intended to make the Pharisees look so bad. The cause of these embellishments is traceable to the tension that existed between Matthew's community and "a noticeable Jewish presence" in which Matthew wrote his gospel.[72] It was this hostility between the late first-century church and the synagogue that left its impact on the material found in Matthew 23.[73]

This type of reasoning once again highlights the implications of theorizing a form of literary dependence among the Synoptic Gospel writers. In trying to explain why Matthew changed his source material to convey new emphases, the historical critic must postulate that the writers took editorial liberties that exceeded the limits of historical precision. In the case of the Pharisees, that liberty included reading into the life of Jesus circumstances that prevailed in the surroundings of Matthew when he wrote his gospel.[74]

Creation of Material

The third kind of editorial change is that of creativity. In this case, according to historical critics the writer inserted new material that was not a part of the source(s) from which he worked. Examples 8, 9, and 10 come under this classification.

8. The Genealogies.

In regard to the two genealogies in Luke and Matthew, Marshall and Gundry assume that the two writers worked from a common source, presumably "Q." Marshall detects that Luke's genealogy is not historically accurate through comparing it with the one in Matthew.[75] Gundry, on the other hand, finds that Matthew has made more revisions in the traditional material than Luke when he compares Matthew's genealogy with the one in Luke.[76] This leads Gundry to the conclusion that Matthew's "genealogy has become a large figure of speech for Jesus' messianic kingship,"[77] thereby removing it from the realm of historical data. Marshall concludes that it is impossible "to be sure that the genealogy in Luke is accurate in detail," and may have resulted from Luke's use of midrashic techniques.[78]

Here are two evangelical treatments that dehistoricize the genealogies. The starting point for both is apparently the assumption that the two gospel writers used a common source. In other words, the two commentators feel compelled to explain discrepancies in the genealogies as traceable to editorial liberties taken by the gospel writers, liberties that injected nonhistorical elements into the apparent ancestral lists. They choose the assumption that the writers worked from a common source rather than the possibility that they worked from different sources and that the genealogies lend themselves to rational harmonization.[79]

9. Visit of the Magi. Because of his assumption that Matthew follows the same tradition as represented in Luke 2:8–20 (presumably the tradition found in Q), Gundry concludes that Matthew 2:1–12 transforms the visit of local Jewish shepherds into adoration by Gentile magi from foreign parts.[80] He sees the necessity of a transformation because of his foregone conclusion that literary collaboration must explain the origin of the Synoptic Gospels.

Such compulsion forces the conclusion that the author of Matthew takes editorial liberty with his sources, a liberty justified by allowing that Matthew incorporated lessons for the church of his day into his gospel. Gundry alleges that for Matthew the coming of the magi previews the bringing of Gentiles into the church at a later time.[81] To further his emphasis on Jesus as the star of David, Matthew also replaces the tradition about the angel and the heavenly host (Luke 2:8–15a) with that of a star.[82] Here is another example of the extremes to which an assumption of literary dependence among the synoptists will drive a scholar.

10. The Beatitudes. Opinion is also widespread among evangelical advocates of Historical Criticism that Jesus is not the source of all the beatitudes in Matthew 5:3–12. Hagner allows that eight of them (5:3–10) may have originated with Jesus Himself—though Jesus spoke them in the second person rather than the third as Matthew has them—but that the ninth (5:11–12) is probably an addition by Matthew himself.[83] Guelich is of the opinion that the core beatitudes (5:3–4, 6; also 5:11–12) go back to Jesus Himself, but that four more (5:5, 7–9) developed in church tradition after Jesus and before Matthew wrote. The gospel writer himself created one beatitude (5:10).[84] Gundry's approach has four beatitudes coming from the lips of Jesus (5:3–4, 9–10) and four resulting from Matthew's redaction (5:5–8).[85]

Gundry assumes Matthew's source (Q?[86]) had only four beatitudes because Luke's Sermon on the Plain has only four. So, he concludes, Matthew must have added the other four.[87] Guelich understands several stages in the growth of three to eight beatitudes. Jesus originated the first three for the sake of the "desperate ones of his day."[88] Tension between what Jesus was accomplishing and the future consummation was the cause for adding the fourth (5:11–12) to the list. The Christian community later added four more (5:5, 7–9) through use of the Psalms and Jesus' sayings. Finally, Matthew added the last (5:10) as he adapted the rest to Isaiah 61.[89] Hagner sees the first eight beatitudes as a unity in themselves, with the ninth probably being added by Matthew himself.[90]

In one way or another the positions of all three men arise through the assumption that Matthew worked from the same source (presumably Q) as Luke did in creating the Sermon on the Plain. So they must explain Matthew's differences from Luke under the assumption that they arose through Matthew's editorial activity. This assumption forces them to grant Matthew unusual liberties in attributing to Jesus either one, four, or five of the beatitudes that He never spoke, which amounts to a dehistoricizing of the gospel accounts. Even the Jesus Seminar has allowed that Jesus probably spoke three of the beatitudes, the same number granted by Guelich.[91]

The above ten "tip-of-the-iceburg" illustrations are revealing. The hazards of Historical Criticism have entered the evangelical camp, raising questions about how much of the Gospels is accurate history and how much is editorial embellishment. McKnight's rejoinder that redaction is not a matter that impinges on history, but that it is a matter of style[92] makes an "either—or" issue out of one that is rightly a matter of "both—and." If authorial style introduces historical inaccuracy, it is not "contorted historiography and logic"—as McKnight contends—to conclude that it is *both* authorial style *and* historical distortion.[93] A factual misrepresentation is an inaccuracy, regardless of its cause.

THE REMAINING ALTERNATIVE

In view of the consequences of assuming literary dependence among the Synoptists, a balancing of evidence seems to rule against such an assumption. Yet it is not so with most who specialize in this field. Despite their acknowledgment that no solution to the Synoptic Problem is without its problems, they still cling to the theory that the gospel writers depended on the works of each other in some manner. Without such literary collaboration, the Synoptic Problem does not exist,[94] but they practice a wholesale neglect of that possibility. They are content to cite the theory of Matthew's and Luke's dependence on Mark and Q as the majority opinion and to build on that as a foundation. They acknowledge the absence of absolute proof of the theory,[95] but are unable to provide any widely accepted solution to plug its holes. This is why McKnight must admit, "But we can never be totally certain about some of these matters since we can never be totally confident of a solution to the Synoptic Problem."[96] The consequence of that theory's being wrong is a trashing of most of the research done on the Synoptic Gospels over the last hundred years.[97]

Is it not more reasonable to drop the ill-supported and dubious assumption of literary dependence and thus dispense with the insoluble difficulties it creates?[98] Would this not furnish a better basis for responding to the destructive conclusions publicized by the Jesus Seminar? It is futile for evangelicals to attempt responses to this Seminar when they employ the same tainted methodology.[99] The difference between them and the Jesus Seminar is only a matter of one person's opinion against another's. For both a gulf is fixed between historical precision and the gospel records. Subjective criticisms of the Seminar's findings are at best peripheral. Those of radical persuasion merely turn the tables and show how evangelicals are dehistoricizing just as they are, though perhaps not to the same extremes.[100]

The only way to objectify historical reliability is to accept the historical accuracy of Scripture throughout. J. Gresham Machen insisted on historical precision and would have been extremely perturbed if he had known evangelicals would eventually embrace historical-critical methodology. He voiced his objection to those who in his day advocated a Christianity independent of history when he wrote, "Must we really wait until the historians have finished disputing about the value of sources and the like before we can have peace with God?"[101] To this he responded, ". . . If religion be made independent of history there is no such thing as a gospel. . . . A gospel independent of history is a contradiction in terms."[102] In an endorsement of Machen's position, Lippmann writes,

> The veracity of that story was fundamental for the Christian Church. For while all the ideal values may remain if you impugn the historic record set forth in the Gospels, these ideal values are not certified to the common man as inherent in the very nature of things.[103]

He continues, "The liberals have yet to answer Dr. Machen when he says that 'the Christian movement at its inception was not just a way of life in the modern sense, but a way of life founded upon a message.'"[104]

Harrisville and Sundberg correctly analyze Machen's response to Historical Criticism when they note, "Christianity is wed inextricably to the particularities of a history that are open to investigation and have the specificity and integrity to risk falsification."[105] Christianity in its fundamental nature is "grounded in a historical narrative; it depends upon the claims of external events. To separate the ideas and values of the faith from their history is to cut the nerve of Christianity."[106] Cutting that nerve is precisely what Historical Criticism does, as Machen seems to have seen years ago. The methodology therefore has no place in evangelical scholarship.

The inerrancy of the gospel records is a guarantee that they are accurate in every detail. Divine and human elements entered into composing the biblical record. The prevalence of the divine over the human guarantees the precision of every part of Bible history.

ENDNOTES

[1] A work entitled *The Jesus Crisis: The Inroads of Historical Criticism into Evangelical Scholarhip* (Grand Rapids: Kregel, 1998) incorporates material from this essay along with other analyses and implications of Historical Criticism.

[2] Robert W. Funk, Roy W. Hoover, and the Jesus Seminar, *The Five Gospels: The Search for the Authentic Words of Jesus* (New York: Macmillan, 1993).

[3] The ensuing discussion will not attempt a close definition of the term "evangelical." The loose sense envisioned allows the word to apply to individuals who probably think of themselves as being in the evangelical camp.

[4] E.g., D. A. Carson, "Five Gospels, No Christ," *Christianity Today* 38, no. 5 (April 25, 1994): 30–33; Ben Witherington III, *The Jesus Quest: The Third Search for the Jew of Nazareth* (Downers Grove, Ill.: InterVarsity, 1995), 42–43; James R. Edwards, "Who Do Scholars Say That I Am?" *Christianity Today* 40, no. 3 (March 4, 1996): 14–20.

[5] E.g., Michael J. Wilkins and J. P. Moreland, eds., *Jesus Under Fire: Modern Scholarship Reinvents the Historical Jesus* (Grand Rapids: Zondervan, 1995); Gregory A. Boyd, *Cynic, Sage or Son of God?* (Wheaton: Victor, 1995); Witherington, *Jesus Quest,* 42–57. *Jesus Under Fire* includes chapters by Craig L. Blomberg, Scot McKnight, and Darrell L. Bock, among others.

[6] Benjamin Breckinridge Warfield, *Christology and Criticism* (New York: Oxford, 1929), 115 n.

[7] Carson alludes to such a possibility ("Five Gospels," 30).

[8] See below for a detailed discussion of and the documentation for the same ten issues enumerated here.

[9] Marshall comments regarding Ernst Käsemann, "Many people who read his works may well be highly shocked by the amount of material in

the Gospels which even he regards as unhistorical" (I. Howard Marshall, *I Believe in the Historical Jesus* [Grand Rapids: Eerdmans, 1977], 12). The same observation would hold true regarding many evangelical scholars if Christians in evangelical churches were to have access to an exhaustive compilation of their conclusions about unhistorical facets in the Gospels.

[10] See "How Should the Jesus Seminar's Conclusions Be Viewed?" *Los Angeles Times,* 6 April 1991, F18–F19.

[11] See "Did the Jesus Seminar Draw from Faulty Assumptions?" *Los Angeles Times,* 13 April 1991, F18–F19.

[12] Craig L. Blomberg argues for an "evidentialist" approach in responding to radical excesses in dehistoricizing the Gospels (*The Historical Reliability of the Gospels* [Downers Grove, Ill.: InterVarsity, 1987], 9–10). He contrasts this with a "presuppositionalist" approach which assumes the inspiration of the Scriptures. What he means by "evidentialist"—i.e., defending the accuracy of Scripture on purely historical grounds—includes an embracing of the same methodology as those of radical persuasions (cf. ibid., 12–18). That is the methodology outlined below in this section.

[13] I. Howard Marshall, "Historical Criticism," in *New Testament Interpretation,* ed. I. Howard Marshall (Grand Rapids: Eerdmans, 1977), 126–27.

[14] E.g., William W. Klein, Craig L. Blomberg, and Robert L. Hubbard Jr., *Introduction to Biblical Interpretation* (Dallas: Word, 1993), 95; Robert H. Stein, *The Synoptic Problem, An Introduction* (Grand Rapids: Baker, 1987), 217–18; Blomberg, *Historical Reliability,* 20; Edwards, "Who Do Scholars," 20.

[15] E.g., Klein et al., *Biblical Interpretation,* 164.

[16] E.g., Stein, *Synoptic Problem,* 96, 149–50, 219–20.

[17] The proposal of Markan priority originated relatively recently. France recalls that Matthean priority was the unanimous opinion of the church for seventeen hundred years, until the theory of Markan priority emerged (R. T. France, *Matthew: Evangelist and Teacher* [Grand Rapids: Zondervan, 1989], 25–27).

[18] See Eta Linnemann, "Is There a Gospel of Q?" *Bible Review* (August 1995): 19–23, 42, for strong evidence that Q never existed.

[19] E.g., Darrell L. Bock, "Luke 1:1–9:50," in *Baker Exegetical Commentary on the New Testament,* ed. Moisés Silva (Grand Rapids: Baker, 1994), 7; D. A. Carson, "Matthew," in *Expositor's Bible Commentary,* ed. Frank E. Gaebelein (Grand Rapids: Zondervan, 1984), 8:13; John Nolland, *Luke, Volume 1: 1:1–9:50,* vol. 35A of *Word Biblical Commentary,* ed. David A. Hubbard, Glenn W. Barker et al. (Dallas: Word, 1989), xxix.

[20] Robert H. Stein, *Synoptic Problem,* 29–44. Scot McKnight builds a case for literary dependence similar to Stein's (*Interpreting the Synoptic Gospels* [Grand Rapids: Baker, 1988], 37–40).

[21] See Robert L. Thomas, "The Agreements Between Matthew and Luke Against Mark," *Journal of the Evangelical Theological Society* 19 (1976): 110–11; idem, "The Rich Young Man in Matthew," *Grace Theological Journal* 3, no. 2 (fall 1982): 244–48.

[22] Thomas, "Agreements," 112; see also idem, "Rich Young Man," 249–51, 259.

[23] Stein, *Synoptic Problem,* 34–37.

[24] E.g., Robert H. Gundry, *Matthew: A Commentary on His Handbook for a Mixed Church under Persecution,* 2d ed. (Grand Rapids: Eerdmans, 1994), 481.

[25] Cf. Stein, *Synoptic Problem,* 42, 194; idem, *Luke,* vol. 24 of *The New American Commentary* (Nashville: Broadman, 1992), 28–29, 63.

[26] E.g., see Wayne A. Meeks, "Hypomnēmata from an Untamed Skeptic: A Response to George Kennedy," in *The Relationships Among the Gospels,* ed. William O. Walker Jr. (San Antonio: Trinity University, 1978), 171.

[27] E.g., Albert B. Lord, "The Gospels as Oral Tradition Literature," in *The Relationships Among the Gospels,* 82; Leander E. Keck, "Oral Tradition Literature and the Gospels," in *The Relationships Among the Gospels,* 116; Eta Linnemann, *Is There a Synoptic Problem?* (Grand Rapids: Baker, 1992), 155–91; cf. France, *Matthew,* 25.

[28] A closely related theory goes by the name Four-Source, the two additional documents being "M" on which Matthew relied and "L" on which Luke relied. Like "Q," these two documents are also phantoms. No one in modern times—if indeed at any time during the Christian era—has ever seen them.

[29] Everett F. Harrison, *Introduction to the New Testament* (Grand Rapids: Eerdmans, 1964), 145.

[30] Scot McKnight, *Interpreting the Synoptic Gospels,* 84, 87.

[31] Cf. Donald A. Hagner, "Interpreting the Gospels: The Landscape and the Quest," *Journal of the Evangelical Theological Society* 24, no. 1 (March 1981): 30–31.

[32] In which category each example belongs is a subjective judgment. Recategorizing from one category to another does not affect the thrust of this discussion. As they stand, perhaps the order of the categories reflects an increasing degree of departure from historical accuracy, with arrangement having the smallest impact on historicity. Nevertheless, even with arrangement a degree of dehistoricization is present.

[33] Robert A. Guelich, *The Sermon on the Mount: A Foundation for Understanding* (Dallas: Word, 1982), 33.

[34] Robert H. Mounce, "Matthew," in *A Good News Commentary,* ed. W. Ward Gasque (San Francisco: Harper & Row, 1985), 34.

[35] Stein, *Luke,* 198; cf. also idem, *Synoptic Problem,* 96, 219–20.

[36] Donald A. Hagner, *Matthew 1–13,* vol. 33A of *Word Biblical Commentary,* ed. David A. Hubbard, Glenn W. Barker et al. (Dallas: Word, 1993), 83. Regarding the conclusion of the Sermon on the Mount (Matt. 7:28–29), Hagner writes, "Matthew will not miss the opportunity here at the end of a *masterful distillation* of the teaching of Jesus to call his readers' attention to the supreme authority of this Teacher" (194, emphasis added). He means the Sermon is "masterful" because of Matthew's knack for distillation, not because of Jesus' preaching.

[37] E.g., William W. Klein, Craig L. Blomberg, and Robert L. Hubbard Jr., *Introduction to Biblical Interpretation,* 164 n. 10; C. R. Blomberg, "Gospels (Historical Reliability)," in *Dictionary of Jesus and the Gospels,* ed.

Joel B. Green, Scot McKnight, and I. Howard Marshall (Downers Grove, Ill.: InterVarsity, 1992), 295; G. R. Osborne, "Round Four: The Redaction Debate Continues," *Journal of the Evangelical Theological Society* 28, no. 4 (December 1985): 406; France, *Matthew,* 162–64. McKnight writes, "I would suggest that Matthew (or a previous Christian teacher) has thematically combined two teachings on prayer for reasons other than strict chronology, augmenting 6:5–6 with 6:7–13 (14–15)" (*Synoptic Gospels,* 53 n. 2). In other words, Jesus did not utter 6:7–13 on the same occasion as He gave the words of 6:5–6.

[38] Michael J. Wilkins, *The Concept of Disciple in Matthew's Gospel, As Reflected in the Use of the Term* Μαθητής (Leiden: E. J. Brill, 1988), 149–50. Gundry is similar in treating the introduction and conclusion to the Sermon, observing that "and seeing the crowds" (Matt. 5:1) is a Matthean addition that makes Jesus' teaching applicable to the universal church, that Matthew derives "He went up a mountain" (Matt. 5:1) from Mark 3:13a, that "it came about when He completed these words" (7:28) is a rewording of Luke 7:1a, and that "the crowds were amazed at His teaching" is the writer's reworking of Mark 1:22 (*Matthew,* 65–66, 136).

[39] D. A. Carson comments on those who see the introductory and concluding notes that frame each of Matthew's five discourses as "artistic, compositional devices" ("Matthew," 124). He objects to this premise because such introductory and concluding brackets do not appear in any other first-century literature. This means they were not merely artistic devices to show the reader that they meant anything other than to furnish the historical setting they profess to describe (124–25).

[40] Carson, "Matthew," 243. When Carson sees the effect of this theory on historical accuracy as "not much," he in essence concedes that it does make *some* difference. Yet he endorses the theory anyway. The effect on the meaning of the words is significant rather than "not much," when he casts them in a different historical context.

[41] Ibid., 241–42; cf. Blomberg, *Historical Reliability,* 145–46.

[42] Carson, "Matthew," 241.

[43] See R. Morosco, "Redaction Criticism and the Evangelical: Matthew 10 a Test Case," *Journal of the Evangelical Theological Society* 22 [1979]: 323–31, for an attempt to prove that "seams" in the discourse are a sign of such a compilation. Except for the last two centuries, Morosco's proposed

clues have escaped readers since the time of Christ, however. The reason is they are nonexistent in the discourse. See also idem, "Matthew's Formation of a Commissioning Type-Scene out of the Story of Jesus' Commissioning of the Twelve," *Journal of Biblical Literature* 103 (1984): 539–56.

[44] Wilkins, *Matthew,* 131.

[45] Ibid., 145.

[46] Craig L. Blomberg, *Matthew,* vol. 22 of *The New American Commentary,* ed. David S. Dockery (Nashville: Broadman, 1992), 166.

[47] Gundry, *Matthew,* 190–91.

[48] Bock, *Luke 1:1–9:50,* 718, 742–43. R. T. France also views the parables of Matthew 13 as a compilation, not uttered by Jesus on the same occasion: "This is hardly a 'single sermon,' and it seems that the larger part of it is not addressed to the audience stated in verse 2 at all" (*Matthew,* 157).

[49] Blomberg concludes that the parables of Matthew 13:1–52 came on a single occasion, but that Mark and Luke redistributed them elsewhere in their gospels. He gives Mark and Q as Matthew's source for the parables, but then says that Mark along with Luke have scattered these parables elsewhere. He evidences a lack of concern for Mark's introduction and conclusion that bracket his section of parables, two of which parallel those in Matthew 13 (cf. Mark 4:1–2, 33) (*Matthew,* 211).

[50] James A. Brooks, *Mark,* vol. 23 of *The New American Commentary,* ed. David S. Dockery (Nashville: Broadman, 1991), 82–83.

[51] Stein, *Luke,* 243–44.

[52] Stein, *Synoptic Problem,* 36.

[53] Ibid. Cf. also Gundry, *Matthew,* 250; Klein, Blomberg, and Hubbard, *Biblical Interpretation,* 164.

[54] Brooks, *Mark,* 205.

[55] Blomberg, "Gospels (Historical Reliability)," 295. Blomberg attributes a higher degree of accuracy to modern historians than to Spirit-inspired writers of the Gospels in ancient times.

[56] Stein, *Luke,* 510 n. 57.

[57] Ibid., 510.

[58] Ibid.

[59] Ibid., 522.

[60] Hagner, *Matthew 1–13,* cf. xlvii–xlviii.

[61] Ibid., 123.

[62] Gundry, *Matthew,* 90.

[63] Stein, *Synoptic Problem,* 152.

[64] Frederick Dale Bruner, *The Christbook: A Historical/Theological Commentary: Matthew 1–12* (Dallas: Word, 1987), 191.

[65] Stein, *Synoptic Problem,* 67, 75–76; cf. also Gundry, *Matthew,* 385; Blomberg, *Matthew,* 297; Carson, "Matthew," 421–23.

[66] Ned B. Stonehouse, *Origins of the Synoptic Gospels* (Grand Rapids: Eerdmans, 1963), 108–9.

[67] Warfield, *Christology and Criticism,* 115 n.

[68] Cf. Thomas, "Rich Young Man," 251–56; cf. also Carson, "Matthew," 423.

[69] D. A. Hagner, "Pharisees," in *The Zondervan Pictorial Encyclopedia of the Bible,* ed. Merrill C. Tenney (Grand Rapids: Zondervan, 1975), 4:750.

[70] R. J. Wyatt, "Pharisees," in *The International Standard Bible Encyclopedia,* ed. Geoffrey W. Bromiley (Grand Rapids: Eerdmans, 1986), 3:823.

[71] Hagner, "Pharisees," 752.

[72] S. Westerholm, "Pharisees," in *Dictionary of Jesus and the Gospels,* ed. Joel B. Green, Scot McKnight, I. Howard Marshall (Downers Grove, Ill.: InterVarsity, 1992), 613.

[73] Donald A. Hagner, *Matthew 14–28,* vol. 33B of *Word Biblical Commentary* (Dallas: Word, 1995), 654–55.

[74] Westerholm expresses the position of Historical Criticism thus: "The Gospels' depictions of Pharisees reflect both memories from the career of Jesus *and subsequent developments in the Christian communities*" (Westerholm, "Pharisees," 613, emphasis added).

[75] I. Howard Marshall, "The Gospel of Luke, Commentary on the Greek Text," in *The New International Greek Testament Commentary* (Grand Rapids: Eerdmans, 1978), 157–60.

[76] Gundry, *Matthew,* 13–14.

[77] Ibid., 15.

[78] Marshall, *Luke,* 160. Nolland sees difficulty in reading biblical genealogies with a strict historical and biographical interest. He concludes that this difficulty precludes ancestry as the exclusive factor in interpreting the Lukan genealogy (*Luke 1:1–9:50,* 169).

[79] For possible ways to harmonize the genealogies, see Robert L. Thomas, ed., and Stanley N. Gundry, assoc. ed., *A Harmony of the Gospels with Explanations and Essays, Using the Text of the New American Standard Bible* (San Francisco: Harper & Row, 1978), 313–19; idem, *The NIV Harmony of the Gospels* (San Francisco: Harper & Row, 1988), 304–10.

[80] Gundry, *Matthew,* 26–27, 651 n. 25.

[81] Ibid., 27.

[82] Ibid.

[83] Hagner, *Matthew 1–13,* 90.

[84] Guelich, *Sermon on the Mount,* 117–18. Bock calls Guelich's analysis "helpful," but is less confident than Guelich as to whether Matthew and

his sources are responsible for additional beatitudes beyond what Jesus actually spoke (Bock, *Luke . . . 1:1–9:50,* 552).

[85] Gundry, *Matthew,* 67–70. Hagner, Guelich, and Gundry differ conspicuously among themselves regarding which beatitudes came from Jesus, which from church tradition, and which from Matthew.

[86] See Robert H. Gundry, *Mark: A Commentary on His Apology for the Cross* (Grand Rapids: Eerdmans, 1993), 17, for an indication that Gundry understands Q to have been a written source.

[87] Ibid.

[88] Guelich, *Sermon on the Mount,* 17.

[89] Ibid.

[90] Hagner, *Matthew 1–13,* 90.

[91] Funk, Hoover et al., *Five Gospels,* 138.

[92] McKnight, *Synoptic Gospels,* 89–90.

[93] Marshall crystalizes the issue in the following: "It is certainly impossible to practice the historical method without concluding that on occasion the correct solution to a difficulty lies in the unhistorical character of a particular narrative. Several cases of this kind have been cited above, but in many of them we have claimed that to establish that a particular statement is unhistorical is not to establish the presence of an error which would call into question the reliability of the NT writer. Very often the reader may be demanding a kind of historical truth from the narrative which it was never intended to provide" ("Historical Criticism," 136). He proceeds to admit that the ordinary reader would view matters differently from the way scholars would. When Marshall and Blomberg speak of "reliable," they obviously distinguish the word from "accurate" or "errorless." When a writer says something happened that did not happen, he can still be reliable even though he has reported the event inaccurately or erroneously (Blomberg, *Historical Reliability,* 151–52; cf. also Marshall, *I Believe,* 19). These writers distinguish sharply between what is *generally reliable* and what is *historically factual* as does Graham Stanton who writes, "Gospel truth cannot be confirmed by historical evidence, but it does depend on *general reliability* of the evangelists'

portraits of Jesus. . . . I have chosen the term 'general reliability' deliberately. We do not have precise historical *records* in the Gospels . . ." (*Gospel Truth? New Light on Jesus and the Gospels* [Valley Forge, Pa.: Trinity Press International, 1995], 193, emphasis in the original).

[94] Linnemann, *Synoptic Problem,* 149–52.

[95] E.g., McKnight, *Synoptic Gospels,* 37; R. H. Stein, "Synoptic Problem," in *Dictionary of Jesus and the Gospels,* ed. Joel B. Green, Scot McKnight, I. Howard Marshall (Downers Grove, Ill.: InterVarsity, 1992), 790; Carson, "Matthew," 13–14; Hagner, *Matthew 1–13,* xlvii–xlviii; Blomberg, *Matthew,* 40–41.

[96] McKnight, *Synoptic Gospels,* 89. Robert H. Stein expresses the uncertainty of the two-document solution by calling it the "least worst!" of the proposed theories ("Is It Lawful for a Man to Divorce His Wife?" *Journal of the Evangelical Theological Society* 22 [June 1979]: 117 n. 8).

[97] A. J. Bellinzoni describes the situation thus: "Since Markan priority is an assumption of so much of the research of the last century, many of the conclusions of that research would have to be redrawn and much of the literature rewritten if the consensus of scholarship were suddenly to shift. . . . Were scholars to move to a position that no consensus can be reached about the synoptic problem or that the synoptic problem is fundamentally unsolvable, we would then have to draw more tentatively the conclusions that have sometimes been drawn on the basis of what were earlier regarded as the assured results of synoptic studies" (*The Two-Source Hypothesis: A Critical Appraisal,* ed. Arthur J. Bellinzoni Jr. [Macon, Ga.: Mercer University, 1985], 9). Such a shift is in progress (cf. France, *Matthew,* 25, 29–49). It remains to be seen how long it will take for the consensus to change.

[98] Cf. France, *Matthew,* 41–46.

[99] For reminders that evangelical respondents to the Jesus Seminar employ the same flawed methodology, see for example Carson, "Matthew," 15–17; Blomberg, *Matthew,* 37; Wilkins, *Matthew,* 8; Bock, *Luke 1:1–9:50,* 9; idem, "The Words of Jesus in the Gospels: Live, Jive, or Memorex?" in Wilkins and Moreland, *Jesus Under Fire,* 90, 99; McKnight, *Synoptic Gospels,* 37–40; Gregory A. Boyd, *Cynic, Sage or Son of God?* 136–37, 204, 295–96 n. 13; Witherington, *Jesus Quest,* 46–47, 50–52, 96, 187, 260–61 nn. 29–30, 32. Compare these with the

methodology of the Jesus Seminar (Funk, Hoover et al., *Five Gospels,* 9–14). The Jesus Seminar's addition of the Gospel of Thomas to the sources Mark, Q, M, and L is the only exception to the parallelism in methodology.

[100] John Dart's article about evangelical responses to the Jesus Seminar, "Holy War Brewing over Image of Jesus," illustrates how unconvinced the radical wing remains in spite of the responses (*Los Angeles Times,* 28 October 1995, B12–B13). In assessing the effectiveness of recent evangelical efforts to refute the Seminar, Dart concludes, "That traditional [i.e., evangelical] viewpoint may also be an increasingly hard sell to a skeptical American public." He adds, "Biola University's Michael Wilkins, co-editor of the first book to take on the Jesus Seminar, said it will be harder to promote orthodox Christianity in the next century, and perhaps easier for the notion of Jesus as a non-divine sage to gain a following."

[101] J. Gresham Machen, *Christianity and Liberalism* (Grand Rapids: Eerdmans, 1946), 121.

[102] Ibid.

[103] Walter Lippmann, *A Preface to Morals* (New York: Macmillan, 1929), 32.

[104] Ibid., 33.

[105] Roy A. Harrisville and Walter Sundberg, *The Bible in Modern Culture: Theology and Historical-Critical Method from Spinoza to Käsemann* (Grand Rapids: Eerdmans, 1995), 195.

[106] Ibid., 201; cf. Lippmann, *Preface to Morals,* 32f.

CHAPTER ELEVEN

God's Love

The Love of God for Humanity[1]

John F. MacArthur Jr.

John 3:16 declares God's love for the whole world, but in recent times some have insisted that God does not love everyone. The OT and the NT repeatedly indicate that God's love extends to everyone. The immediate context of John 3:16 supports this fact. Further, no grounds exist for questioning God's sincerity in showing mercy to the nonelect. Though difficult for humans to understand, God can love and be the Savior of those whom He does not save. His love for the elect may be somewhat different from that for the nonelect, but His love for the latter is still genuine. God demonstrates His love for all people in four ways: through His common grace, through His compassion, through His admonitions to the lost, and through His gospel offer to them.

* * * * *

Perhaps you have noticed that someone shows up at almost every major American sporting event, in the center of the television camera's view, holding a sign that usually reads "John 3:16." At the World Series, the sign can normally be spotted right behind home plate. At the Super Bowl, someone holding the sign inevitably has seats between the goalposts. And in the NBA playoffs, the ubiquitous "John 3:16" banner can be seen somewhere in the front row seats. How these people always manage to get prime seats is a mystery. But someone is always there, often wearing a multicolored wig to call attention to himself.

A couple of years ago, one of the men who had gained some degree of fame from displaying these "John 3:16" signs barricaded himself in a Los Angeles hotel and held police at bay until he was permitted to make a statement on television. It was a surrealistic image—here was someone who felt his mission in life was declaring John 3:16, and he was waving a gun and threatening police, while spouting biblical slogans. His career of attending major sporting events ended when police took him into custody without further incident.

As I watched the sordid episode unfold on television, I was embarrassed that someone whom the public identified as a Christian would so degrade the gospel message. It occurred to me that I was watching someone whose approach to "evangelism" had never really been anything more than a quest for publicity. This stunt, it seemed, was nothing more than a large-scale attempt to get himself into the camera's eye once more. Sadly, he brought a horrible reproach on the very message he was seeking to publicize.

I also realized while watching that episode that John 3:16 may be the most familiar verse in all of Scripture, but it is surely one of the most abused and least understood. "God so loved the world"—waved like a banner at a football game—has become a favorite cheer for many people who presume on God's love and who do not love Him in return. The verse is often quoted as evidence that God loves everyone exactly the same and that He is infinitely merciful—as if the verse negated all the biblical warnings of condemnation for the wicked.

That is not the point of John 3:16. One has only to read v. 18 to see the balance of the truth: "He that believeth not is condemned already, because he hath not believed in the name of the only begotten Son of God" (AV). Surely this is a truth that needs to be proclaimed to the world at least as urgently as the truth of John 3:16.

DOES GOD LOVE THE *WHOLE* WORLD?

Nevertheless, though acknowledging that some people abuse the notion of God's love, we cannot respond by minimizing what Scripture says about the extent of God's love. John 3:16 is a rich and crucial verse. Perhaps a closer look at this subject is warranted. I am encountering more and more Christians who want to argue that the only correct interpretation of John 3:16 is one that actually limits God's love to the elect and eliminates any notion of divine love for mankind in general.

Arthur Pink's argued that "world" in John 3:16 "refers to *the world of believers*" rather than "*the world of the ungodly.*"[2] This notion seems to have gained popularity in recent years. A friend recently gave me seven or eight articles that have circulated in recent months on the Internet. All of them, written and posted in various computer forums by Christians, deny that God loves everyone. It is frankly surprising how pervasive this idea has become among evangelicals. Here are some excerpts taken from these articles:

- The popular idea that God loves everyone is simply not to be found in the Scripture.

- God does love many, and those whom He loves, He will save. What about the rest? They are loved not at all.
- *Sheer logic alone* dictates that God save those whom He loves.
- If God loved everyone, everyone would be saved. It is as simple as that. Clearly not everyone is saved. Therefore God does not love everyone.
- Scripture tells us that the wicked are an abomination to God. God Himself speaks of hating Esau. *How can anyone who believes all of Scripture claim that God loves everyone?*
- God loves His chosen ones, but His attitude toward the nonelect is pure hatred.
- The concept that God loves all humanity is contrary to Scripture. God clearly does not love everyone.
- All who are not keeping the Ten Commandments of God can be certain that God does not love them.
- Not only does God *not* love everyone, there are multitudes of people whom He utterly loathes with an infinite hatred. Both Scripture and consistent logic force us to this conclusion.

But neither Scripture *nor* sound logic support such bold assertions.

I want to state as clearly as possible that I am in no way opposed to logic. I realize there are those who demean logic as if it were somehow contrary to spiritual truth. I do not agree; in fact, to abandon logic is to become irrational, and true Christianity is not irrational. The only way any spiritual matter is understandable is through applying careful logic to the truth that is revealed in God's Word. Sometimes logical deductions are necessary to yield the full truth on matters Scripture does not spell out explicitly. (The doctrine of the Trinity, for example, is implicit in Scripture but is never stated explicitly. It is a truth that is deduced from Scripture by good and necessary consequence—and therefore it is as surely true as if it were stated explicitly and unambiguously.)[3] Certainly nothing whatsoever is wrong with sound logic grounded in the truth of Scripture; in fact, logic is essential to understanding.

But surely *"sheer logic alone"* may lead to a conclusion that runs counter to the whole thrust and tenor of Scripture. Applying logic to an incomplete set of propositions about God has often yielded the bitter fruit of false doctrine. Logical conclusions need checking by comparison with the more sure word of Scripture. In this case, the notion that God reserves His love for the elect alone does not survive the light of Scripture.

Scripture clearly says that God *is* love. "The LORD is good to all, and His mercies are over all His works" (Ps. 145:9).[4] Christ commands Christians to love even their enemies, and the reason He gives is this: "In order that you may be sons of your Father who is in heaven; for He causes His sun to rise on the evil and the good, and sends rain on the righteous and the unrighteous" (Matt. 5:45). The clear implication is that in some sense *God* loves *His* enemies. He loves both "the evil and the good," both "the righteous and the unrighteous" in precisely the same sense He commands Christians to love their enemies.

In fact, the second greatest commandment, "You shall love your neighbor as yourself" (Mark 12:31, cf. Lev. 19:18) is a commandment to love *everyone*. It is certain the scope of this commandment is universal, because Luke 10 records that a lawyer, "wishing to justify himself . . . said to Jesus, 'And who is my neighbor?'" (Luke 10:29)—and Jesus answered with the Parable of the Good Samaritan. The point? Even Samaritans, a semi-pagan race who had utterly corrupted Jewish worship and whom the Jews generally detested as enemies of God, were neighbors whom Jesus commanded to love. In other words, the command to love one's "neighbor" applies to *everyone*. This love commanded here is clearly a universal, indiscriminate love.

Consider this: Jesus perfectly fulfilled the law in every respect (Matt. 5:17–18), including this command for universal love. His love for others was surely as far-reaching as His own application of the commandment in Luke 10. Therefore surely He loved *everyone*. He *must* have loved everyone in order to fulfill the Law. After all, the apostle Paul wrote, "The whole Law is fulfilled in one word, in the statement, 'You shall love your neighbor as yourself'" (Gal. 5:14)— and, "He who loves his neighbor has fulfilled the law" (Rom. 13:8). Therefore Jesus must have loved His "neighbor." His definition of "neighbor" in universal terms demonstrates that His love while on earth was universal.

Is it possible that Jesus as perfect man loved those whom Jesus as God does not love? Would God command Christians to love in a way that He does not? Would God demand that Christian love be more far-reaching than His own? And did Christ, having loved all humanity during His earthly sojourn, then revert after His ascension to pure hatred for the nonelect? Such is unthinkable; "Jesus Christ is the same yesterday and today, yes and forever" (Heb. 13:8).

Those who approach John 3:16 determined to suggest that it *limits* God's love miss the entire point of the verse's context. No delimiting language is anywhere in the context. Nothing relates to how God's love is distributed between the elect and the rest of the world. It is a statement about God's demeanor toward mankind in general. It is a declaration of *good* news to the effect that Christ came into the world on a mission of salvation, not a mission of condemnation: "For God did not send the Son into the world to judge the world, but that the world should be saved through Him" (v. 17). To convert it into an expression of divine hatred against those whom God does not save is to turn the passage on its head.

John Brown, the Scottish Reformed theologian, known for his marvelous studies on the sayings of Christ, has written,

> The love in which the economy of salvation originates, is love *to the world.* "God so loved the world, as to give his only begotten Son." The term "world," is here just equivalent to mankind. It seems to be used by our Lord with a reference to the very limited and exclusive views of the Jews. . . .
>
> Some have supposed that the word "world" here, is descriptive, not of mankind generally, but of the whole of a particular class, that portion of mankind who, according to the Divine purpose of mercy, shall ultimately become partakers of the salvation of Christ. But this is to give the term a meaning altogether unwarranted by the usage of Scripture.[5]

B. B. Warfield takes a similar position:

> Certainly here "the world" and "believers" do not seem to be quite equipollent terms: there seems, surely, something conveyed by the one which is not wholly taken up by the other. How, then, shall we say that "the world" means just "the world of believers," just those scattered through the world, who, being the elect of God, shall believe in His Son and so have eternal life? There is obviously much truth in this idea: and the main difficulty which it faces may, no doubt, be avoided by saying that what is taught is that God's love of the world is shown by His saving so great a multitude as He does save out of the world. The wicked world deserved at His hands only total destruction. But he saves out of it a multitude which no man can number, out of every nation, and of all tribes, and peoples and tongues. How much must, then God love the world! This interpretation, beyond question, reproduces the fundamental meaning of the text.[6]

Warfield continues and makes the crucial point that the primary concern in interpreting the word "world" in John 3:16 should not be not to limit the *extent* of God's love, as much as to magnify the rich *wonder* of it:

> The key to the passage lies . . . you see, in the significance of the term "world." It is not here a term of extension so much as a term of intensity. Its primary connotation is ethical, and the point of its employment is not to suggest that it takes a great deal of love to embrace it all, but that the world is so bad that it takes a great kind of love to love it at all, and much more to love it as God has loved it when He gave His Son for it.[7]

In fact, if the word "world" holds the same meaning throughout the immediate context, verse 19 cannot refer to the "world of the elect" alone: "This is the condemnation, that light is come into the world, and men loved darkness rather than light, because their deeds were evil" (KJV). About this, Robert L. Dabney wrote,

> A fair logical connection between verse 17 and verse 18 shows that "the world" of verse 17 is inclusive of "him that believeth" and "him that believeth not" of verse 18. . . . It is hard to see how, if [Christ's coming into the world] is in no sense a true manifestation of divine benevolence to that part of "the world" which "believeth not," their choosing to slight it is the just ground of a deeper condemnation, as is expressly stated in verse 19.[8]

So the context of John 3:16 requires the verse to speak of God's love to sinful mankind in general. Calvin's interpretation is worth summarizing here. He saw two main points in John 3:16: "Namely, that faith in Christ brings life to all, and that Christ brought life, because the Father loves the human race, and wishes that they should not perish."[9]

A fresh look at John 3:16 helps to absorb the real sense: "God so loved *the world,*" wicked though it was, and despite the fact that nothing *in* the world deserved His love. He nevertheless loved the world of humanity so much "that He gave His only begotten Son," the dearest sacrifice He could make, so "that *whoever believes in Him* should not perish, but have eternal life." The end result of God's love is therefore the gospel message—the free offer of life and mercy to anyone who believes. In other words, the gospel—an indiscriminate offer of divine mercy to everyone without exception—manifests God's compassionate love and unfeigned lovingkindness to all humanity.

And unless one ascribes unrighteousness to God, His offer of mercy in the gospel is sincere and well-meant. Surely His pleas for the wicked to turn from their evil ways and live must in some sense reflect a sincere desire on God's part. As indicated below, however, some deny that this is the case.

IS GOD SINCERE IN THE GOSPEL OFFER?

Of course, people who assert that God's love is exclusively for the elect will usually acknowledge that God nevertheless shows mercy, long-suffering, and benevolence to the unrighteous and unbelievers. But they will insist that this apparent benevolence has nothing whatsoever to do with *love* or any sort of sincere affection. According to them, God's acts of benevolence toward the nonelect have no other purpose than to increase their condemnation.

Such a view appears to impute insincerity to God. It suggests that God's pleadings with the reprobate are artificial and that His offers of mercy are mere pretense.

Often in Scripture, God makes statements that reflect His yearning for the wicked to repent. For instance, in Psalm 81:13 He says, "Oh that My people would listen to Me, that Israel would walk in My ways!" Ezekiel 18:32 says, "'I have no pleasure in the death of anyone who dies,' declares the Lord GOD. 'Therefore, repent and live.'"

Elsewhere, God freely and indiscriminately offers mercy to all who will come to Christ: "Come to Me, all who are weary and heavy-laden, and I will give you rest. Take My yoke upon you, and learn from Me, for I am gentle and humble in heart; and you shall find rest for your souls. For My yoke is easy, and My load is light" (Matt. 11:28–30). "And the Spirit and the bride say, 'Come.' And let the one who hears say, 'Come.' And let the one who is thirsty come; let the one who wishes [whosoever will—AV] take the water of life without cost" (Rev. 22:17).

God Himself says, "Turn to Me, and be saved, all the ends of the earth; for I am God, and there is no other" (Isa. 45:22). And, "Ho! Every one who thirsts, come to the waters; and you who have no money come, buy and eat. Come, buy wine and milk without money and without cost" (Isa. 55:1). "Let the wicked forsake his way, and the unrighteous man his thoughts; and let him return to the Lord, and He will have compassion on him; and to our God, for He will abundantly pardon" (v. 7).

Some flatly deny that such invitations constitute a sincere offer of mercy to the nonelect. As far as they are concerned, the very word *offer* smacks of Arminianism (a name for the doctrine that makes salvation hinge solely on a human decision). They deny that God would "offer"

salvation to those whom He has not chosen. They deny that God's pleadings with the reprobate reflect a real desire on God's part to see the
wicked turn from their sins. To them, suggesting that God could have
such an unfulfilled "desire" is a direct attack on His absolute sovereignty. God is sovereign, they suggest, and He does whatever pleases
Him. Whatever He desires, He does.

To be completely honest, this poses a difficulty. How can unfulfilled
desire be compatible with a wholly sovereign God? For example, in Isaiah
46:10, God states, "My purpose will be established, and I will accomplish
all My good pleasure." He *is,* after all, utterly sovereign. Is it not improper
to suggest that any of His actual "desires" remain unfulfilled?

This issue was the source of an intense controversy within some Reformed and Presbyterian denominations about fifty years ago. It is sometimes referred to as the "free offer" controversy. One group denied that
God loves the nonelect. They also denied the concept of common grace
(God's nonsaving goodness to mankind in general). And they denied
that divine mercy and eternal life are offered indiscriminately to everyone who hears the gospel. The gospel offer is not free, they claimed, but
extends to the elect alone. That position is a form of hyper-Calvinism.

Now let's acknowledge that Scripture clearly proclaims God's absolute and utter sovereignty over all that happens. Scripture says He declared the end of all things before time even began, and whatever comes
to pass is in perfect accord with the divine plan. What God has purposed, He will also do (Isa. 46:10–11; Num. 23:19). God is not at the
mercy of contingencies. He is not subject to His creatures' choices. He
"works all things after the counsel of His will" (Eph. 1:11). Nothing
occurs but that which is in accord with His purposes (cf. Acts 4:28).
Nothing can thwart God's design, and nothing can occur apart from His
sovereign decree (Isa. 43:13; Ps. 33:11). He does all His good pleasure:
"Whatever the Lord pleases, He does, in heaven and in earth, in the seas
and in all deeps" (Ps. 135:6).

But that does not mean God derives pleasure from every aspect of
what He has decreed. God explicitly says that He takes no pleasure in
the death of the wicked (Ezek. 18:32; 33:11). He does not delight in evil
(Isa. 65:12). He hates all expressions of wickedness and pride (Prov.
6:16–19). Since none of those things can occur apart from the decree of
a sovereign God, the inevitable conclusion is that there is a sense in
which His *decrees* do not always reflect His *desires;* His *preferences* do
not necessarily dictate His *purposes.*

The language here is necessarily anthropopathic (i.e., ascribing human emotions to God). To speak of unfulfilled desires in the Godhead is
to employ terms fit only for the finite human mind. Yet such expressions

communicate some truth about God that human language cannot express otherwise. God uses anthropopathisms in His Word to convey truth about Himself that no other means can represent adequately. To give an example, consider Genesis 6:6: "The LORD was sorry that He had made man on the earth, and He was grieved in His heart." Yet God does not change His mind (1 Sam. 15:29). He is immutable; "with [Him] there is no variation, or shifting shadow" (James 1:17). So whatever Genesis 6:6 means, it cannot suggest any changeableness in God. The best way to approach such an anthropopathism is try to grasp the essence of the idea, then reject any implications that lead to ideas about God that are unbiblical.

That same principle applies when grappling with the question of God's expressed desire for the wicked to repent. If God's "desire" remains unfulfilled (and in some cases it does—Luke 13:34), it is wrong to conclude that God is somehow less than sovereign. He is fully sovereign; it is impossible to understand why He does not turn the heart of every sinner to Himself. Further, speculation in this area is futile. It remains a mystery, the answer to which God has not seen fit to reveal. "The secret things belong to the LORD our God"; only "the things revealed belong to us" (Deut. 29:29). At some point, finite humans join the psalmist in saying, "Such knowledge is too wonderful for me; It is too high, I cannot attain to it" (Ps. 139:6).

CAN GOD REALLY LOVE WHOM HE DOES NOT SAVE?

I realize, of course, that most have no objection whatsoever to the idea that God's love is universal. Most were weaned on this notion, being taught as children to sing songs like, "Jesus loves the little children; all the children of the world." Many may never even have encountered a person who denies that God's love is universal.

Yet dwelling on this issue is necessary because it poses a perplexing difficulty to combine it with other aspects of God's revealed truth. Frankly, the universal love of God is hard to reconcile with the doctrine of election.

Election is a biblical doctrine, affirmed with the utmost clarity from beginning to end in Scripture. The highest expression of divine love to sinful humanity is evident in the fact that God set His love on certain undeserving sinners and chose them for salvation before the foundation of the world. There *is* a proper sense in which God's love for His own is a unique, special, particular love determined to save them at all costs.

It is also true that when Scripture speaks of divine love, the focus is *usually* on God's eternal love toward the elect. God's love for mankind reaches fruition in the election of those whom He saves. And not every aspect of divine love extends to all sinners without exception. Otherwise, all would be elect, and all would ultimately be saved. But Scripture clearly teaches that *many* will *not* be saved (Matt. 7:22–23). Can God sincerely love those whom He does not save?

British Baptist leader Erroll Hulse in dealing with this very question has written,

> How can we say God loves all men when the psalms tell us he hates the worker of iniquity (Ps. 5:5)? How can we maintain that God loves all when Paul says that he bears the objects of his wrath, being fitted for destruction, with great patience (Rom. 9:22)? Even more how can we possibly accept that God loves all men without exception when we survey the acts of God's wrath in history? Think of the deluge which destroyed all but one family. Think of Sodom and Gomorrah. With so specific a chapter as Romans [1,] which declares that sodomy is a sign of reprobation, could we possibly maintain that God loved the population of the two cities destroyed by fire? How can we possibly reconcile God's love and his wrath? Would we deny the profundity of this problem?[10]

Yet Hulse realizes that when taking Scripture at face value, he cannot escape the conclusion that God's love extends even to sinners whom He ultimately will condemn. "The will of God is expressed in unmistakable terms," Hulse writes. "He has no pleasure in the destruction and punishment of the wicked (Ezek. 18:32; 33:11)." Hulse also cites Matthew 23:37, where Jesus weeps over the city of Jerusalem, and then says, "We are left in no doubt that the desire and will of God is for man's highest good, that is his eternal salvation through heeding the Gospel of Christ."[11]

It is crucial to accept the testimony of Scripture on this question, for as Hulse points out:

> We will not be disposed to invite wayward transgressors to Christ, or reason with them, or bring to them the overtures of the Gospel, unless we are convinced that God is favorably disposed to them. Only if we are genuinely persuaded that he will have them to be saved are we likely to make the effort. If God does not love them it is hardly likely that we will make it our business to love them. Especially is this the case when there is so much that is repulsive in the ungodliness and sinfulness of Christ-rejecters.[12]

Biblically, it is an inescapable conclusion that God's benevolent, merciful love is unlimited in extent. He loves the *whole* world of humanity. This love extends to all people in all times. It is what Titus 3:4 refers to: "the kindness of God our Savior and His love for mankind." God's singular love for the elect quite simply does not rule out a universal love of sincere compassion—and a sincere desire on God's part to see every sinner turn to Christ.

Mark 10 relates a familiar story that illustrates God's love for the lost. It is the account of the rich young ruler who came to Jesus and began asking Him, "Good Teacher, what shall I do to inherit eternal life?"— a great question. Scripture tells us,

> And Jesus said to him, "Why do you call Me good? No one is good except God alone. You know the commandments, 'Do not murder, Do not commit adultery, Do not steal, Do not bear false witness, Do not defraud, Honor your father and mother.'" (vv. 18–19)

Jesus designed every aspect of His reply to confront the young man's sin. Many people misunderstand the point of Jesus' initial question: "Why do you call Me good?" Our Lord was not denying His own sinlessness or deity. Plenty of verses of Scripture affirm that Jesus was indeed sinless—"holy, innocent, undefiled, separated from sinners and exalted above the heavens" (Heb. 7:26). He is therefore also God incarnate (John 1:1). But Jesus' reply to this young man had a twofold purpose: first, to underscore His own deity, confronting the young man with the reality of who He was; and second, to chide gently a brash young man who clearly thought of *himself* as good.

To stress this second point, Jesus quoted a section of the decalogue. Had the young man been genuinely honest with himself, he would have admitted that he had not kept the law perfectly. But instead, he responded confidently, "Teacher, I have kept all these things from my youth up" (Mark 10:20). This was unbelievable impertinence on the young man's part. It shows how little he understood of the demands of the law. Contrast his flippant response with how Peter reacted when he saw Christ for who He was. Peter fell on his face and said, "Depart from me, for I am a sinful man, O Lord!" (Luke 5:8). This rich young ruler's response falls at the other end of the spectrum. He is not willing to admit he has ever sinned.

So Jesus gave him a second test: "One thing you lack: go and sell all you possess, and give to the poor, and you shall have treasure in heaven; and come, follow Me" (Mark 10:21).

Sadly, the young man declined. Here were two things he refused to do: he would not acknowledge his sin, and he would not obey Christ's command. In other words, he shut himself off from the eternal life he seemed to be seeking so earnestly. As it turned out, some things were more important to him than eternal life. His pride and his personal property took priority in his heart over the claims of Christ on his life. So he turned away from the only true Source of the life he thought he was seeking.

That is the last we ever see of this man in the NT. According to the biblical record, he remained in unbelief. But notice a significant phrase, tucked away in Mark 10:21: "Looking at him, Jesus felt a love for him." Here is an explicit statement that Jesus loved an overt, open, nonrepentant, nonsubmissive Christ-rejecter. He loved him.

Other Scriptures also speak of God's love for those who turn away from Him. In Isaiah 63:7–9 the prophet describes God's demeanor toward the nation of Israel:

> I shall make mention of the lovingkindnesses of the LORD, the praises of the LORD, according to all that the LORD has granted us, and the great goodness toward the house of Israel, which He has granted them according to His compassion, and according to the multitude of His lovingkindnesses. For He said, "Surely, they are My people, Sons who will not deal falsely." So He became their Savior. In all their affliction He was afflicted, and the angel of His presence saved them; in His love and in His mercy He redeemed them; and He lifted them and carried them all the days of old.

Someone might object that the passage talks about God's redemptive love for His elect alone. No, this speaks of a love that spread over the entire nation of Israel. God "became their Savior" in the sense that He redeemed the entire nation from Egypt. He suffered when they suffered. He sustained them "all the days of old." This speaks not of an eternal salvation, but of a temporal relationship with an earthly nation. How do we know? Look at verse 10: "But they rebelled and grieved His Holy Spirit; therefore, He turned Himself to become their enemy, He fought against them."

That is an amazing statement! Here we see God defined as the Savior, the lover, the redeemer of a people who make themselves His enemies. They rebel against Him. They grieve His Holy Spirit. They choose a life of sin.

Now notice verse 17: "Why, O LORD, dost Thou cause us to stray from Thy ways, and harden our heart from fearing Thee?" That speaks of God's judicial hardening of the disobedient nation. He actually hardened the hearts of those whom He loved and redeemed out of Egypt.

Forward one chapter in Isaiah's prophecy are these shocking words in Isaiah 64:5: "Thou wast angry, for we sinned, we continued in them a long time; and shall we be saved?"

How can God be Savior to some who will not be saved? Yet these are clearly unconverted people. Verses 6–7 which begin with a familiar passage read,

> For all of us have become like one who is unclean, and all our righteous deeds are like a filthy garment; and all of us wither like a leaf, and our iniquities, like the wind, take us away. And there is no one who calls on Thy name, who arouses himself to take hold of Thee; for Thou hast hidden Thy face from us, and hast delivered us into the power of our iniquities.

These are clearly unconverted, unbelieving people. In what sense can God call Himself their Savior?

Here is how He can do it: God revealed Himself as Savior. He manifested His love to the nation. "In all their affliction He was afflicted" (Isa. 63:9). He poured out His goodness, lovingkindness, and mercy on the nation. That divine forbearance and long-suffering should have moved them to repentance (Rom. 2:4). But instead they responded with unbelief, and their hearts were hardened.

Isaiah 65 takes it still further:

> I permitted Myself to be sought by those who did not ask for Me; I permitted Myself to be found by those who did not seek Me. I said, "Here am I, here am I," to a nation which did not call on My name. I have spread out My hands all day long to a rebellious people, who walk in the way which is not good, following their own thoughts. (vv. 1–2)

In other words, God turned away from these rebellious people, consigned them to their own idolatry, and chose a people for Himself from among other nations.

Isaiah reveals the shocking blasphemy of those from whom God turns away. They considered themselves holier than God (v. 5); they continually provoked Him to His face (v. 3), defiling themselves (v. 4), and scorning God for idols (v. 7). God judged them with the utmost severity, because their hostility to Him was great, and their rejection of Him was final.

Yet these were people on whom God had showered love and goodness! He even called Himself their Savior.

In a similar sense Jesus is called "Savior of the world" (John 4:42; 1 John 4:14). Paul wrote, "We have fixed our hope on the living God, who is the Savior of all men, especially of believers" (1 Tim. 4:10). The point is not that He actually saves the whole world (for that would be universalism, and Scripture clearly teaches not all will be saved). The point is that He is the only Savior to whom anyone in the world can turn for forgiveness and eternal life—and therefore He urges all to embrace Him as Savior. Jesus Christ is proffered to the world as Savior. In setting forth His own Son as Savior of the world, God displays the same kind of love to the whole world that was manifest in the OT to the rebellious Israelites. It is a sincere, tenderhearted, compassionate love that offers mercy and forgiveness.

IN WHAT SENSE IS GOD'S LOVE UNIVERSAL?

What aspects of God's love and goodwill are seen even in His dealings with the reprobate? God manifests His love universally to all people in at least four ways:

Common grace. Common grace is a term theologians use to describe the goodness of God to all mankind universally. Common grace restrains sin and the effects of sin on the human race. Common grace is what keeps humanity from descending into the morass of evil that would exist if the full expression of man's fallen nature had free reign.

Scripture teaches that people are totally depraved—tainted with sin in every aspect of their being (Rom. 3:10–18). People who doubt this doctrine often ask, "How can people who are supposedly totally depraved enjoy beauty, have a sense of right and wrong, know the pangs of a wounded conscience, or produce great works of art and literature? Aren't these accomplishments of humanity proof that the human race is essentially good? Don't these things testify to the basic goodness of human nature?"

The answer is no. Human nature is utterly corrupt. "There is none righteous, not even one" (Rom. 3:10). "The heart is more deceitful than all else and is desperately sick" (Jer. 17:9). Unregenerate men and women are "dead in . . . trespasses and sins" (Eph. 2:1). All people are by nature "foolish . . . disobedient, deceived, enslaved to various lusts and pleasures, spending [their lives] in malice" (Titus 3:3). This is true of all alike, "For all have sinned and fall short of the glory of God" (Rom. 3:23).

Common grace is what restrains the full expression of human sinfulness. God has graciously given humans a conscience, which enables them to know the difference between right and wrong and which to some degree places moral constraints on evil behavior (Rom. 2:15). He sovereignly maintains order in human society through government (Rom. 13:1–5). He enables people to admire beauty and goodness (Ps. 50:2). He imparts numerous advantages, blessings, and tokens of His kindness indiscriminately on both the evil and the good, the righteous and the unrighteous (Matt. 5:45). All of those things are the result of common grace, God's goodness to mankind in general.

Common grace *ought* to be enough to move sinners to repentance. The apostle Paul rebukes the unbeliever: "Do you think lightly of the riches of His kindness and forbearance and patience, not knowing that the kindness of God leads you to repentance?" (Rom. 2:4). Yet because of the depth of depravity in the human heart, all sinners spurn the goodness of God.

Common grace does not pardon sin or redeem sinners, but it is nevertheless a sincere token of God's goodwill to mankind in general. As the apostle Paul said, "In Him we live and move and exist . . . 'For we also are His offspring'" (Acts 17:28). That takes in everyone on earth, not just those whom God adopts as sons. God deals with all as His offspring, people made in His image. "The Lord is good to all, and His mercies are over all His works" (Ps. 145:9).

If anyone questions the love and goodness of God to all, he should look again at the world in which we live. Someone might say, "There's a lot of sorrow in this world." The only reason the sorrow and tragedy stand out is because there is also much joy and gladness. The only reason the ugliness is recognizable is that God has given so much beauty. The only reason a person feels disappointment is that there is so much that satisfies.

An understanding that all of humanity is fallen and rebellious and unworthy of any blessing from God's hand helps give a better perspective. "Because of the LORD's great love we are not consumed, for his compassions never fail" (Lam. 3:22 NIV). The only reason God ever gives anything to laugh at, smile at, or enjoy is because He is a good and loving God. If He were not, His wrath would immediately consume humanity.

Acts 14 contains a helpful description of common grace. Paul and Barnabas were ministering at Lystra, when Paul healed a lame man. The crowds saw it and someone began saying that Paul was Zeus and Barnabas Hermes. The priest at the local temple of Zeus wanted to organize a sacrifice to Zeus. But when Paul and Barnabas heard about it, they said,

Men, why are you doing these things? We are also men of the same nature as you, and preach the gospel to you in order that you should turn from these vain things to a living God, who made the heaven and the earth and the sea, and all that is in them. And in the generations gone by *He permitted all the nations to go their own ways; and yet He did not leave Himself without witness, in that He did good and gave you rains from heaven and fruitful seasons, satisfying your hearts with food and gladness.* (vv. 15–17, emphasis added)

That is a fine description of common grace. Though allowing sinners to "go their own ways," God bestows on them temporal tokens of His goodness and lovingkindness. It is not saving grace. It has no redemptive effect. Nevertheless, it is a genuine and unfeigned manifestation of divine lovingkindness to all people.

Compassion. God's love to all humanity is a love of compassion. To say it another way, it is a love of pity. It is a brokenhearted love. He is "good, and ready to forgive, and abundant in lovingkindness to all who call upon [Him]" (Ps. 86:5). "To the Lord our God belong compassion and forgiveness, for we have rebelled against Him" (Dan. 9:9). He is "compassionate and gracious, slow to anger, and abounding in lovingkindness and truth" (Exod. 34:6). "God is love" (1 John 4:8, 16).

Of course, nothing in any sinner compels God's love. He does not love sinners because they are lovable. He is not merciful to them because they in any way deserve His mercy. They are despicable, vile sinners who if not saved by the grace of God, will be thrown on the trash heap of eternity, which is hell. They have no intrinsic value, no intrinsic worth—there's nothing in them to love.

I recently overheard a radio talk-show psychologist attempting to give a caller an ego-boost: "God loves you for what you are. You *must* see yourself as someone special. After all, you are special to God."

That approach misses the point entirely. God does *not* love people "for what we are." He loves them *in spite of* what they are. He does not love them because they are special. Rather it is only His love and grace that give their lives any significance at all. That may seem like a doleful perspective to those raised in a culture where self-esteem is the supreme virtue. But it is, after all, precisely what Scripture teaches: "We have sinned like our fathers, we have committed iniquity, we have behaved wickedly" (Ps. 106:6). "All of us have become like one who is unclean, and all our righteous deeds are like a filthy garment; and all of us wither like a leaf, and our iniquities, like the wind, take us away" (Isa. 64:6).

God loves because He *is* love; love is essential to who He is. Rather than viewing His love as proof of something worthy in mankind, people ought to be humbled by it.

God's love for the reprobate is not the love of value; it is the love of pity for that which *could* have had value and has none. It is a love of compassion. It is a love of sorrow. It is a love of pathos. It is the same deep sense of compassion and pity humans feel when they see a scab-ridden derelict lying in the gutter. It is not a love that is incompatible with revulsion, but it is a genuine, well-meant, compassionate, sympathetic love nonetheless.

Frequently the OT prophets describe the tears of God for the lost:

> Therefore my heart intones like a harp for Moab, and my inward feelings for Kir-hareseth. So it will come about when Moab presents himself, when he wearies himself upon his high place, and comes to his sanctuary to pray, that he will not prevail. This is the word which the LORD spoke earlier concerning Moab. (Isaiah 16:11–13)

> "And I shall make an end of Moab," declares the LORD, "the one who offers sacrifice on the high place and the one who burns incense to his gods. Therefore My heart wails for Moab like flutes; My heart also wails like flutes for the men of Kir-heres. Therefore they have lost the abundance it produced. For every head is bald and every beard cut short; there are gashes on all the hands and sackcloth on the loins." (Jeremiah 48:35–37)

Similarly, the NT gives the picture of Christ, weeping over the city of Jerusalem: "O Jerusalem, Jerusalem, who kills the prophets and stones those who are sent to her! How often I wanted to gather your children together, the way a hen gathers her chicks under her wings, and you were unwilling" (Matt. 23:37). Luke 19:41–44 gives a more detailed picture of Christ's sorrow over the city:

> And when He approached, He saw the city and wept over it, saying, "If you had known in this day, even you, the things which make for peace! But now they have been hidden from your eyes. For the days shall come upon you when your enemies will throw up a bank before you, and surround you, and hem you in on every side, and will level you to the ground and your children within you, and they will not leave in you

one stone upon another, because you did not recognize the time of your visitation."

Those are words of doom, yet they are spoken in great sorrow. It is genuine sorrow, borne out of the heart of a divine Savior who "wanted to gather [them] together, the way a hen gathers her chicks under her wings," but they were "unwilling."

Those who deny God's love for the reprobate usually suggest that it is the human side of Jesus here, not His divinity. They say that if this were an expression of sincere desire from an omnipotent God, He would surely intervene on their behalf and save them. Unfulfilled desire such as Jesus expresses here is incompatible with a sovereign God, they say.

That view has problems. Is Christ in His humanity *more* loving or *more* compassionate than God? Is tenderness perfected in the humanity of Christ, yet somehow lacking in His deity? When Christ speaks of gathering the people of Jerusalem as a hen gathers her chicks, is this not deity speaking, rather than humanity? Do not these pronouncements of doom necessarily proceed from His deity as well? And if the words are the words of deity, how can anyone assert that the accompanying sorrow is the product of Christ's human nature only, and not the divine? Does not intuition dictate that if God is love—if His tender mercies are over all His works—then Jesus' words *must* be an echo of the divine?

Admonition. God's universal love is revealed not only in common grace and His great compassion, but also in His admonitions to all sinners. God is constantly warning the reprobate of their impending fate, and pleading with them to repent. Nothing demonstrates God's love more than the various warnings throughout the pages of Scripture, urging sinners to flee from the wrath to come.

If God really did *not* love the reprobate, nothing would compel Him to warn them. He would be perfectly just to punish them for their sin and unbelief with no admonition whatsoever. But He does love and He does care and He does warn.

Anyone who knows anything about the Bible knows it is filled with warnings about the judgment to come, warnings about hell, and warnings about the severity of divine punishment.

God obviously loves sinners enough to warn them. Sometimes the warnings of Scripture bear the marks of divine wrath. They sound severe. They reflect God's hatred of sin. They warn of the irreversible condemnation that will befall sinners. They are unsettling, unpleasant, even terrifying.

But they are admonitions from a loving God who weeps over the destruction of the wicked. They are necessary expressions from the heart of a compassionate Creator who takes no pleasure in the death of the wicked. They are further proof that God is love.

The gospel offer. The final proof that God's love extends to all lies in the gospel offer. The gospel invitation is an offer of divine mercy. The breadth of that offer is unlimited. It excludes no one from the gospel invitation. It offers salvation in Christ freely and indiscriminately to all.

In Matthew 22:2–14 Jesus told a parable about a king who had a marriage celebration for his son. He sent his servants to invite the wedding guests. Scripture says, "They were unwilling to come" (v. 3). The king sent his servants again with the message, "Behold, I have prepared my dinner; my oxen and my fattened livestock are all butchered and everything is ready; come to the wedding feast" (v. 4). But even after that second invitation, the invited guests remained unwilling to come. In fact, Scripture says, "But they paid no attention and went their way, one to his own farm, another to his business, and the rest seized his slaves and mistreated them and killed them" (vv. 5–6). This was outrageous, inexcusable behavior! And the king judged them severely for it.

Then Scripture says he told his servants, "The wedding is ready, but those who were invited were not worthy. Go therefore to the main highways, and as many as you find there, invite to the wedding feast" (vv. 8–9). He opened the invitation to all comers. Jesus closes with this: "Many are called, but few are chosen" (v. 14).

The parable represents God's dealing with the nation of Israel. They were the invited guests. But they rejected the Messiah. They spurned Him and mistreated Him and crucified Him. They would not come—as Jesus said to them, "You search the Scriptures, because you think that in them you have eternal life; and it is these that bear witness of Me; and *you are unwilling to come to Me,* that you may have life" (John 5:39–40, emphasis added).

The gospel invites many to come who are unwilling to come. Many are called who are not chosen. The invitation to come is given indiscriminately to all. Whosoever will may come—the invitation is not issued to the elect alone.

God's love for mankind does not stop with a warning of the judgment to come. It also invites sinners to partake of divine mercy. It offers forgiveness and mercy. Jesus said, "Come to Me, all who are weary and heavy-laden, and I will give you rest. Take My yoke upon you, and learn from Me, for I am gentle and humble in heart; and you shall find rest for your souls" (Matt. 11:28–29). And Jesus said, "The one who comes to Me I will certainly not cast out" (John 6:37).

It should be evident from these verses that the gospel is a *free offer* of Christ and His salvation to all who hear. Those who question the free offer therefore alter the nature of the gospel itself and deny that God's love extends to all humanity, thereby obscuring some of the most precious truth in all Scripture about God and His lovingkindness.

God's love extends to the whole world. It covers all humanity. Common grace demonstrates it, as do His compassion, His admonitions to the lost, and the free offer of the gospel to all.

God *is* love, and His mercy is over all His works.

That is not all there is to know about God's love, but it is a very significant aspect of it, especially in light of recent declarations to the contrary. Those who contend that God does not love everyone are unbiblical and illogical. Who God is requires that His love extends to all mankind.

ENDNOTES

[1] The source of this essay is the volume entitled *The Love of God* (Dallas: Word, 1996). It is adapted and used here by permission.

[2] Arthur W. Pink, *The Sovereignty of God* (Grand Rapids: Baker, 1930), 314.

[3] This is the formulation of the Westminster Confession of Faith with regard to the sufficiency of Scripture: "The whole counsel of God, concerning all things necessary for His own glory, man's salvation, faith, and life, is either expressly set down in Scripture, *or by good and necessary consequence may be deduced from Scripture*: unto which nothing at any time is to be added, whether by new revelations of the Spirit, or traditions of men" (1:6, emphasis added).

[4] All Scripture quotations in this chapter are from the New American Standard Bible unless otherwise indicated.

[5] John Brown, *Discourses and Sayings of Our Lord,* 3 vols. (reprint, Edinburgh: Banner of Truth, 1990), 1:34.

[6] B. B. Warfield, *The Saviour of the World* (reprint, Edinburgh: Banner of Truth, 1991), 114.

[7] Ibid., 120–21.

[8] R. L. Dabney, *Discussions: Evangelical and Theological,* 3 vols. (reprint, Edinburgh: Banner of Truth, 1982), 1:312.

[9] John Calvin, *Commentary on a Harmony of the Evangelists: Matthew, Mark, and Luke,* trans. William Pringle (reprint, Grand Rapids: Baker, 1979), 123.

[10] Erroll Hulse, "The Love of God for All Mankind," *Reformation Today,* November–December 1983, 18–19.

[11] Ibid., 21–22.

[12] Ibid., 18.

Index of Authors

Abbott, Walter M. 185, 186
Adams, Jay E. 27
Alford, Henry 92
Allis, Oswald T. 74
Ankerberg, John 126, 128
Aune, David E. 49, 52–53

Bacchiocchi, Samuele 132, 148, 154
Bahnsen, Greg L. 74
Baldessarini, Ross 20
Balyeat, Joseph R. 93
Bancroft, Emery H. 76
Barker, Kenneth L. 74
Barron, Bruce 148
Bass, Clarence B. 74
Bellinzoni, Arthur J. 219, 230
Black, Matthew 52
Blaising, Craig L.
    on Dispensationalism, 73
    on hermeneutics, 89
    on Progressive
      Dispensationalism, 188,
        189, 191, 195, 198–203
Blomberg, Craig
    on evangelical feminism, 134,
      141, 150, 153–155
    on Historical Criticism, 202,
      212, 214, 221–22, 224,
      226–27, 229–30

Blumhofer, Edith L. 100, 110
Bobgan, Deidre 16, 27, 28
Bobgan, Martin 16, 27, 28
Bock, Darrell L.
    on Dispensationalism, 73, 74
    on Historical Criticism, 188,
      189, 191, 193, 195,
      198–203, 221, 223, 228
Boomsma, Clarence 136, 151, 152
Boyd, Gregory A. 221, 230
Bretscher, Paul M. 125
Brodeur, Nicole 25
Brooks, James A. 213, 226
Brown, John 236
Bruce, F. F. 133, 149
Bruner, Frederick D. 215, 227
Burton, Ernest De Witt 127
Buswell, J. Oliver 111

Caird, G. V. 90
Campbell, Donald 73
Carlson, Ron 126
Carson, D. A. 43, 53, 212,
    221, 223, 225, 227, 230
Casriel, Daniel 29
Chantry, Walter J. 111
Chilton, David 90, 93
Clutter, Ronald T. 73
Collins, Gary R. 18, 27

Index of Scriptures

Index of Subjects

antinomianism 59, 62, 67, 70, 173
apostle(s) 77, 87–88, 117, 170,
    194, 196
  distinct from prophets, 36–38,
    38–40, 42, 44, 46–47
  miracles by, 97–99, 103–5
  Paul 23–24, 142, 235, 246
  prophets, 36
application 130
  of grammatical rules, 34, 36,
    38–39, 51 n. 33
  versus interpretation, 140, 189
    191, 193–95
article-noun-καί-noun plural
  construction 38, 50 n. 21
Ashlar 112, 118, 120
attempted proof of literary
  dependence 207–8
authority 32–34, 42–43, 46–47
  of Scripture, 95, 98, 129, 136,
    143, 147 n. 9, 150 n. 32,
    158, 161, 170–71, 180
  of the Catholic church, 170–71,
    181, 195

Blue Lodge 114–15

Celestial Lodge 117–18
cessationism
  miraculous gifts, 94, 96–100,
    104–8, 109 nn. 1 & 4

prophecy, 31–33, 48 n. 2
Chafer, Lewis S. 63, 65, 67, 70
Christian
  gospel 116–17, 127 n. 35
  membership in Lodge
    112, 120, 123
  mission 156, 159,
    161–62, 167
  Reconstructionism 89 n. 1
church 57, 62, 76 n. 31, 84–87,
    88, 113, 123, 124
  and counseling, 14–19, 21–23,
    24–26, 27 n. 3, 29 n. 11
  early, 208, 213, 216–18, 220,
    222 n. 17, 225 n. 38
  Israel and the, 58, 66, 68,
    80–82, 191–92, 194, 197
  miracles in the, 95–98, 100–105,
    107–9
  prophecy in the, 31–34, 36, 42,
    44–45
  Roman Catholic, 157–61, 164,
    166–68, 170–74, 176–77,
    179, 180–81, 183
  women's role in the, 129–138,
    140–41, 144, 146, 147 nn.
    8 & 9, 148 n. 14
Common Gavel 112, 119–20
common mission 156, 161
concluding discourse formula 211,
    213–14, 225 n. 39